Post-Enlightenment Society

Markus Tiedemann

Post-Enlightenment Society

What we are losing and what lies ahead

BRILL | MENTIS

This publication was produced as part of the author's work at the Dresden University of Technology, Chair of Didactics of Philosophy and Ethics, and was financially supported by the Dresden University of Technology.

Cover illustration: Rubjerg Knude lighthouse, M. ullmann 2003, cropped. Creative Commons, License CC BY-SA 2.0 DE (https://creativecommons.org/licenses/by-sa/2.0/de/deed.en)

Bibliographic information published by the Deutsche Nationalbibliothek

The Deutsche Nationalbibliothek lists this publication in the Deutsche Nationalbibliografie; detailed bibliographic data available online: http://dnb.d-nb.de

All rights reserved. No part of this publication may be reproduced, translated, stored in a retrieval system, or transmitted in any form or by any means, electronic, mechanical, photocopying, recording or otherwise, without prior written permission from the publisher.

© 2025 by Brill mentis, Wollmarktstraße 115, 33098 Paderborn, Germany, an imprint of the Brill-Group (Koninklijke Brill BV, Leiden, The Netherlands; Brill USA Inc., Boston MA, USA; Brill Asia Pte Ltd, Singapore; Brill Deutschland GmbH, Paderborn, Germany; Brill Österreich GmbH, Vienna, Austria) Koninklijke Brill BV incorporates the imprints Brill, Brill Nijhoff, Brill Schöningh, Brill Fink, Brill mentis, Brill Wageningen Academic, Vandenhoeck & Ruprecht, Böhlau and V&R unipress.

www.brill.com
E-Mail: info@fink.de

Copy editing: Josephin Schneller, Dresden
Cover design: Anna Braungart, Tübingen
Production: Brill Deutschland GmbH, Paderborn

ISBN 978-3-95743-339-8 (paperback)
ISBN 978-3-96975-339-2 (e-book)

For the three of you

Contents

Introduction and the concept of Enlightenment IX

1 Looking back in gratitude 1
   1.1   An amazing coincidence 1
   1.2   A titanic project and its wonderful consequences 4
   1.3   Rare, proud and fragile 11

2 Simply the Best! 23
   2.1   Related, but not identical 23
   2.2   Facts and arguments of a higher order: not ultimate,
but best justified 25
   2.3   Freedom: not absolute, but transcendental 35
   2.4   Ethical universalism: European, but not Eurocentric 39
   2.5   Racism: despite, not through, Enlightenment 45
   2.6   Alternatives: possible, but inhumane 53
   2.7   Take it or leave it 64

3 Transience 67
   3.1   The eternal competition 67
   3.2   The reproduction problem 73
   3.3   The self-destructive tendencies of freedom 77
       3.3.1   *The instrumental shortening* 78
       3.3.2   *Uprising of the masses* 80
       3.3.3   *Education without Humanism* 86
       3.3.4   *Wrong use for the right thing. Cancel Culture and
language loss* 99
   3.4   Current stress factors 118
       3.4.1   *Destruction of natural resources* 118
       3.4.2   *Extremism* 122
       3.4.3   *Migration* 131
   3.5   The digital catalyst 140
       3.5.1   *The aestheticization of the living environment and the
problem of unequal acceleration* 140
       3.5.2   *Structural loss of the public sphere* 146

4	And now? The Post-Enlightenment Society	155
4.1	The return of the classics	155
	4.1.1 *Child-adults*	156
	4.1.2 *Autocracy*	161
4.2	Marginal existence: surviving on the periphery	168
4.3	Speculative consolation	170
	4.3.1 *Speculation 1: Putin, the savior of the West*	170
	4.3.2 *Speculation 2: bad for freedom, but good for the climate*	171
	4.3.3 *Speculation 3: digital options*	172

Ciao Bella 176

Postface to the second German edition 177

Literature 181

Introduction and the concept of Enlightenment

This essay argues that we are witnessing a paradigm shift in the history of mentalities and culture. We are observing the end of the second Enlightenment era and the beginning of the Post-Enlightenment Society.

The term 'Post-Enlightenment Society' seems to be justified because the few societies that are still committed to the ideals of the Enlightenment are in a state of self-dissolution or find themselves on the edge of global insignificance. Moreover, this term does not imply that a majority of the world's population lived in societies guided by Enlightenment ideals until recently. That was never the case.

The Post-Enlightenment Society is a historical epoch or a form of society in which the achievements and ideals of the Enlightenment are no longer effective as guiding principles. Instances, structures and ideas that owe their genesis to the Enlightenment will not disappear completely overnight, but they will lose their primacy. In moments of critical decision-making, society will no longer rally firmly behind these values.

The Post-Enlightenment Society is best understood in terms of the absence or erosion of Enlightenment ideals. This is why Enlightenment needs to be narrowed down. In the Historical Dictionary of Philosophy alone, the corresponding article fills 15 pages.[1] The following use of the term Enlightenment therefore does not claim to do justice to all facets of the phenomenon or even all analytical or hermeneutic interpretations.

This essay understands the essence of the Enlightenment as the always unfinished cultivation of a way of life that strives for objectivity and normative justification. This form of life is incomplete because it is subject to immanent self-criticism. The reason for this is the realization that one never or only rarely fully lives up to one's own expectations. It is a form of cultivation because the potential for rational self-discipline is inherent in human beings, but can only unfold through nurturing and support. Humans are gifted with reason. Unfortunately, they have little affinity to use this talent.

---

[1] Article "Aufklärung". In: Joachim Ritter (ed.): *Historisches Wörterbuch der Philosophie*, Volume 1 A-C. Wissenschaftliche Buchgesellschaft, Darmstadt 1971. pp. 620–635.

At the same time this exit of man from his self-inflicted immaturity and the endeavor to overcome the determination of nature and tradition by means of reason is also the core substance of humanism. Rationality enables autonomy. Autonomy enables responsibility and, in sum, the dignity of a being capable of morality arises. Ideals such as maturity and objectivity have far-reaching consequences for social and political organization. However, they are not bound to any cultural morphology. Enlightenment is a civilizational project that is compatible with many cultural forms and ways of life. The only binding commonality is the principle of rational justification striving for objectivity.

It is a system of thought closely linked to the historical and systematic development of democracy, the separation of powers, and human rights. However, there is neither a necessary nor a sufficient connection.

As an individual act, Enlightenment can manifest itself at any place and at any time, at least in theory. A critical mass of individuals striving for Enlightenment may necessarily give rise to demands for democracy, human rights and the rule of law. Unfortunately, this does not automatically imply the realization of these principles. The causalities are controversial. From the perspective of historical materialism, bourgeois freedom is not the result of Enlightenment, but rather the consequence of productivity increases in the social substructure. It was the economic change from feudalism to capitalism that brought about the ideas of the Enlightenment, not the other way around. Of course, the materialist interpretation of history is not necessarily a refutation of the idealism of the Enlightenment. A dialectical interlocking of the forces can also still be defended. However, it is important to note that none of the possible interpretations can be proven to be necessarily right or wrong.

It is of central importance for this essay that all mentioned achievements can also be conceived and realized without the essence of the Enlightenment as defined above. Law can be reduced to positive law, which is why it is possible for the worst dictatorships to call themselves a constitutional state. Science orientation can be reduced to feasibility, mechanics and efficiency. This is why theocracies can also push ahead with the construction of atomic bombs, even though the physical explanation of the world is diametrically opposed to their own dogmas. Democracy can be reduced to majority law. This is exactly what happens in so-called illiberal democracies, such as Hungary, Poland or Turkey. Even human rights, the declaration of which is inextricably linked to the history of the Enlightenment, are currently being reinterpreted. China in particular is aggressively promoting an understanding of human rights which in their core include the right to economic development. Liberal civil rights and liberties, on the other hand, are being neglected. In the communist one-party state of China, it is not the bourgeois who is in danger, but the citoyen.

For this reason, many interpretations of the current crisis fall short. They speak of the death of democracies or of a war against science.[2] In reality, however, only those forms of democracy, science or society that are rooted in the principles of the Enlightenment are in danger. The driving force behind the current erosion lies in deeper layers. The pursuit of objectivity and rational justification are either declared impossible, normatively discredited or simply ignored. For example, we are not primarily in a crisis of democracy. Rather, it is the case that "an erosion of enlightened culture has taken place, affecting the way in which democracies 'function'".[3]

Enlightenment is not, however, a *culture* in the sense of an arbitrary expression of customs and traditions. Nor should it be understood as a diffuse, emancipation-friendly attitude. Rather, the essence of the Enlightenment consists of a feat of self-discipline or submission to the principle of rational justification and the greatest possible objectivity. Following this definition, it becomes clear to what extent erosion pervades all social and political structures. This process is omnipresent and leads to what will be called a Post-Enlightenment Society in the following.

This is not about advocating a historical-philosophical model. Ever since humanity became aware of its own history, there have been different models for interpreting it. A rough distinction can be made between chaotic, teleological and circular models. Those who interpret world history as chaos deny the existence of any kind of structure. Teleological models assume that human history is heading towards a final state. This can be both utopian and apocalyptic in the truest sense of the word. Social reformist theories, such as communism, saw the end of history in the creation of a perfect society. Religious beliefs interpreted the end as the last judgment. The historical image of the modern Enlightenment understood human history as a never-ending quest that, despite all setbacks, was heading towards greater freedom and humanity in the long term. Circular models, as represented by Plato among others, understand history as a cycle of processes of development and decline. Even the most just kingship eventually mutates into a tyranny, which is then overthrown and replaced by a just aristocracy. Unfortunately, the few good people

---

[2] See: Steven Levitsky & Daniel Ziblatt: Wie Demokratien sterben: Und was wir dagegen tun können. DVA Verlag, Munich 2018.

[3] Michael Hampe: Die dritte Aufklärung. Nicolai Publishing & Intelligence GmbH, Berlin 2018. p. 9.

who want to serve the common good gradually develop into selfish oligarchs who are also overthrown. This is followed by a phase of just democracy which, however, also mutates. The result is the rule of the mob, in which everyone is only interested in personal advantage and loses sight of the common good. Out of this chaos comes the call for the strong man and the cycle begins again with the sole rule of a righteous man or a tyrant.

This essay is not intended to take sides in the dispute between historical-philosophical models. The matter is decided by physics alone. The history of our entire planet will end in five billion years at the latest with the apocalyptic collapse of our solar system. It remains questionable whether humanity will remain in chaos until then, experience a steady rise to the better, a final self-destruction or a circular succession of good and bad phases remains.

The central concern of the essay is to defend the following theses:

1. The project of Enlightenment was and is the noblest thing that mankind has ever produced.
2. It is an elitist minority project that is dependent on favorable framework conditions which it cannot guarantee itself.
3. The Post-Enlightenment Society is a return to the authoritative standard models of humanity, accompanied by the technical possibilities of modernity.
4. For the current generations, the decline of Enlightenment values will be an irreversible reality

The point is to show that we are not observing the crisis of individual social instances, but the demise of a way of life. Of course, nothing would be less enlightened than to present one's own convictions as unquestionable knowledge. This essay is an essay in the original meaning of the word. It is a polemic, borne by the fading hope that I am wrong.

CHAPTER 1

Looking back in gratitude

1.1 An amazing coincidence

The ideals of the Enlightenment are among the most breathtaking achievements of mankind. The fact that the human species was able to produce and develop such a jewel in the first place is the result of fortunate coincidences and impressive performances. At the heart of this guiding principle is the pursuit of rational orientation. And the criterion for rational orientation is objectivity.

This was not one of the many fantasies invented by the clever human animal, but the realization of an astonishing ability and an act of impressive self-discipline. The attempt to elevate knowledge and not inclination or power to a yardstick for right and wrong, for good and evil, was a titanic intellectual and cultural achievement. It formed the basis for what was probably the noblest project of mankind: the overcoming of biological animality and cultural determination, the exit from a found and self-inflicted immaturity. Human dignity, if it exists, is based on this very achievement.

By no means does this advocate naïve idealism. Humanity did not discover a free-floating, platonic idea, but developed criteria that, under normal conditions, could be made comprehensible to the vast majority of members of the species. This development was not incidental but the result of numerous evolutionary, economic, and social factors.

It required a brain capable of conceiving abstract concepts such as objectivity. The fact that humans developed such an organ is an evolutionary coincidence. According to one theory, the development of the upright gait caused a narrowing of the pelvis, which in turn necessitated a shortening of the gestation period and a reduction in the circumference of the intestine. The energy saved in the intestinal winds could have benefited the growth of the neuronal system, which was exposed to immense stimulation through the constant grasping of the now freely acting hands. The rapidly increasing complexity of human language was no less crucial.

Essentially, this is based on the interaction of the tongue and vocal cords, which provide a rare range of sound combinations. In this way, it became possible to name an almost unlimited number of objects. However, human sounds are not only used to describe things in a differentiated way. They can also be used to name things that do not exist at all, or at least not physically. In this context, Yuval Noah Harari speaks of the cognitive revolution in human history.[1] At some point, our ancestors not only began to describe the location, position and nature of food sources that were beyond sensory perception. Numerous animals are also able to do this. Humans also began to communicate about things that did not exist or did not yet exist. For example, they could not only communicate where specific prey animals were actually located, but they were also able to speculate about what to do if the herds were to take a different direction. This development enabled increasingly abstract objects and concepts such as hunts, animal breeding, calendars, Gods, economic systems, constitutions and quantum physics. The concept of objectivity is also one of these abstractions.

The use of abstract language was promoted by the growth of social communities. In the small tribal communities of the Old Stone Age, there was little need for abstract communication. The things to be settled were probably mostly concrete. In addition, emotional family ties may have made a large number of formulated conventions superfluous. This quickly changed in the Neolithic period. In villages of over 100 inhabitants, there were numerous concrete and abstract topics of conversation. Around 4500 BC, cities such as Jericho probably had over 10,000 inhabitants. This means that the majority of citizens did not know each other. Their relationship itself was abstract. The citizens had to think theoretically about what to do if they met or even came into conflict with one of the many unknown people. Abstract concepts such as work, wages, trade or law became necessary. Emotional ties may be enough to enable the success of a group of hunters and gatherers. However, they are insufficient for economic success and peaceful coexistence in a small town. This is especially true when the community sets out to build a defensive fence, an irrigation system, a pyramid, a legal system or a global economic system.

The progression of the economic substructure promoted the discovery of objectivity as well. Before complex social and communication communities develop, it must be ensured that the corresponding land unit provides sufficient food. Without agriculture there would be no permanent settlements and without production surpluses there would be no systemic division of labor, without stockpiling there would be no large-scale projects. The example of slavery illustrates how differentiated the achievements of the Neolithic period

---

[1] Cf: Yuval Noah Harari: *Eine kurze Geschichte der Menschheit*. Pantheon, Munich 2015, Chapter I.

are. Slavery is likely to have played only a minor role in the Palaeolithic period. Overpowered opponents were either beaten to death, eaten, left to fend for themselves or integrated into the tribe. Slavery is only logical if a person's labor can at least feed himself and his master. Initially, only very few people benefited massively from the innovations of the Neolithic. It is likely that, if at all, the quality of life of the average person only improved in very small steps. The advantage of permanent housing was offset by the increased confrontation with animal pathogens and a one-sided diet. To this day, four crops (sugar cane, maize, wheat and rice) feed the majority of the world's population. Above all, however, the race between food production and human reproduction began. Poor harvests, famines and epidemics took their toll. Nevertheless, more and more surpluses made it possible to increase the population and differentiate society. The profitability of slavery facilitated further divisions of labor.

In addition to farmers and craftsmen, the class of usufructuaries soon emerged, who claimed the majority of the profits for themselves and cultivated a life of idleness on the backs of slaves and fellahin. The most honest among them simply lived the law of the strongest. They demanded services of all kinds and, at best, offered protection from other usufructuaries of their ilk. The second group of usufructuaries justified themselves through a special relationship with the divine. They were probably helped to their special position by coincidental conformities of predictions and factuality or even just rhetoric and personal nimbus. For example, anyone who had repeatedly observed the coincidental parallelism of a celestial constellation such as the star Sirius with the subsequent Nile flood was able to impress his contemporaries by reading supposedly divine signs. In addition, elaborate narratives were spread that told of rewards and punishments in the future or a world beyond. Basically, it was just a more perfidious version of the intimidation technique already used by the first group of usufructuaries. The third group of usufructuaries called themselves researchers, wise men or philosophers. They cultivated something they called *theoria*, which at first glance must also have looked like idleness. With a view to the production of society as a whole, the following also seemed to apply to scientists: "The work is done by others!"[2].

Nevertheless, there was a serious difference to the first two groups of usufructuaries: the investment in the apparent idleness of the researchers was supposed to yield returns. Behind the *theoria* lay ideas such as objectivity, truth, predictive power and natural causality. And these categories were to bring

---

2 Helmut Schelsky: Die Arbeit tun die anderen. Klassenkampf und Priesterherrschaft der Intellektuellen. Westdeutscher Verlag, Leverkusen 1975.

about unimagined economic, epistemic and normative progress for humanity as a whole. The philosophers began to pay back.

1.2 A titanic project and its wonderful consequences

The philosophers' titanic project is maturity, understood as the rational self-empowerment of human beings.

The first and most fundamental revolution was of a mental nature. It was the "birth of the Logos"[3], a previously unknown rationalization of the individual and collective understanding of the world, which opened up the possibility of escaping the self-inflicted immaturity towards nature, tradition and religion. This enormous intellectual achievement can be attributed to numerous mothers and fathers. It was a long and difficult pregnancy and the labor pains can be traced back to the most diverse cultures in human history. However, the final delivery undoubtedly took place in Greece. We still have the birth certificate today: Plato's *Theaetetus*.

According to the British philosopher and mathematician Alfred North Whitehead, the entire intellectual history of Europe consists of "a series of footnotes to Plato".[4] This statement is certainly an exaggeration. Nevertheless, Plato's work in general and *the Theaetetus* in particular stand for a revolutionary mental paradigm shift. The distinction found there between *doxa* and *episteme*, between opinion and knowledge, is the essence of the modern man striving for objectivity.

Almost all of the ideas expressed in *Theaetetus* can be found scattered in earlier texts from ancient Greece. However, it was only with Plato that the pursuit of knowledge became an epistemic and normative program. Knowledge, according to Plato, is true justified conviction. It is not enough to win one's case, it is about actually being right. It is not enough to overpower, intimidate or persuade. The goal is to convince. Knowledge has three central characteristics. Copernicus knows that the earth is round precisely when (1) the earth really is round; (2) Copernicus is convinced that his assertion is correct and (3) Copernicus can plausibly justify his theses. The ancient Egyptian priest mentioned above, who owed his position to the prediction of the Nile flood,

---

3   Arno Schmidt: *Die Geburt des Logos bei den alten Griechen*. Logos Verlag, Berlin 2003.
4   "The safest general characterization of the European philosophical tradition is that it consists of a series of footnotes to Plato.", Alfred North Whitehead: Process and Reality. The Free Press, New York 1979. p. 39.

does not meet these requirements. Although the flood really did follow the appearance of the star Sirius (criterion 1) and perhaps the priest really was convinced of his assumption (criterion 2), he was unable to offer a plausible explanation (criterion 3). The requirements of the *Theaetetus* drew a clear dividing line between the priests and the philosophers. It was not enough for the latter to notice something. They always asked the question of why. A claim to knowledge can only be made when the answer and the eyplanation are succesful. Since then, intersubjective verifiability, consistency, coherence as well as premise parsimony and falsifiability have been identified as quality criteria.

It is difficult to assess whether all the historical protagonists were aware of the scope of their debate. Reading the *Theaetetetus*, however, it quickly becomes clear that even then, as in any real educational process, "everything was at stake."[5] Truth cares neither for traditions and myths nor for the randomness of opinions. For anyone who has understood the origin of the rainy season in the East African highlands, the prediction of the Nile flood with the help of the Sirius star is just a droll auxiliary construction. Priests become superfluous. Plato's *Theaetetus* was written at an academy, not in a temple. At the same time, the philosophers succeeded in pushing back the religions without succumbing to relativism. Religions make claims to truth without being able to justify them. Relativists negate the possibility of truth claims. Both result in immaturity. Socrates fell victim to the accusation of blasphemy. Nevertheless, his teachings continued to have an effect and argument began to triumph over ritual. Plato struggled with a sophistical understanding of the Homo Mensura theorem, according to which man with his individual opinion is elevated to the measure of all things. Plato countered this relativism with the possibility of knowledge. Man and his needs are an important yardstick of practical philosophy and deserve consideration in political and social questions, but the mere opinion of the individual is not the final authority in deciding right and wrong. Regardless of feelings and ideas, objectivity exists and recognizing it is man's most noble task. There is no need for a Platonic theory of ideas to pursue this approach. It is enough to accept that truth is not in the eye of the beholder and can at least be partially inferred. The project of Enlightenment begins with the distinction between *doxa* and *episteme*.

Over two thousand years after the *Theaetetus*, a second epoch drove the project of rationalization forward. Kant's distinction between opinion, belief

---

5 Peter Bieri: Wie wäre es, gebildet zu sein? In: Hans-Ulrich Lessing, Volker Steenblock (eds.): *"Was den Menschen eigentlich zum Menschen macht. ...". Klassische Texte einer Philosophie der Bildung.* Verlag Karl Albert, Freiburg im Breisgau 2010. p. 217.

and knowledge became famous. According to Kant, these are three modes of subjective and/or objective belief. 'Opinion' refers to an assumption that is neither subjectively nor objectively considered to be sufficiently justified. I think that the US will eventually introduce civilized gun laws, but I would not put my money on it. 'Belief' stands for an assumption that is based on sufficiently convincing subjective grounds. Peter believes that all living beings were created on a single day. For him, the religious evidence is sufficient. This is legitimate as long as he is aware that there is no objective evidence for his assumption and therefore he cannot claim any knowledge. Only *'knowledge'* denotes a subjective and objectively sufficiently substantiated assumption. We know that coelacanths populated the oceans for over 400 million years. Numerous fossils do not allow any other conclusion.[6]

Step by step, criteria for rational justification were differentiated and many of these findings are now part of general knowledge. The distinction between deductive reasoning from general principles and inductive deduction of general principles from concrete observations already became more pronounced with Plato and Aristotle. The degree of scientific quality increases with the reduction of presupposed axioms and premises. Superfluous assumptions should be removed as with the intellectual razor named after Ockham. Accordingly, an explanation of the cosmos that necessarily presupposes a religious worldview is unscientific. In any case, it is clearly inferior to a system that uses gravity alone as an axiom. Radical criticism is capable of explicating evidence. Descartes Methodological Doubt is rightly one of the classic contents of philosophy lessons. A statement is only considered self-evident when it is beyond doubt. According to Popper, pure science must specify the criteria for falsifying its own statements.

It becomes evident that the scientific pursuit of objectivity is rooted in the principle of intersubjective communicability. Science employs methodologies and language designed to allow any rational individual to understand, replicate, and verify cognitive processes. It remains both critical and self-critical in evaluating the validity of its knowledge claims.

Cultivated rationality, the differentiation of *doxa* and *episteme* from opinion, belief and knowledge, frees us from the shackles of myth and protects us from relativistic arbitrariness. What was driven forward was a rational

---

[6] My colleagues in epistemology in particular may forgive me this exaggeration. Of course, a radical, Cartesian doubt can also be applied to the last statement. However, the premise of an evil demon that deceives us must be introduced. An exciting philosophical exercise. But let's be honest: can you find a colleague who takes this possibility seriously?

understanding of the physical world and formal logical consistency as well as a special appreciation for the subject of the cognitive process: the human being.

For this process, the humanities and natural sciences worked hand in hand. The humanities questioned the status quo and developed criteria and concepts for objective knowledge. The natural sciences proved that these criteria could be met in full or at least approximately.

True, well-founded opinion must be empirically verifiable, capable of prognosis, but at least free of presuppositions and contradictions. The myth cannot meet these requirements. It does not become worthless as a result, but it remains *doxa*. This can be illustrated by two examples: "Lightning is an expression of divine wrath!". A nice idea, but it cannot be compared epistemologically with the research results of a physicist, who is not only able to derive them theoretically, but also to demonstrate them through predictions and model experiments. Physicists are able to attract lightning, redirect it and reproduce it in miniature. Admirers of Thor or Zeus can pray and tell stories. "Do X because this is the will of God as it has been handed down to us in the Holy Scriptures." This is statement with numerous prerequisites: *God is. God is good. God's will should be observed. The Holy Scriptures correctly reflect God's will. We understand the Holy Scriptures correctly*. All these premises must be *believed* without any evidence so that a claim to truth or a norm can be derived from them. This is precisely the dividing line between mythical explanations of the world and science, as well as between religious morality and philosophical ethics. While the former rely on revelation and narration, the latter strive for arguments and intersubjective and intercultural evidence. Those who consider objectivity to be possible look for reasons that are comprehensible to all rational beings. Religion and myth fill this void with dogmas. Critical reason often encounters obstacles, much like the wolf in the fable with the seven young goats. It has to swallow so many cobblestones that it finally sinks into dogmatic abysses.

The enormous upheavals of this mental revolution can also be illustrated by the categories of being and ought. Man likes to interpret as God-given what he is unable to change. On the other hand, the progression of the natural sciences provides factual evidence that man does not have to submit to his natural being. Short-sightedness has always existed, but that does not mean that it should or must exist. Infant mortality, floods, darkness or lack of water are by no means necessary conditions. Pregnancy is not the inevitable consequence of an active sex life, and toothlessness is not a necessary event of old age. All cultivation is a questioning of natural conditions and the construction of a counter-design. Being is contrasted with what should be. Options and alternative courses of action increase. Anyone bitten by a rattlesnake in Arizona today does not have to die or rely on the mercy of a deity. They can get an antidote. This is quite different from a prayer. Injected in time, the antidote will help, regardless of whether the patient believes in it or not or whether he is able to communicate with his ancestors.

This progress was achieved through endless diligence, willingness to experiment, ingenuity and courage. The step from pure experiential knowledge to science is already described by Aristotle. A master craftsman has learned that something works and how it works. The scientist can also explain why exactly this is the case. Only the architect, the scientist, is able to present calculations that explain why the dome of the Pantheon does not collapse despite an opening. Furthermore, he is able to formulate abstract laws of statics and physics and make them usable for the creation of other buildings. His forecasts are no longer *trial and error*, but the application of objective findings. They enable reliable a priori statements to be made about the resilience of bridges, the spread of disease or the occurrence of a solar eclipse. Without these epistemic certainties, numerous human projects would never have been undertaken. Who would invest huge sums of money in a project if the builder merely declared that something similar had always worked before? It takes science to calculate that it *will* work. Theodor Storm's *Schimmelreiter* is an impressive account of how offerings and spells were still regarded as a sensible method of coastal protection in the 18th century. Today, physical knowledge about wave dynamics, force transmission and outlet slopes determine dyke construction and thus the safety of human lives. The repayment of natural scientists consists of light bulbs, pacemakers, vaccinations, fertilizers, dentures, refrigerators, water filters, condoms and much more.

What applies to the relationship between the natural sciences and quality of life also applies to the relationship between the humanities and moral-political progress. Slavery, oppression of women, destruction of the environment: all these evils have existed since the dawn of time. However, this does not mean that they should or even must exist. It certainly does not follow that we are allowed to practice them. In ethics, the juxtaposition of being and ought reaches the essence of man himself. The second nature of man is to be able to relate to his biological and social imprint. This is precisely the core idea behind the human dignity advocated by the Enlightenment and humanism. Those who muster the courage to use their own intellect do not cease to be a being determined in many ways, but they do open up the possibility of making decisions according to criteria of their own choosing. A freedom option that only exists if the criteria do not arise solely from a random, cultural context, but strive for the highest degree of objectivity. It is not necessary to know everything correctly, but to be able to put information and explanations in relation to each other, guided by criteria. According to Herder, it is the shedding of dogmatic constraints and trust in one's own reason that elevates people to "the first freedmen of creation"[7]. This second nature is not a trifle, but the core of human dignity. Man is by no means subject to his instincts and inclinations alone. Traditions and imprints are not absolute determinants either. Of course, freedom and emancipation are extremely difficult. Furthermore, neuropsychology proves how complex biological, physical, psychological and social determinants areinterlocked (see chapter 3.3). Nevertheless, the conditions for the possibility of freedom remain. They already lie in the medium of language, which makes it possible to formulate the problem as an abstraction and thus open up a new level. The person who submits to all these efforts, who tries not to allow judgments and actions to be determined by inclinations or traditions, but tries to bind them to criteria that can be communicated intersubjectively and interculturally, cultivates his second nature. He elevates himself to what Kant called a *causa noumenon*. A being that is capable of freedom and thus of goodness. A being that possesses dignity and deserves respect.

On the basis of the mental paradigm shift, a revolution in political thinking was the necessary conclusion. It was only logical, although unspeakably courageous, to demand a political order that took account of the special freedom of man. Both the theoretical legitimization and the concrete exercise of rule became the focus of criticism. The claim to be God and king in one person, to belong to a family of Gods or at least to have been chosen by God, has legitimized rule for thousands of years and still serves, in a slightly weakened form, as a justification for dictatorships such as North Korea. Nevertheless, this narrative loses all justification in the face of the barriers of reason. Divine right is based on a premise without an objective foundation. The same applies to a practice of rule that does not see itself as a service to the ruled.

In the fourth century BC in Athens, not only the legitimization of rule but also political decision-making was linked to voting processes. Democracy was born. From today's perspective, many things seem deficient: patriarchy and slavery remained untouched. The ethical universalism of Plato or the humanistic approaches of the Stoa or Epicurus were unable to change this practice. A comparison with parallel civilizations, on the other hand, illustrates the enormous progression that manifested itself in Athens. While elsewhere claims to power and political decisions were legitimized by bloodlines, the will of the

---

7 Johann Gottfried Herder: *Ideen zur Philosophie der Geschichte der Menschheit*. Vol. 1, Johann Friedrich Hartknoch, Leipzig 1784, p. 231.

Gods or visceral inspection, the Athenians organized election campaigns, invented voting machines, compulsory voting and the rotation of offices.

Two thousand years later, the liberation movement, driven by the claim to rational justification, developed a far greater and more sustainable dynamic. If Copernicus, Galileo and Columbus overthrew the world view of the Christian Middle Ages, Thomas Hobbes did the same with the concept of rule. The revolutionary concept that changed everything was the theory of contract. Legitimate rule does not come about through religious consecration, bloodlines or force. It is the result of a contract in which reciprocal claims are guaranteed.

Contract theory belongs to a Janus-faced understanding of justice. Its second face is the philosophical natural law which is no less innovative. It is a natural law that did not refer to a divine plan. Mere existence implies the right to use existing abilities. A renunciation of these natural rights can only be expected on the basis of an attractive consideration. This is exactly what the contract means. The parties to the contract assure each other that they will refrain from using force. In order to guarantee compliance with the contract, an initially absolute ruler, the Leviathan, was established. The latter was not sent by God, but appointed by humans to protect them. Just like Attic democracy, the contract theory also had massive teething problems. These included the control of Leviathan, who was created by the contract without being a party to it. However, these shortcomings were overcome with impressive intellectual and political dynamism. When Thomas Hobbes died in 1679, John Locke was 47 years old. In 1690, *The Second Treatise of Civil Government* was published, in which the idea of the separation of powers was developed. A principle that Locke's contemporary, Charles de Montesquieu, perfected in the same year. When Montesquieu died in 1755, a private tutor named Immanuel Kant submitted his doctorate in Königsberg. As a world-famous professor, he was to elevate the theory of contract to the principle of international justice and the approach to perpetual peace. Revolutions and wars of independence were the result. In 1776, the Declaration of Independence of the United States of America was published. The French Revolution led to the declaration of human and civil rights on 26 August 1789. When Jefferson, the author of the Declaration of Independence and eyewitness to the French Revolution, died at his country estate Monticello in 1826, the treaty theory had become a reality. The USA had achieved a democracy legitimized by elections, guaranteed by a constitution and controlled by a system of *checks and balances*, which is still in place today.

Serious injustices persisted for far too long. Slavery was not abolished in the USA until 29 years after Jefferson's death. Racial segregation persisted until the 1960s. Genocides against the indigenous population were made possible under democratic governments. In Europe, slavery was successfully condemned, but at the same time democracy and republicanism failed. At the Congress of Vienna, the European ruling houses established a renaissance of divine right. Further revolutions were necessary to implement the ideas of the Enlightenment.

Gender equality proved to be a tough struggle. Women were denied the right to vote in Germany until 1918, in the USA until 1920, in France until 1944 and in Switzerland even until 1971. However, the agonizingly slow overcoming of all these evils does not alter the value of the intellectual and political paradigm shift. Enlightenment, contract theory and natural law are incompatible with any kind of discrimination. The elimination of injustices from real social life remained a grueling and often agonizingly slow process. However, the right to freedom and equal treatment was established. This revolutionary achievement is still alive today in political liberalism and elevates the principles of free and equal deliberation as well as rational and intersubjective justification to a criterion of legitimacy for political institutions and decisions.[8]

Hence, the humanities scholars paid back as well. Their gifts consisted of constitutions, human rights, the separation of powers, education systems, equal rights, the rule of law and international law.

1.3   Rare, proud and fragile

From a historical perspective, the Enlightenment is one thing above all: rare. The quest for objectivity and intersubjective justification achieved social dominanceonly twice. At no time has the majority of humanity been won over to the project. Moreover, there is no master plan, no recipe of sociological and political ingredients with which an enlightened way of life could be reliably created and maintained. Nevertheless, two epochs demonstrate not only the exclusivity and fragility of Enlightenment, but also its at least partial realization. One coincides with Attic democracy, the other with the liberal societies of the modern era.

The dating alone is already a thankless business. What began tentatively in Athens in the 6th century BC ended at the latest in 262 BC with the renewed

---

8 Cf.: Jürgen Habermas: *Die Einbeziehung des Anderen. Studien zur politischen Theorie.* Suhrkamp, Frankfurt am Main 1996; Rainer Forst: *Das Recht auf Rechtfertigung.* Suhrkamp, Frankfurt am Main 2007; John Rawls: Gerechtigkeit als Fairneß: politisch und nicht metaphysisch. In: Axel Honneth (ed.): *Kommunitarismus,* Campus, Frankfurt am Main 1993. pp. 37–67.

occupation by Macedonia. During this period, the pursuit of rational orientation occasionally succeeded in shaping society. Time and again, there were relapses into tyranny, into dogmatic traditionalism or egomania. A society that organized itself primarily according to the principle of rational justification rarely existed for more than a few decades. Nevertheless, two great feats were achieved: Attic democracy and systematic philosophy.

In standard encyclopaedias, the Enlightenment of the modern era is often presented as a closed epoch of intellectual history in the period between 1650 and 1800.[9] There is nothing to be said against this dating with regard to the development of the theoretical foundations and the first political implementations. Hobbes' *Leviathan* was published in English in 1651. The work did not appear in Latin, the language of scholars, until 19 years later. Between 1781 and 1790, the understanding of criticism as the essence of rational thought reached its peak in the major Kantian works. In addition, the political ideas of Enlightenment were put into practice by the Declaration of Independence of the 13 American colonies in 1776 and the French Revolution of 1789. Nevertheless, there is no need to regard this era as having ended at the beginning of the nineteenth century. While there were massive political setbacks due to monarchies and dictatorships, principles such as the pursuit of objectivity and maturity had not disappeared and were able to gain dominance in many places. A large and influential number of societies are still oriented and organized according to the principle of rational justification. We may be witnessing the downfall, but it is not yet complete.

Both eras did not fall from the sky, but were made possible by a complex structure of framework conditions, innovations and synergy effects.

The cultural upheavals that preceded the ancient Enlightenment have been described by Karl Jaspers as the "Axis Era".[10] In fact, fundamental technical and cultural changes can be traced in numerous independent cultures between 800 and 200 BC. Confucius and Lao Tzu taught in China, Buddhism emerged in India and Iran was shaped by the teachings of Zarathustra. Prophets such as Elijah, Isaiah and Jeremiah were active in Israel and Greek mythology reached its literary peak through Homer. But in Greece alone, humanity went a decisive step further and elevated the pursuit of objectivity and autonomy to a guiding principle.

---

9 Article "Aufklärung". In: Joachim Ritter (ed.): *Historisches Wörterbuch der Philosophie – Volume 1 A-C*. Wissenschaftliche Buchgesellschaft, Darmstadt 1971. pp. 622–632.

10 Karl Jaspers: Vom Ursprung und Ziel der Geschichte. In: Kurt Salamun (ed.): *Karl Jaspers Complete Edition*, I/10. Schwabe Verlag, Basel 2017. p. 50.

An important reason for this special position arises from the unusual nature of Hellenic myth, which had a certain inherent affinity for the Logos. It was already the very plurality of the Olympians and their constant competition that threw man back on his individual power of judgment. This was particularly evident in normative questions. Before embarking on a voyage, it seemed prudent to offer a sacrifice to Poseidon. Whether this attempt at bribery was normatively desirable was another matter. Added to this was the capricious unpredictability of the worshipped and the constant competition from other deities. For example, it was important to please Poseidon without angering Helios. Few tales illustrate this dilemma more clearly than the story of the choice of Paris. The poor young man is supposed to decide which of three Goddesses is the most beautiful by giving her an apple. The trap is perfect: whatever Paris does, he will win a girlfriend as well as two equally powerful enemies. Furthermore, the Greek Goddesses do not act in an exemplary manner at all. Instead, they use secret promises to prove their even too earthly vanity. These anthropomorphisms did not go unnoticed:

> But if the cattle and horses and lions had hands and could paint with these hands and create sculptures like humans, then the horses would depict and paint the Gods in the shape of horses, the cattle with the figure of cattle. They would carve statues that correspond to the shape of their own bodies. But if the oxen and horses and lions had hands or could paint with their hands and form works like men, the horses would paint figures of the Gods like horses, the oxen like oxen, and form such bodies as each species itself would have the appearance of.[11]

Furthermore, the Logos had its own voice within Greek mythology. In his work *The Rebirth of Tragedy from the Spirit of Music*, Nietzsche diagnoses a dualism of the Apollonian and Dionysian principles. Apollo embodies the rule of reason, of order, in short, the Logos. Dionysus stands for pleasure, intoxication and chaos. Nietzsche regrets that Greek philosophy, namely Socrates, brought about the absolute dominance of the Apollonian principle. However, he overlooks a dialectical interlocking of both tendencies. The central example of this is the wise Silen, the companion and tutor of Dionysus. As he is not averse to the experience of pleasure himself, Silen takes advantage of numerous opportunities to encourage instinctive pupils to reflect. The Dionysus cult practiced in reality also knew both elements.

---

11   Xenophanes, DK 11 B 15.

In addition to various intoxicating experiences, the celebrations also included rational challenges such as solving puzzles or competing with speakers.

According to Nietzsche, Socrates is the historical figure who helped the Apollonian principle to victory. In fact, this transition can be understood as a harsh confrontation. After all, the forefather of philosophy was accused of godlessness and executed. On the other hand, there is some evidence that his contemporaries understood Socrates as a combination of logos and myth.[12]

Shortly after his death, the Athenians erected a statue of atonement for Socrates. On this statue, the face of Socrates resembles the depictions of the wise Silen in an astonishing way.[13]

Another important factor was the experience of a military, political and intellectual crisis. Although the wars against the Persians had strengthened the Hellenes' sense of unity and pride in independence and democracy, they had also shown what military superiority non-Greeks were capable of. The leaders of such formidable armed forces were equally unsuitable for the cliché of the stupid barbarian as the builders of pyramids reported by traders and adventurers. Additionally, only few Greeks proved to be exemplary leaders. Rather, they themselves often stood for treachery and tyranny. The Peloponnesian Wars and the onset of the plague did the rest to call their own way of life into question. The myth was no longer able to offer satisfactory legitimization. War and suffering had given rise to a critical generation for whom the ideal of an Achilles plowing through the battle lines was no longer enough. In the search for a new orientation, mythical heroism seemed far less appealing than argumentative persuasiveness.

The third important aspect is the favorable geographical, technical and economic conditions. In the rugged valleys and bays of the Peloponnese, independent but trade-friendly city-states had emerged in which civic self-government proved to be economically profitable and organizationally practicable. In addition, trade, fishing and agriculture ensured stable prosperity, at least in times of peace. The production of surpluses made the use of slaves profitable, who again increased the surplus value as a means of production. In this way, slaveholders were able to participate in political opinion-forming and the scientific search for truth. Additionally, the participation of all free male citizens in the still manageable city-states was practicable even without general literacy. Public discourse on collective decisions or controversial issues led to the cultivation

---

12   Plato, The Banquet, [215a].
13   Cf.: Ekkehard Martens: *Die Sache des Sokrates*. Reclam, Stuttgart 1992. pp. 24–45.

of rhetoric and the art of argumentation. The result was a self-reinforcing process. In the classical reading of the Platonic dialogues, the Sophists appear as pure teachers of rhetoric, whose art of persuasion is exposed by the analytical acumen of Socrates. In fact, both stand together for the cultivation of the *logos*. *Myth* comes from the Greek 'mýein', which means 'to inaugurate' or 'to reproduce' and can also be translated as 'to repeat'. Like the legend, the myth is also something taken over, reproduced. *Logos*, on the other hand, is derived from 'légein' (legain), which means 'self-talk' and includes independent explanation and justification. The essence of myth is therefore the reproduction of other people's thoughts and that of logos is the production of one's own thoughts. Anyone who wanted to triumph in the popular assembly had to develop independent concepts and present them in a rhetorically appealing manner. The corresponding skills can of course be misused, but are in no way contradictory to the principle of argumentative justification.

The second era of the Enlightenment was also preceded by a long phase of intellectual uncertainty and existential threat. Political events, discoveries and inventions had shaken the world. While the Reconquista was completed on the Iberian Peninsula, Constantinople fell in the East. Both events resulted in the import of education. Countless scholars left the lost Eastern Rome for Italy, and in cities such as Córdoba or Granada, the Christian conquerors stood in amazement at the cultural testimonies of the "infidels". The library of Córdoba alone contained more books than the rest of Western Europe put together. Technical achievements and scientific insights shook and changed the world view. After Copernicus, Galileo and Columbus, the geocentric view of the world was falsified, as was the idea of the earth as a bell jar. These findings resonated all the more because their theories and evidence were disseminated in unprecedented speed and quantity via printed books. Even seemingly small inventions had a big impact. These included the Venetian glass mirror produced by the Dal'Gallo brothers in 1516.

From then on, a rapidly growing proportion of the European population became familiar with their own face. Looking in the mirror is not just an aesthetic check, it is also always a phenomenological affirmation of the self and a moral challenge.

The advance of the Ottomans to the gates of Vienna strengthened the much-invoked unity of Christendom in the short term. More profound, however, was the disillusionment regarding an alleged Christian superiority. If there had been a viable sense of unity in Christendom at all, this was permanently destroyed by the French Wars of Religion, the English Civil Wars and the Thirty Years' War.

All of this contributed to a considerable change in mentality. Michelangelo's *David* can rightly be regarded as a symbol of the Renaissance. He stands there with perfect beauty of form and sensuality. What a difference to the understanding of the body in the Middle Ages, in which the body was generally presented as ugly, sinful and unacceptable. The connection to antiquity is abundantly clear. In purely visual terms, Michelangelo's *David* could be presented between Roman or Greek statues of Hermes or Heracles without any break in style. The biblical context has almost disappeared and can only be identified by the sling thrown over his shoulder.

In antiquity, resistance to the Persians and criticism of myth gave rise to philosophy and popular rule. In modern times, religious intolerance, dogmatism and absolute rule were confronted with the humanism and knowledge affinity of the Renaissance. The synthesis of the Enlightenment was the orientation towards reason, science, natural law and republicanism.

Another thing that both Enlightenment eras have in common is that they should neither be idealized nor romanticized. As great as the intellectual liberation may have been, real life was anything but paradisiacal. The normative achievements of the Attic heyday were limited to free Hellenic men. Women, children, foreigners and slaves benefited indirectly at best. The ethical universalism of Plato or the humanistic approaches of the Stoa or Epicurus were unable to change this practice. Even in modern times, intolerance, injustice, dogmatism and fanaticism had not disappeared with the writings of Hume, Voltaire or Locke. On the contrary, they were to shape a large part of the realpolitik for centuries to come and could only be pushed back step by step. At the same time, the awakening of aesthetics, science and self-confidence stood in stark contrast to a world characterized by suffering, war and oppression. The plague ravaged Europe and killed over a third of the population. Witch hunting and religious wars flourished just as cruelly as the exercise of complete and unbridled rule. Extending the phase of the Second Enlightenment to the present day also encompasses the period of political totalitarianism, the two world wars and the Holocaust. Human civilization has never experienced a deeper fall.

Nevertheless, the two Enlightenment eras developed and defended nothing less than an awareness of the maturity, freedom and dignity of all people. Right and wrong, good and evil, all this was no longer to be left to the free play of supremacy, blind tradition or religious dogma, but to the unconstrained compulsion of the better argument. The legacies are science, the education system, private and civic responsibility, the rule of law, constitutions and much more.

In his defense speech, Socrates did not warn of the Gods' resentment, he discussed his position that an unexamined life was not worth living. When Plato opened his academy, the inscription above the gate did not demand a religious confession, but knowledge of geometry. In fact, only two generations of philosophers established the systematic foundations of almost all sciences. The distinction between disciplines, the critique of method, idealism and realism, rationalism and empiricism, deductive reasoning and inductive research; all of this began in the academy.

The principle of rational justification also shaped politics. When Pericles appeared before the Athenians in 430 BC to honor the fallen of the Peloponnesian War, he did not offer sacrifices or invoke mythical traditions. He praised the value of rational decision-making and democratic community.

> We live under a constitution that has not been modeled on foreign laws; on the contrary, we are a model for many rather than imitating others. And because our constitution is not based on a minority, but on the majority of citizens, it bears the name "democracy". [...] We alone do not regard those who take no part in public life as peace-loving citizens, but as lazy and useless members of the state. The citizens as a whole (by casting their votes) bring the affairs of the state to a decision or give them their thoughts. We do not believe that speech is detrimental to action, but rather that it is harmful not to be instructed by speech before taking action.[14]

According to Karl Jaspers, this is where the origin of "all Western awareness of freedom manifests itself, both in the reality of freedom and in the concept of freedom. China and India do not know freedom in this political sense".[15]

2263 years after Pericles, Abraham Lincoln gave a similar speech.

> 87 years ago, our fathers founded a new nation on this continent, conceived in freedom and dedicated to the principle that all men are created equal. Now we are engaged in a great civil war, which is a test of whether this or any other nation so conceived and dedicated to such principles can endure. [...] It is rather for us to be consecrated to the great task that still lies before us [...] that we here solemnly resolve that these dead shall not have died in vain – that this nation, under God, shall experience a rebirth of liberty – and that the government of the people, by the people and for the people, shall not perish from the earth.[16]

---

14   Pericles, Thuc. 2,37 / 2,40.
15   Karl Jaspers: *Vom Ursprung und Ziel der Geschichte*. Piper, Munich 1949. p. 88.
16   Abraham Lincoln: *Gettysburg Address*, Gettysburg Nov. 19, 1863.

The fact that these two speeches were given in honor of fallen soldiers shows how vulnerable and ephemeral Enlightenment eras are.

At least four causes put an end to the ancient Enlightenment: decadence, lack of reproduction, military inferiority and Christianity.

The new ideas of *episteme*, objectivity and civil freedom were young and ambitious. They were opposed by ancient value systems and beliefs. The intellectual potential of women and children remained largely untapped. It was difficult enough to persuade free men to commit themselves to the efforts of the new freedom instead of giving in to the temptations of decadence, patriarchy and irrationality. Plato responded to this Herculean task with the first educational curriculum in history. Nevertheless, the activation of the Logos remained insufficient. Popular assemblies trained the process of rational deliberation, sophists disseminated rhetoric and science, philosophical academies trained elites and invited them to exoteric lectures. However, there was no systematic education of the general population. Athens produced more tyrants and soldiers than philosophers and democrats. One prominent example is the aforementioned Alcibiades. The admired young man grew up in the house of his uncle Pericles and was one of those young people who were fascinated by Socrates. Nevertheless, he went down in history as an unscrupulous man of power who made deals with tyrants. Biographies such as this question Platonic idealism, according to which theoretical insight also entails corresponding behavior. Aristotle's idea that theoretically recognized values must first be acquired as a virtue of character through practice and perseverance seems more convincing. On the other hand, there was a lack of appropriate educational opportunities for the theoretical and practical training of broad sections of the population.

But even if the basic scientific, moral and political orientation had been stable, the military superiority of competing peoples was overwhelming. Macedonians, Spartans and Persians took turns to occupy the city, and eventually the Roman Empire took over supremacy in the entire Aegean. The continuation of Attic Enlightenment ideals was therefore politically dependent on the benevolence of occupiers. The attempt at renewed democratization, even if only as a Roman province, failed to materialize. Enlightenment was forced out of public life and back into the academies. At least the teachings there were able to develop a certain sustainability. Representatives of the Roman elite were taught rhetoric and philosophy. Influences on the Roman legal system and the discourses in the popular assembly and the senate are unmistakable. However, sacrificial offerings, ancestor worship and foundation myths also continued to exist there as instances of justification. With the transition to Caesarism, rational deliberation suffered a further setback. Critical thinking and open-ended research increasingly became an elitist pastime. Nevertheless, two explicit representatives of the Stoa, Seneca (ca. 1–65 AD) and Marcus Aurelius (121–180 AD), acted as administrators and rulers of the Roman Empire.

With the rise of Christianity as the state religion, this influence of Attic philosophy came to an end as well. On a conceptual level, the Logos is either dispensable or threatening for every myth. Paul had elevated "faith, love and hope" to the cardinal virtues of Christianity.[17] There is no longer any talk about reason and *Sophia*, which, according to Plato, should guide the personal soul and the state.[18] "Do not try to understand in order to believe, but believe in order to understand" wrote Augustine to a friend. As a monotheism organized as an official church tangible economic and political interests were also at stake. As a result, Christianity became a persecutor shortly after its own history of persecution. The intolerance was not only directed against real or perceived competitors to the faith, such as heretics or witches, but also against sciences, personalities and institutions that questioned the Christian world view. In 529 AD, Cairo Justinian I ordered the closure of an almost thousand-year-old educational institution on the grounds of pagan doctrines: Plato's Academy.[19] In the same year, the foundation stone was laid on Monte Cassino for what was perhaps the most influential monastery in Christendom.

This brings us to the most important difference between the two Enlightenment eras: the second has not yet ended. The fact that it resisted so many dangers and only seems to be disintegrating today can be attributed to several factors.

Firstly, the second phase of the Enlightenment was able to draw on the ideas and principles of the first phase via the Renaissance. One may argue at length about which was the greater achievement: the primary production of original ideas and concepts or their perfection and dissemination.

---

17   Cor 13, 13.
18   Plato, Phaedrus, [246a-e].
19   However, it is unclear whether this was a deliberate prohibition of the Platonic Academy or the consequence of a general ban on teaching for unbaptized persons. (Cf.: Edward Watts: Justinian, Malalas, and the End of Athenian Philosophical Teaching in A.D. 529. In: *The Journal of Roman Studies* 94/2004. pp. 168–182;

Rainer Thiel: *Simplikios und das Ende der neuplatonischen Schule in Athen*. Franz Stei- ner Verlag, Stuttgart 1999. p. 16f;

Udo Hartmann: Geist im Exil. Römische Philosophen am Hof der Sasaniden. In: Monika Schuol et al. (eds.): *Grenzüberschreitungen. Formen des Kontakts zwischen Orient und Okzident im Altertum*. Franz Steiner Verlag, Stuttgart 2002. pp. 123–160.

Secondly, societies striving for Enlightenment soon had superior weapons technology at their disposal. This unfortunately led to repeated betrayals of Enlightenment ideals in the form of imperialist expansions, but also enabled resistance to totalitarian regimes.

Thirdly, the social alternatives were often so off-putting that support for the ideals of the Enlightenment was strengthened ex negativo. This was true for religious dogmatism and monarchical absolutism in the early modern period and even more so for nationalism and totalitarianism of the twentieth century.

Fourthly, numerous sections of the population were won over affirmatively and intellectually to the ideas of the Enlightenment. Affirmatively, this happened through the right to freedom and equality, intellectually through a rapidly growing education system.

Fifthly, the second Enlightenment succeeded in establishing secularism as a necessary component of liberal ways of life. The achievement was to domesticate myth without becoming barbaric. Rite, myth, religion; all of these have their legitimate place in the private conception of a successful life. For public discourse, however, they remain irrelevant. In the entire history of mankind, there is not a single example in which peace and human dignity could be realized without this separation.

The second Enlightenment era owes its considerable expansion and astonishing resilience to these factors. During this period, it was not only possible to defend against totalitarianism, but also to expand fundamental ideas and concepts of the state. The same applies to the reversal of legal pressure. At the beginning of the twentieth century, democracy was still in need of legitimization in many places. The picture quickly changed. For a short time, the illusion was even nurtured that Enlightenment, human rights and democracy would embark on a global triumphal march. There were plenty of reasons for optimism: the peaceful revolution of 1989 led to the fall of the Berlin Wall and ended the division of Europe. The Cold War was history and the successor states of the USSR were striving towards democracy. Disarmament treaties that had never been hoped for were signed. Parliamentarianism in the Commonwealth of Independent States (CIS) survived the attempted coup in 1991, South Africa overcame apartheid and the world celebrated presidents such as Nelson Mandela and Vaclav Havel. The conflict in Northern Ireland was pacified and Israelis and Palestinians shook hands at Camp David. Carried by the "wind of change", representatives of the "no-future generation" transformed themselves into globally-minded optimists at breathtaking speed.

With the end of the systemic conflict, according to Francis Fukuyama's thesis, history has come to a positive end.[20]

Unfortunately, this is a great miscalculation. Firstly, the so-called liberal democracies were never without competition. The massacre in Tiananmen Square, the genocide in Rwanda and Burundi, the war in Yugoslavia and the catastrophe in Srebrenica, the bloody conflicts in the Kashmir Valley, the rule of the Mujahidin and Taliban in Afghanistan: all these events should have made it clear that ideological, religious and national totalitarianism persisted.

Secondly, the stability and resilience of the Enlightenment structures that have already been achieved was grossly overestimated. As will be shown in Chapter 5, massive erosion is on the horizon, with no turnaround in sight.

It is precisely because the phenomenon of the Enlightenment is so rare that it is sad to see the second era drawing to a close. Nevertheless, there is reason to look back with gratitude. We belong to a small minority that was able to experience the best that humanity has to offer.

---

20   Francis Fukuyama: *Das Ende der Geschichte: Wo stehen wir?* Kindler, Munich 1992.

CHAPTER 2

Simply the Best!

There are numerous objections and accusations against the Enlightenment project. Romantics and theologians complain about the coldness of reason. Enlightenment disregards people's emotional needs and destroys religious certainties without offering any alternative support.[1] According to Max Horkheimer and Theodor W. Adorno, Enlightenment already contains the seeds of self-destruction and the instrumentalization of reason.[2] Freedom as a necessary premise of the Enlightenment idea is disputed by determinists of various stripes. For representatives of postmodernism, constructivism, cultural relativism and postcolonialism, the Enlightenment is epistemically deficient and historically burdened.[3]

All these objections deserve consideration. Nevertheless, they do not prove that Enlightenment is impossible or not worth striving for. The result of the following defense is clear: the Enlightenment project is not perfect, but it is by far the best thing that humanity has ever produced.

2.1 Related, but not identical

The core of the Enlightenment was defined in Chapter 1 as a way of life that is characterized by intellectual and moral self-discipline. The essence of this is the pursuit of objectivity and intersubjective justification. Of course, Enlightenment can also be understood as a historical epoch, a secularization movement or a political program. It is also undisputed that, despite the Enlightenment, terrible crimes were committed time and again. Due to this

---

1 Rüdiger Bubner (1989): Rousseau, Hegel and the Dialectic of Enlightenment. In: Jochen Schmidt (ed.): *Aufklärung und Gegenaufklärung in der europäischen Literatur, Philosophie und Politik von der Antike bis zur Gegenwart.* Wissenschaftliche Buchgesellschaft, Darmstadt 1989. S. 416.
2 Max Horkheimer, Theodor W. Adorno: Dialectic of Enlightenment. In: *Max Horkheimer: Collected Writings.* Vol. 5. Fischer, Frankfurt am Main 1987. p. 25.
3 Cf.: Jean-Francois Lyotard: *Postmodern Knowledge: A report.* Passagen Verlag, Vienna 2015. p. 96; Robert C. Bartlett: *The idea of Enlightenment: a post-mortem study.* University of Toronto Press, Toronto 2001. chapter 9.

fact, the second Enlightenment phase in particular is declared as either causally evil, complicit or useless.

The first two accusations stem from an inadmissible simplification, the third from historical ignorance. Enlightenment is not a synonym for modern times, scientific-technological modernity or even the geopolitical sphere of the so-called West.[4] Of course there are historical, ideological and causal correlations. The rise of the bourgeoisie, individualism, atheism, industrialization, capitalism, world trade: all these phenomena and isms can be regarded as parents, siblings or children of the Enlightenment. Nevertheless, collective punishment is an injustice. This applies to people as well as to ideals and theories. Even twins are not identical and it would be unfair to praise or blame one for the achievements or misdemeanors of the other. The achievements of Pasteur and Koch were a blessing for mankind. This would not have changed even if they had had a criminal brother. It is therefore also inadmissible to blame the Enlightenment for the many negative developments of modern times or the modern age. Sad truths should not be denied: personalities of the Enlightenment were misogynists or even slave owners. Enlightenment, education and humanism were no more able to prevent the totalitarianism of the twentieth century than they were to prevent the current ecological self-destruction. However, it is also true that none of these evils can be justified intersubjectively and that the Enlightenment is its harshest, often even its only critic. The first thing that dogmatists, racists or totalitarian rulers fight against are always the ideas of the Enlightenment. And it is precisely these ideas that have been used against slavery, colonialism and totalitarianism and have pushed them back in bitter wars. For this reason alone, it is ignorant to describe the Enlightenment as useless or ineffective. The principles of the Enlightenment not only formed the resistance against totalitarianism, contempt for humanity and exploitation, they also actively brought about a humanistic progression. This applies not only to fundamental rights and political organizations, but also to the natural sciences, which consciously placed themselves at the service of humanity. Authors such as Steven Pinker never tire of celebrating the Enlightenment as a success despite all the setbacks and criticizing the ingratitude of their contemporaries. The scourge of violence and war has not yet been overcome, but courts, constitutional states and the United Nations do exist. As far as we know, only our species has developed institutions for non-violent conflict resolution. Injustices, diseases and misfortunes still exist, but health systems,

---

4 See: Johannes Rohbeck: Zur Aktualität der Aufklärung. In: *Zeitschrift für Didaktik der Philosophie und Ethik* (*ZDPE*), issue 1/ 2021. p. 4–19.

vaccinations, educational institutions and emergency aid programs have been developed. Pinker's conclusion is clear: thanks to education, more people are living longer, healthier, more peaceful, fairer and safer lives than ever before. "The world has never been as good as it is today." – "The Enlightenment has realized its program. "[5] In fact, there is much evidence that the successes of the Enlightenment were considerable. Unfortunately, it does not follow that they are permanent. Since Pinker published his theories in 2018, the danger of nuclear war, which was thought to have been averted, has returned and the UNHCR has reported the highest number of refugees ever recorded at 100 million people.[6] However, it would be difficult to understand this development as a consequence of the Enlightenment. It is much more obvious to attribute the renewed increase in suffering to a decline in reason, negotiation, cooperation and the rule of law – in short, to an erosion of the principles of Enlightenment.

The accusation that the Enlightenment is the main cause of the horrors of the modern age is unjustified. The fact that all these horrors have occurred does not generate an argument against the Enlightenment. Enlightenment is a necessary prerequisite for identifying and coherently condemning violations of international law or human dignity. Unfortunately, it has never been sufficient to prevent them.

2.2 Facts and arguments of a higher order: not ultimate, but best justified

> Reason comes first. Reason is non-negotiable. As soon as we discuss the meaning of life (or any other question), as long as we insist that our answers, whatever they are, are *reasonable* or *sound* or *true* and that other people should therefore take them at face value as well, we have committed ourselves to reason and to the assumption that our beliefs stand up to objective standards.[7]

Of course, the epistemological and ethical premises of the Enlightenment can be called into question. The Enlightenment itself even explicitly calls for this. The critique of pure reason is and has always been a critique through and of

---

5   Steven Pinker: Die Welt war noch nie so gut wie heute! In: *Philosophiemagazin*. No. 2 /2018. p. 66–71.
6   United Nations High Commissioner for Refugees (ed.): *Global Trends Report 2021*. UNHCR Global Data Service, Copenhagen 2022. p. 7ff.
7   Stephen Pinker, Martina Wiese (transl.): *Aufklärung Jetzt – Für Vernunft, Wissenschaft, Humanismus und Fortschritt*. S. Fischer Verlag, Frankfurt am Main 2018. p. 20.

itself. The most radical form of this self-criticism implies the question of one's own existence. Is there even such a thing as human reason? Well, you could make it easy for yourself and use a variant of Descartes' Meditations. Who, if not reason, is capable of doubting the existence of reason? Ergo: if reason is doubted, this proves reason. However, this does not protect us from the accusation of empty reasoning. Can there be universal truths for all people? Is there even such a thing as objectivity outside of our imagination? If not, the Enlightenment is chasing after a phantom.

The self-criticism of the Enlightenment has given rise to numerous theories that question objectivity in principle. Prominent examples are skepticism, postmodernism and constructivism.

Skepticism emphasizes the unreliability of our experiences. When we let a stone slip from our outstretched hand, we take it for granted that it will fall to the ground. However, we cannot know this, as it cannot be logically ruled out that our stone will be the first of its kind to fall. David Hume exposed induction as a circular argument. Experience teaches us that our stone will fall to the ground. But we also conclude from experience that we can rely on experience. We have been able to rely on it so far. This alone does not prove that it will remain so.

According to Jean-François Lyotard, the father of postmodernism, all knowledge is only supposed knowledge that is always embedded in a meta-narrative. Without the framework or language game of the meta-narrative, knowledge claims lose their validity. Religious theses refer to sacred writings. Cell biologists base their statements on observations, experiments and principles of scientific falsification. The truth claims of both metanarratives cannot be proven by necessity, which is why, according to Lyotard, they must be regarded as epistemically equal. The theory of constructivism states that the content of our reality is produced by the conditions and methods of our observation. In fact, it can hardly be denied that a large part of our world view is constructed. Of course, it makes a difference whether we look at the Andromeda Nebula with the naked eye or through a high-resolution telescope. Our image, our idea of the cosmos, our reality will be different. It is equally undisputed that cultural imprinting plays a dominant role. In Germany, many children are likely to hear the story of a friendly man in the moon when they ask about the optical structures on the lunar surface. On the other hand, in large parts of Tanzania grandparents, tell that "Hänge-Peters", the cruel German colonialist, will receive his eternal punishment up there. Our world view, our truth claims are always constructions of our randomly shaped minds.

But what does this tell us? Do we learn that the human mind produces many very different interpretations and that every claim to truth should be met with skepticism? Or is the doctrine that there is no objective truth at all? If this is the case, then statements about "Hänge-Peters", the "man in the moon" or the existence of the moon as an earth satellite are equally true or false.

Well, this assumption is possible. But that alone does not make it convincing. Is there really any reason to declare the pursuit of objectivity as the "task of all science "[8] obsolete? As a first step, it only seems legitimate to point out the contradictions in which skepticism, constructivism and the theory of postmodernism are entangled. If everything is relative to framing meta-narratives or to the construction of perception, then so are the statements of the theories themselves. Anyone who declares any truth claim to be impossible cannot claim any validity for their own statements.

In order to conceal their own inconsistencies, many authorities of constructivism work with suspicions and questions instead of systematic argumentation. For example, the demand for consistent justifications and logical reasoning is condemned as an exercise of power and Michel Foucault asks: "Is power not simply a form of war-like domination?"[9]

Well, there are good reasons to answer with a confident NO. Firstly, there is the important distinction between power and violence, which we owe to Hannah Arendt, among others. Power can emerge as empowerment from a process of rational justification. Overpowering alone corresponds to martial rule, and numerous instruments of the separation of powers have been devised to avoid this. According to Susan Neiman, even a basic course in logic "would have saved us a lot of confusion. The fact that some people have blue eyes does not mean that there are no other eye colors. From the fact that some moral claims are hidden claims to power, one cannot conclude that every claim to act for the common good conceals a claim to power."[10]

---

8   Gottlob Frege: Der Gedanke – Eine logische Untersuchung. In: *Logische Untersuchungen.* Vandenhoeck & Ruprecht, Göttingen 2003. p. 48.
9   "Isn't power a form of warlike domination? Shouldn't one therefore conceive of all problems of power in terms of relations of war?" – Michel Foucault: Truth and Power. In: Colin Gordon (ed.): Power/Knowledge: Selected Interviews and Other Writings, 1972–1977. Pantheon Books, New York 1980. p. 123.
10 Susan Neiman: Widerstand der Vernunft. Ein Manifest in postfaktischen Zeiten. Ecowin, Salzburg 2017. p. 49.

The second step is to show that, despite all justified objections, the possibility of objective findings has not been refuted. On the contrary, there are many good reasons for continuing to assume the existence of actualities, data and facts.

If someone carelessly throws a stone, we consider this to be negligent. This is because all people in all cultures have experienced that events have consequences. Causality is a necessary category in the thinking of all people. Furthermore, we are able to describe, calculate, diagnose and predict what the stone will do in the culturally independent language of physics. Although different units of measurement may have been developed, the fact that changes in temperature cause water to both freeze and evaporate is more than a convention. The same is true for logical conclusions. All human reason is forced to recognize thinking as sufficient proof of existence. There is much evidence for the fact that structures of the world are at least partially understood correctly. When Ottmar Ammann proposed the idea of a spectacular suspension bridge in 1925, many of his contemporaries thought he was crazy. The possibility of such a structure was incompatible with their world view. However, when Ammann presented his structural calculations, he was able to convince them. The George Washington Bridge was built and has been in place since 1931. This is not because his contemporaries changed their world view, but because there are objective laws of statics.

The fact that we perceive and interpret events and phenomena differently does not mean that they have no factual core. Children in Tanzania and in Germany may have a very different visual and emotional image of the moon. But does this allow the conclusion that no objective statements about the Earth's moon are possible? Is it not rather the case that our different perceptions prove the existence of an object, which in turn triggers the different interpretations? According to Markus Gabriel, constructivism "wrongly [assumes] that what we observe is also a constructed fact."[11]

Suppose I was sitting on a park bench with a stranger and we saw three objects approaching us. Of course, we may experience the situation very differently. My neighbor may be delighted, while I feel uncomfortable. We can also argue about what the objects are: women, men, children, pupils, etc. But we can probably agree very quickly that we are both observing a quantity of objects (probably three) that make a change in space within a certain time frame. From here it is not far from the Kantian theory of knowledge. According to Kant, an objective knowledge of the world is impossible for us

---

11   Markus Gabriel: Kritik am radikalen Konstruktivismus. In: *Warum es die Welt nicht gibt.* Ullstein, Berlin 2013. p. 14.

due to the construction of our perceptual apparatus. The thing in itself, the noumenon, remains sealed to us, but it exists. There is objectively something that affects our perception and gives rise to the thing for us, the phenomenon. Furthermore, there are good reasons to assume that our perceptions are based on a common minimal structure. Otherwise, understanding would not be possible. This minimal structure would also be a fact as an anthropological constant. According to Kant, no human perception can be conceived outside of space and time. Likewise, there are no human statements that do not obey the categories of quantity, quality, relation and modality. According to Herbert Schnädelbach, the philosophical search for truth can be read as a process of increasing self-limitation. The ontological paradigm still hoped to understand the constitution of the world itself. The mentalist and linguistic paradigms are content to explore the structures of human thought and speech.[12] The field of knowledge has thus become more modest. However, this does not change the well-founded claim to objectivity of the statements. And once again: the lack of evidence of facts does not mean that there are no facts. In the 2001 film *A Beautiful Mind*, a mathematics professor exposes his own schizophrenia when he realizes that a child who has been part of his delusions for years has neither grown nor changed. Since this contradicts the space-time continuum, it must be fiction. It does not matter whether the historical model of the movie, the mathematician John Forbes Nash Jr., really got to grips with his problems in this way, what matters is that it would be possible.

Finally, one last example: during a stay in Central Africa, a local doctor told me that he repeatedly had to treat Europeans even though they had only been bitten by a non-poisonous snake. This report is well suited to illustrate constructivism. Apparently, the chain of associations between snake, Africa and bite is so powerful that symptoms requiring treatment are developed. However, the reverse is also illuminating. If I am injected with the venom of a black mamba or an inland taipan far away from human help, I will die. This is also the case if I consider the snake to be non-poisonous, worship it as a lucky charm or – for whatever reason – do not even notice the bite. My death is objectively unavoidable and we all know that this is the case.

Similar to data-based physical facts are man-made facts such as laws, titles, ownership, theories, etc. These may be perfect or flawed, desirable or reprehensible, but they exist. Moreover, truth can also manifest itself in them. A true statement articulates a fact that exists independently of the

---

12 Cf: Herbert Schnädelbach: Philosophie. In: Ekkehard Martens, Herbert Schnädelbach (eds.): *Philosophie. Ein Grundkurs*. Volume 1, Rowohlt, Reinbek bei Hamburg 1985, revised and expanded new edition 1991, pp. 37–76.

statement. Facts are "timelessly true, regardless of whether anyone believes [them] to be true."[13]

Admittedly, there is no final certainty as to whether we are not making a mistake. Nevertheless, there is evidence of varying quality. The statement "Carl Peters atones on the moon" is difficult to accept as true. There is simply a lack of evidence. The thesis "Carl Peters did violence to many people in present-day Tanzania", on the other hand, is confirmed by numerous independent sources.

It is also true that human communication is prone to error. Understanding each other correctly is made more difficult by language barriers, cultural imprints and individual chains of association. We all have very different perspectives on events or statements. However, this does not mean that correct understanding is impossible. Is the history of mankind only to be understood as a series of misunderstandings? Does every translation into another language result in a completely new work that does not correspond to the original statement? For Hilary Putnam, this is not convincing.

> That conceptions differ does not prove the impossibility of ever translating anyone 'really correctly' as is sometimes supposed; on the contrary, we could not say that conceptions differ and how they differ if we couldn't translate.[14]

Of course, everything becomes even more complicated when we are not wrestling with descriptive but normative findings. However, this does not mean that values and norms are arbitrary constructs.

Immanuel Kant's ethics was one of the last systems that claimed to have definitively and objectively established the law of morality. After all, Kant believed that he could derive the moral law as a synthetic, practical proposition a priori, i.e. without recourse to cultural experience. To this day, strong arguments can be put forward that this was actually successful. Nevertheless, it is also doubtful whether such pure practical reason, i.e. the ability to realize moral considerations in complete abstraction from personal and cultural influences, is possible. It is no more ultimately justified than any other premise of the major ethical systems. Nevertheless, it does not follow from this that moral demands are equal in principle. It is still possible to distinguish between better and worse arguments. The necessary criteria have long been made explicit.[15]

13　Frege 2003: p. 48.
14　Hilary Putnam: *Reason, Truth and History*. Cambridge University Press, Cambridge 1998. p. 117.
15　Holm Tetens: *Philosophisches Argumentieren*, Verlag C.H. Beck, Munich 2004. p. 23.

"[Norms] should therefore not be based on premises that are known to be only a fraction of those who understand them – such as members of a particular religion or denomination – will accept, comprehend or understand them."[16]

Good arguments are consistent and coherent, i.e. they consist of logical derivations that fit into a system of statements without contradiction. If the following applies: all animals are equal (P1) and pigs are animals (P2), then the thesis "pigs are more equal" is not compatible with P1. The paradox and the political fraud are logically unmistakable. All witches are women (P1), ergo (conclusion) all women are witches. Even primary school children recognize that this is a false reversal. The second premise (P2) is missing, which should state that the set of all women and the set of all witches are identical. Those who call to arms in the name of peace and mercy create an incoherence that requires explanation. Anyone who claims that women, people of color or whatever target group is being discriminated against is not intelligent enough to take responsibility ignores unambiguous findings. Coherent arguments, on the other hand, weave together the largest possible number of aspects, data and positions into a consistent "web of reasoning."[17] Good arguments are intersubjective and intercultural. They can be exchanged and understood among people of very different backgrounds. The commandment not to show one's teeth when laughing can only be reliably understood as appropriate from an internal cultural perspective. Understanding the prohibition of killing as a necessary prerequisite for peaceful coexistence, on the other hand, requires no cultural conditioning. The stigmatization of cruelty, theft, lying and the like can be found in almost all human communities. Anyone who builds their justification on the basis of an argument can hope to be understood even if their counterpart comes from a different cultural context, belongs to a foreign religion or is of a different gender.

We agree that human lives should not be recklessly endangered (P1).
Method A achieves goal X while endangering human life and method B without endangering human life (P2).
Ergo, method B is better than method A (K).

---

16   Dieter Birnbacher: Religion und Religionskritik – eine Einführung. In: *Zeitschrift für Didaktik der Philosophie und Ethik (ZDPE)* 1/2018. pp. 3–8.
17   Cf. Julian Nida-Rümelin: Veritas Filia Temporis. In: Ders: *Humanistische Reflektionen*. Suhrkamp, Frankfurt am Main 2016; Klaus Goergen: Einleitung. In: Dieter Birnbacher, Klaus Goergen, Markus Tiedemann (eds.): *Normative Integration. Kulturkampf im Klassenzimmer und netzgeprägte Schülerschaft*. Schöningh, Paderborn 2021. p. VII.

This argument is intersubjective and interculturally communicable. It is therefore far better than the following example:

A God who does not like dark clouds lives in Mount T (P1).
Dark clouds have gathered today (P2).
The God can be appeased by the death of virgins (P3) Ergo, we must sacrifice a virgin (K).

Although our second example is logically consistent, P1 and P3 lack any intercultural evidence.

Good arguments are reciprocal. Rainer Forst distinguishes between the reciprocity of content and that of reasons. The reciprocity of reasons emphasizes that one's own values and understanding of the world must not be taken for granted. This is therefore once again a demand for intersubjective and intercultural communicability. Reciprocity of content means "that no one may deny his counterpart certain demands that he himself makes."[18] If I want a chain-link fence, I may not deny it to my neighbor. Strictly speaking, anyone who demands freedom of religion cannot sue for freedom of speech, etc.

Good arguments are universally valid. This refers to adherence to principles regardless of the situation. The validity and comprehensibility of a good argument are independent of changing social situations or personal preferences.

We share the conviction that the abuse of people is an evil. (P1)
Slavery is an abuse of human beings (P2)
Ergo, slavery is an evil (K).

This conclusion is universally valid. It is neither tied to a particular era nor to a personal perspective. Its validity is independent of the fact whether current jurisdiction approves of slavery or not. It is equally irrelevant whether I am in the role of a potential slave or a slave owner. Slavery is morally wrong and always has been.

Higher-order ethical arguments make it possible to include the other. This term, borrowed from Jürgen Habermas[19], stands for both consideration and participation. Ideal discourse conditions are not required for this. Active

---

18   Rainer Forst: *Toleranz im Konflikt: Geschichte, Gehalt und Gegenwart eines umstrittenen Begriffs*. Suhrkamp, Frankfurt am Main 2012. p. 171.
19   Cf.: Jürgen Habermas: *Die Einbeziehung des Anderen. Studien zur politischen Theorie.* Suhrkamp, Frankfurt am Main 1996.

participation is not always possible. This applies, for example, to minors or unborn generations. At the same time, the question arises as to what extent these others are at least given the best possible consideration. Furthermore, deliberation must be designed in such a way that the barriers to active participation are as low as possible. If participation is tied to preconditions such as gender or skin color, if the arguments exchanged there require an internal cultural perspective or if there is an exclusionary subtext, the results will be of low ethical quality.

Measured by the inclusion of the other, four qualitative levels can be distinguished. The highest level of ethical legitimization would be a universal morality a priori. A concept that must be understood and recognized by all rational beings. Kant was convinced that he had achieved precisely this. Unfortunately, his evidence is not unassailable. The status of an ultimate justification cannot be attributed to him.

The lowest level of justification can actually only be regarded as moral by hard-core egoists or people with a very optimistic view of human nature. These are actions and decisions that are dominated by our instincts and inclinations. There is no inclusion of the other. Often not even the personal self-image is compatible with the resulting actions.

The second level of the ethical hierarchy is dominated by concepts of the good life, as manifested in cultures, religions and ways of life. As these are generally collective concepts, many people gather here behind common ideas of good and evil. Nevertheless, ethical commitment remains limited to the radius of those who share this concept of the good. Strictly speaking, it is a gathering of equals, not an inclusion of others. There is also no external regulator. From a common internal perspective, a brutal crusade can be justified just as well as humanistic assistance.

The third level stands for a genuine inclusion of the other and thus for the central ethical difference in quality. These are concepts of justice that strive to unite different life plans and ideas of the good life. *Your Pursuit of Happiness – my Pursuit of Happiness*. Thomas Jefferson was well aware that justice must not be derived from individual or collective concepts of the good, but must nevertheless make them possible.[20] A state in which the arbitrariness of the one can be united with the arbitrariness of the other according to a general law of freedom.[21] The inclusion of the other is constitutive for this level.

---

20   Cf.: Thomas Jefferson, *letter to Major John Cartwright dated June 5, 1824*, available online at: http://www.let.rug.nl/usa/presidents/thomas-jefferson/letters-of-thomas-jefferson/jefl278.php [last accessed August 15, 2022].
21   Cf.: Kant: AA VI, p. 230.

Insofar as the highest level of morality, a moral law a priori, remains unattained, it does not follow that the distinction between the other qualitative levels of ethical argumentation is also invalid. A coherent ethics, understood as the consistent inclusion of as much information and perspective as possible[22], is still possible. In particular, the qualitative ascent from purely random preferences via conceptions of the good to conceptions of justice can be illustrated on the basis of the above-mentioned criteria.

In this way, it is also possible to break through the supposed equality of narratives. My great-grandfather was part of the so-called 'Schutztruppe' in the colony of German South West Africa. For the adventurous Müller, this seems to have been an opportunity to escape the stuffy confines of the German Empire. His adventurous descriptions of "wild Africa" became part of the family narrative for generations. It was not until I was a 10th grade student that I learned that my great-grandfather was active in what is now Namibia immediately after the genocide of the Herero and Nama. The survivors of this genocide certainly tell a completely different story about the years 1908 and 1909. As representatives of subjective experience, both stories are equally true in the sense of being real. But there are very good reasons why the accounts of the victims are more important, more relevant and more representative of the real events and deserve to be taken into account. The murder of 40,000 to 60,000 Herero and about 10,000 Nama[23] is both an empirical event and a normative crime that is supported by physical evidence and the most elementary ethical principles. To deny this and speak of equal narratives is evidence of ignorance, loss of reality or malice.

The epistemic and normative hierarchies described above adhere to the premises of the Enlightenment. Objectivity exists and rationality enables people to come close to it.

No one can be forced to recognize the existence of rationality, the existence of facts or the differences in quality between better and worse argumentation. However, there is also no reason to grant such positions equal rights. They are neither well-founded nor do they coincide with our daily life practice. "Outside the philosophical seminar room, everyone becomes a realist again."[24]

---

22   Dietmar von der Pfordten: Moralischer Realismus? Zur kohärentistischen Metaethik Julian Nida-Rümelins. Brill/mentis, Paderborn 2015.
23   See: George Steinmetz: *Von der "Eingeborenenpolitik" zur Vernichtungsstrategie: Deutsch-Südwestafrika, 1904*. In: *Peripherie: Zeitschrift für Politik und Ökonomie in der Dritten Welt*. Vol. 97–98, vol. 25, 2005. p. 195.
24   Julian Nida-Rümelin: *Unaufgeregter Realismus. Eine politische Streitschrift*. Brill/mentis, Paderborn 2015. p. 138.

Therefore, the following applies to both the epistemic and the normative principles of Enlightenment: they are not ultimate, but best justified.

2.3   Freedom: not absolute, but transcendental

Anyone who accepts the possible existence of facts and arguments of a higher order can still deny that the human mind has the freedom to orient itself towards them. This would also jeopardize an important premise of the Enlightenment. What use is it if we can theoretically distinguish between better and worse arguments, but none of this has any effect on our intentions and actions? Where would the dignity of man, so stubbornly defended by the Enlightenment, be if he is a determined thing? Anyone who denies freedom of will turns Kant's "You can, because you should" into "You should, but you cannot".

The attacks on free will are as old as philosophy itself and stem essentially from its scientific self-criticism. Stoics and Epicureans argued in a breathtakingly modern debate about how a cosmos determined by the movement of atoms could leave room for freedom. Schopenhauer and Nietzsche argued that man can do what he wants; but he cannot want what he wants.[25] For Marx, every judgment about the world is shaped by an ideological superstructure, which in turn emerges from the economic substructure, the production processes. Freud saw the human being as a creature controlled by unconscious processes. Neurologists such as Gerhard Roth, Wolfgang Prinz and Wolf Singer believe they can observe the mechanics of will formation. Gerhard Roth came up with the often quoted thesis: "It was not my conscious act of will, but my brain that decided!"[26]

However, many of these objections overlook how modestly the Enlightenment's idea of freedom is conceived, despite all its pathos. Kant wrote what is probably the most important book in the history of philosophy, the *Critique of Pure Reason*, because he primarily wanted to answer one question: Is freedom at least theoretically possible to think without contradiction? If the answer had been negative there would have been no need for further

---

25   Cf.: "You can do what you want: but you can, at any given moment of your life, only want one thing in particular, and nothing else at all but this one thing." Arthur Schopenhauer: *Die beiden Grundprobleme der Ethik*. Joh. Christ. Hermannsche Buchhandlung, Frankfurt am Main 1841. p. 24.
26   Gerhard Roth: Worüber dürfen Hirnforscher reden – und in welcher Weise? In: Christian Geyer (ed.): *Hirnforschung Und Willensfreiheit*. Suhrkamp, Frankfurt am Main 2004. p. 73.

discussion of morality, duty and dignity. Works such as the *Critique of Practical Reason* or the *Metaphysics of Morals* would never have been written. The actual result was as clear as it was modest: Yes, freedom can be thought without contradiction, but only as a possibility, not as a practical certainty or social action. The modesty remained, although Kant was able to show in subsequent writings that the theoretical possibility can also develop practical relevance. Nevertheless, the nature of freedom always remains transcendental. It can be thought of as theoretically and practically possible. However, its factual reality remains unproven and unrefuted simply because reasons have no physical appearance. What we measure, observe or feel are the dispositions that can contribute to the realization of reasons or the actions that are carried out for reasons. The reasons themselves remain intelligible.

The quality of this transcendental idea of freedom had grandiose consequences. They range from criminal law and the separation of powers to human dignity. "The protection of human dignity is based on the idea of man as a spiritual and moral being who is designed to determine and develop himself in freedom."[27] Nevertheless, the scope of potential human freedom has always been assessed very modestly. The "crooked wood" of which man is made offers little reason to hope for an unrestricted rule of reason. In any case, the idea of absolute free will is absurd. An absolutely free will would also have to be free from us. Strictly speaking, it would not be our will. It would be a metaphysical entity that takes possession of us.

> Let's assume that you have unconditional free will. It would be a will that depended on nothing: a completely detached will, free from all causal connections. Such a will would be a ludicrous, abstruse will. Its detachment would mean that it would be independent of your body, your character, your thoughts and feelings, your fantasies and memories. In other words, it would be a will with no connection to anything that makes you a particular person. In a substantial sense of the word, therefore, it would not be your will at all.[28]

Of course, the development of free will is linked to biological and social determinants. You must be conceived, born, nourished, raised and educated in order to develop free will.

---

27 BVerfG, Judgment of the Second Senate of June 30, 2009 – 2 BvE 2/08 -, para. 1–421. para. 364.
28 Peter Bieri: *Das Handwerk der Freiheit. Über die Entdeckung des eigenen Willens*. Fischer, Frankfurt 2003. p. 230.

However, none of this precludes you from rising above anything you may have been conditioned to do throughout the process. It is unlikely and rare, but not impossible. Of course every observed action can be interpreted as an unfree stimulus-response scheme from an external perspective. However, this does not change the fact that we can experience ourselves as free from an internal perspective. This is particularly the case when we decide against our desires and inclinations and in favor of our moral convictions. It remains open, which of the two perspectives can more often be declared as an illusion. Of course, we are subject to immanent influences. Nevertheless, evolution has created an organ in our brain that is capable of astonishing linguistic abstractions. "What would it be like if everyone acted like you?" Even very young children understand this question. The invitation to adopt the perspective of a neutral observer, to calculate a utilitarian calculation of happiness or to consider the validity of a moral law a priori are further steps on this ladder of abstraction. Of course they are demanding, but they are obviously possible. The abstractions our brain is capable of are revealed in such simple expressions as 'indifferent' or 'blasé'. Let's suppose we were completely determined so that there would always be a dominant, inclination-driven impulse. How do these terms come about then? However, if these terms describe a balance of determinants and people still make decisions, it is reasonable to conclude that our neural system is able to take a bird's eye view of its own motives.

Of course, activities in our brain can be measured before we make a decision. The famous Libet experiment is regarded by many neurologists as the ultimate refutation of free will. In fact, the neuronal readiness for a movement can be measured in the motor center of the brain on average 50 ms before the conscious decision to execute the movement. However, for Libet himself this by no means disproved free will. Several subsequent experiments confirmed his assumption that although neuronal structures cause a predisposition, consciousness has a kind of veto or control function.[29] There is even a time window of approx. 100 ms for correcting actions that have already been initiated.[30] These findings fit well with several philosophical theories. Harry G. Frankfurter

---

29 Benjamin Libet: Unconscious cerebral initiative and the role of conscious will in voluntary action. In: *The Behavioral and Brain Sciences*, 8, 1985. pp. 529–566.
30 Matthias Schultze-Kraft, Daniel Birman, Marco Rusconi, Carsten Allefeld, Kai Görgen, Sven Dähne, Benjamin Blankertz, John-Dylan Haynes: Point of no return in vetoing movements. In: William T. Newsome (ed.): *Proceedings of the National Academy of Sciences of the United States of America*, 113(4), 2016. pp. 1080–1085.

distinguishes between first- and second-level desires.[31] First-level volitions are the unfree desire to satisfy our inclinations or drives. Second-level volitions represent a principled desire and enable a normative assessment of first-level desires. For example, we may feel a strong impulse to act violently. At the same time, it is possible to condemn this urge and force ourselves to renounce it. In this case, there would be a second-order desire to be a civilized person. Of course, such concepts do not fall from the sky. A minimum degree of rationality is indispensable in order to be able to abstract from first-order inclinations. The mere insight into the ethical goodness of non-violence is not enough either. Only a naïve Platonist assumed that knowledge of the good automatically entails good behavior. According to Aristotle, it takes a long period of training to make something that has been recognized as a desirable part of one's own character. Peter Bieri speaks of a *craft of freedom* that involves shaping one's own second-order will. According to Frankfurter, a person possesses a will precisely when they have second-order values and want them to guide their actions. Measurable brain activity prior to conscious acts of will is therefore neither surprising nor incompatible with the assumption of freedom. Of course, brain activity is a necessary prerequisite for both conscious and unconscious decisions. The brain-dead have no will. Human decisions are not made by a free-floating spirit being. They require a functioning neuronal network. However, the provision of an activity is not identical with the decision to carry it out. Determination only exists if the provision also prescribes the content of the decision without any alternative. This is precisely what has not yet been proven by any experiment and, according to authors such as Brigitte Falkenburg or Peter Roth, will never be proven.[32] Brain screening, hormone levels and psychoanalysis allow astonishingly reliable predictions. For example, it is possible to prove that due to a lack of intelligence, an excess of aggression or a lack of imagination, someone is only capable of limited judgment and guilt. However, this only shows that this person has no or only limited freedom of will. The possibility that other people are certainly in control of their own decisions has not been eliminated. Let's do a quick thought experiment: you are shipwrecked and two islands are exactly the same distance away from you. A hungry lion is pacing up and down the beach on the first island. On the second beach there is a hungry man with a club. The majority of us would swim

---

31 Harry G. Frankfurt (1971): Freedom of the Will and the Concept of a Person. In: *Journal of Philosophy* 68. pp. 5–20.
32 Cf. inter alia: Peter Rohs: Geist und Gegenwart. Entwurf einer analytischen Transzendentalphilosophie. Brill/mentis, Paderborn 2016. p. 159–160; Brigitte Falkenburg: Mythos Determinismus: Wieviel erklärt uns die Hirnforschung? Springer, Berlin 2012.

to the human. The chance of being spared there is very small, but it exists. A human can choose to starve next to you, a lion cannot.

Another aspect should be particularly emphasized. The Enlightenment's understanding of freedom focuses on decisions made for moral reasons. Strictly speaking, freedom can only become a reality through submission to a self-imposed moral duty. The Enlightenment never denied that our drives, instincts and inclinations are unfree. What we desire, our first-order preferences, are determined by a complex biological, physical and social network. The freedom thesis merely states that we have the potential to behave normatively to these conditionings. In the Libet experiment, test subjects are asked to raise or rest a finger. There are no ethical criteria for evaluating these options; they have no moral relevance. There can therefore be no decision based on (moral) reasons and it is not surprising that a completely determined process is observed.

The assumption of free will would only become obsolete if neurologists were able to observe how the brain carries out an ethical deliberation without the person being aware of it. This would require showing, for example, how the brain decides in favor of a utilitarian benefit calculation and against a deontological moral law without the person being aware of the corresponding considerations. At present, such proof seems inconceivable.[33]

So there are good reasons to hold on to a modest concept of transcendental freedom. Man's first nature is animalistic and unfree. However, people are able to relate to their own nature and cultivate their second nature. It is precisely this process that describes and confirms the condition of the possibility of freedom.

2.4 Ethical universalism: European, but not Eurocentric

Eurocentrism, understood as the culturally chauvinistic dominance of the so-called West, is an evil. It has laid the ideological groundwork for the perpetration of colonialism and continues to blind us to a fair global economy or the appreciation of otherness and cultural diversity.

Allegedly, the ethical universalism of the Enlightenment is the main reason for this tradition. In fact, the cultural tolerance of the Enlightenment is limited. Human rights, equal rights, republicanism or the separation of powers are not understood as possible alternatives, but as the dictates of a general practical

---

33 Christian Geyer (ed.): *Hirnforschung und Willensfreiheit. Zur Deutung der neuesten Experimente*. Suhrkamp, Frankfurt am Main 2004.

reason. Patriarchies, class societies or hereditary monarchies are seen as objectively in need of reform. It does not matter in which parts of the world they are located. So does one culture want to dominate all others?

No! As long as we hold on to the premise that objective facts and arguments of a higher order exist and that human reason is capable of recognizing them, the answer is: no and no again! The essence of Enlightenment is to overcome cultural imprints through reason and self-criticism and to strive for a universally valid justification. As seen above, there are far better arguments for adhering to this premise than abandoning it. Admittedly, there is the threat of a circle. The cat bites its own tail. After all, the idea that there should be criteria-based justifications at all comes from the rational paradigm of the Enlightenment itself. This is precisely why there can be no ultimate justification.

Nevertheless, there is no reason to understand Enlightenment and reason as an "eurocentric machination of a post-colonialist system of oppression".[34] At least the following four objections seem appropriate: first, it is hard to see why classic authors of postcolonialism such as Charles W. Mills or Achille Mbembe must be read as accusers of ethical universalism. If one reads, for example, *Black Rights/White Wrongs*[35] or the *Critique of Black Reason*[36], the following core statements can be formulated: the power of ethical universalism has not been able to prevent the colonialism of an economically truncated liberalism. Collective experiences of degradation continue to have an impact and are difficult or impossible to comprehend from an external perspective. Capitalist processes of exploitation persist, whereby the category of "race" can increasingly be understood as "class". The injustices described can only be overcome through a new global humanism.

With the exception of the equation of "race" and "class", these statements can be agreed with in their entirety. However, any humanism, whether old or new, cannot be realized without Enlightenment and without rationality and ethical universalism.

Secondly, a claim that only Europeans are rational would be both racist and implausible. It is precisely this figure that has made racism, apartheid and delusions of superiority possible in the first place. Anyone who seriously claims that people from non-white cultures do not have the same rational capacity has not understood that they are stumbling over the dialectic of their alleged

---

[34] The wording comes from a flyer calling for a demonstration against human rights in the canteen of Freie Universität Berlin in 2014.
[35] Charles W. Mills: *Black Rights/White Wrongs: The Critique of Racial Liberalism*. Oxford University Press, Oxford 2017.
[36] Achille Mbembe: *Kritik der schwarzen Vernunft*. Suhrkamp, Berlin 2013.

tolerance. Furthermore, such a statement is simply empirically false. Rational analysis, the exchange of reasons or the expectation of justification are not uniquely European phenomena. If a person X has promised to build a wall of four meters, but stops work after two meters, then justification is expected around the globe. This can be of a different nature: "Look, I have used all the bricks. It was objectively impossible to continue!", "The work is so difficult that it would be unfair to let me continue without help!", "The green spaghetti monster has appeared to me. It demands that I pull out a molar at the next full moon. Only then can the work continue." Some of these justifications can be understood by all people, others only from the internal perspective of a culture. Some of them may not be understood by anyone. The decisive factor is something else: the giving and taking of reasons is an anthropological constant. It is the very condition of the possibility of human community. Moreover, we are all familiar with the compelling power of logical conclusions. X has been stabbed in the back. Y was demonstrably the only person in contact with X for days. At all times, in all cultures and religious communities, Y will be suspected. Arithmetic, playing chess, elementary logic: all of these have been developed in various places on earth and can be mastered by any averagely gifted member of humanity. Furthermore, they are based on fundamental structures that are constitutive for the thinking of the human species. In other words:

In the tradition of Gottlob Frege, a distinction is made between ideas and thoughts. Ideas are products of individual consciousness and cannot be reliably reproduced by others. My conception of a novel heroine will always differ from yours. Thoughts, on the other hand, are the manifestations of identical insights that can be produced by different subjects at different times and in different places. Examples would be the functions of the wheel, arithmetic or criteria for fair sharing. However, if thoughts in Frege's sense exist, then there is also the possibility of inter-subjective and intercultural understanding.

Thirdly, a distinction must be made between the genesis and the validity of ethical universalism. These are two completely different categories. Yes, the Enlightenment developed primarily in Europe. However, this does not mean that the insights gained lost their validity beyond Gibraltar. Numerous authors from Aristotle to Leibniz to Reichenbach have sufficiently demonstrated that the local and methodological genesis of an insight must be distinguished from its claim to validity. The "context of discovery" may have been chaotic, local or accidental. The decisive factor for the claim to truth remains the "Context of justification". Wilhelm Conrad Röntgen discovered the x-rays named after him through a chance observation. The same applies to Alexander Flemming and the development of penicillin. However, the circumstances of the discovery are merely amusing anecdotes. What is crucial for epistemic relevance is that the processes were understood, analyzed and explained. A current example: the CRISPR/Cas method (*Clustered Regularly Interspaced Short Palindromic Repeats*) will change all our lives. Suppose Emmanuelle Charpentier and Jennifer Doudna had not developed this method in meticulous basic research in Berlin and California but had discovered it by chance and in a drunken state in the laboratory of a Chinese colleague in Beijing. What difference would that make? Would the results be unusable under these conditions? When assessing the technical feasibility and the normative implications, it is not the context of discovery that is decisive, but the rational context of justification. Moreover, nobody would think of claiming that the use of CRISPR is only possible in Berlin, California or Beijing.

It has to be admitted that normative claims such as human rights are different from scientific processes. Nevertheless, genesis a priori has no effect on the scope of application. However, if we argue posteriori, we should also take a closer look. Human rights are a good example of this. First of all, human rights also have non-European roots. The Cyrus Cylinder, the oldest proclamation of human rights ideas known to us, is known to have originated in Babylon.[37] The Golden Rule, the basic idea of fairness and reciprocity, can be found in almost all languages and human cultures.[38] Subsequently, the adjective "European" or "white" is a truly rough generalization. We can thank the Stoic school of philosophy for the first discussions about universal human rights. At this time around 300 BC., there was no European identity, and the reality of a Germanic man's life was just as far removed from that of the Greeks as that of most other inhabitants of the earth. The mentality of an Egyptian or a woman from Babylon was probably even closer to that of the Attic philosophers than that of our Germanic people. According to the logic presented above, human rights would therefore only be Greek, no, actually only Athenian.

When, almost 2000 years later, the Enlightenment thinkers of the modern age began to argue for universal and egalitarian human rights, they faced a powerful opponent: organized Christianity. It should not be forgotten that human rights were fought for against and not by the churches. Pope Pius VI officially condemned the Declaration of the Rights of Man and of the Citizen of 1789 because of its incompatibility with the Christian doctrine of natural law. Bishops were demonstratively withdrawn from France. However, it

---

37 Rykle Borger: Der Kyros-Zylinder. In: Otto Kaiser (ed.): *Texte aus der Umwelt des Alten Testaments*. Volume 1: *Alte Folge*. Gütersloher Verlagshaus, Gütersloh 1985. pp. 407–410.

38 Heinz-Horst Schrey, Hans-Ulrich Hoche: Regel, goldene. In: Joachim Ritter, Karlfried Gründer (eds.): *Historisches Wörterbuch der Philosophie*. Volume 8, Schwabe & Co, Basel 1992. pp. 450–464.

can hardly be doubted that Christianity is one of the most formative components of European identity. According to the logic presented above, the Enlightenment and human rights would therefore have been anti-European. Incidentally, the conflict persists: to this day, the Vatican has not signed the United Nations Charter of Human Rights. An obvious diagnosis would be that European identity contains a good deal of schizophrenia. Equally obvious is the conclusion that a distinction must be made between local genesis and universal aspirations. The genesis of the Enlightenment is primarily European. Its principles are not.

Fourthly, the normative principles of the Enlightenment are not a threat, but the only effective protection of cultural diversity. Once again:

It is undisputed that the worst atrocities and evils were committed and spread under the guise of Enlightenment and human rights. Exploitative structures of all kinds, decadence, destruction of natural resources: the list is long. However, this is a shameless disguise and not human rights themselves. If a trickster has posed as a policeman, it is still wrong to send the real police away.

The ethical universalism of Enlightenment is the only reliable instrument to castigate the above-mentioned evils. The statement that everything is culturally relative and that everyone should do what they want is tantamount to absolution for oppression and cruelty. The demand for universal human rights, self-determination and freedom, on the other hand, creates a compulsion to justify oneself. This demand has always been particularly inconvenient for oppressors. It is therefore hardly surprising that the values of the Enlightenment played an important role in the process of de-colonization.[39]

Furthermore, authors such as John Rawls and Otfried Höffe have convincingly argued that human rights are not only understood interculturally, but are also wanted interculturally.

We have John Rawls to thank for one of the most famous thought experiments in the history of ideas, the *Veil of Ignorance*.[40] Let us assume that we are all born again tomorrow. We know nothing about our future identity. We can be old or young, healthy or ill, clever or in need of support, female or male. Nor do we know anything about our social status, income opportunities or anything else. However, we now have the opportunity to define the rules of future society. According to Rawls, every participant in this thought experiment is

---

39 Steven Jensen: *The Making of International Human Rights: The 1960s, Decolonization, and the Reconstruction of Global Values*, Cambridge University Press, Cambridge 2016. p. 334 ff.
40 John Rawls: *A Theory of Justice*. Harvard University Press, Cambridge 1971. p. 118 ff.

forced to abstract from their concrete conception of the good. Perhaps I have not yet questioned the rules of my racist and misogynistic society. But can I also wish these rules for the world of tomorrow if the option exists that I will be reborn as a black woman? Perhaps I have enjoyed my privilege as a millionaire heir so far without question. But will I also be against an inheritance tax tomorrow if there is a possibility that I will be dependent on state social benefits? If the rules for the future society are decided collectively, a rule-free discourse community will emerge.

Out of strategic self-interest alone, everyone is interested in all opinions, perspectives and information. Idealistically speaking, the *Veil of Ignorance* gives rise to intelligent personalities in Kant's sense and a legislation of "pure practical reason".[41] A somewhat more sober diagnosis could be made of a necessarily enlightened self-interest.[42]

Two aspects are particularly important for our context. Firstly, if all people from all cultures on earth can understand and carry out the thought experiment, then rational abstraction is not a European specificity, even in questions of ethics, but an anthropological constant. Secondly, the rules decided behind the veil of ignorance describe universal justice. According to Rawls, people behind the *Veil of Ignorance* are the first to decide on an equal right for everyone to the most comprehensive system of equal basic freedoms that is compatible with the same system for all others.[43] According to Rawls, this principle of freedom includes above all the inviolability of the person, protection against arbitrariness, the right to political participation as well as freedom of speech, thought, conscience and assembly. In short: the participants in the thought experiment represent the principles of the Enlightenment. They decide on human rights.

Ottfried Höffe builds his defense of ethical universalism and human rights on an anthropological minimalism. Regardless of how different our individual life plans may be, we can agree that we are all bodily, rational, social and political beings. Taking into account the resulting basic needs does not yet result in a specific concept of the good life. Rather, it is a question of the necessary conditions for the possibility of a desirable life in general.

---

41   Kant: AA V, p. 33.
42   Stefan Gosepath: *Aufgeklärtes Eigeninteresse – Eine Theorie theoretischer und praktischer Rationalität*. Suhrkamp, Frankfurt am Main 1992.
43   "Each person is to have an equal right to the most extensive total system of equal basic liberties compatible with a similar system of liberty for all", Rawls 1971. p. 266.

"What is to be addressed as transcendental is what one already implicitly affirms, insofar as one always wants when one wants something; transcendental means the condition for being able to have and pursue ordinary interests at all."[44]

In order to be able to practice your own ideas of a successful life, you need the ability to act. However, agency is only possible if the basic needs mentioned above are protected. Anyone who agrees to this and at the same time is prepared to accept a minimum of reciprocity comes to the conclusion that people should promise each other the integrity of their basic needs. Höffe speaks of a transcendental exchange. Human rights are just that.

In other words: in order to be self-determined, to be able to practice one's own culture or one's own idea of a successful life, we need the ability to act. Disregarding our basic physical, social, rational and political needs destroys this ability to act. Human rights protect basic needs. Ergo, they protect our ability to act. Ergo: anyone who wants to be different wants ethical universalism, wants human rights.

It is important to understand "that there is only one alternative to tribalism: universalism."[45]

2.5   Racism: despite, not through, Enlightenment

The matter is actually quite simple. Enlightenment demands critical thinking and requires us to accept only what meets scientific standards. Racism as a normative concept is an ideology without any scientific legitimacy. Enlightenment is therefore not a cause of racism, but its most effective prevention. Moreover, Enlightenment should not be understood as a synonym for all phenomena of the modern era (see chapter 3.1). The Enlightenment's thirst for knowledge acted as a catalyst for moral and legal liberation movements, as well as for technical innovations. The latter also prepared the ground for European expansion and the oppression of other peoples. Enlightenment, however, is neither identical with these phenomena nor responsible for their encroachments. The same applies to the unpleasant fact that the history of science is full of examples of misguided reason and ideological aberrations. This view is

---

44   Cf.: Otfried Höffe: Menschenrechte. In: Ders. (ed.), *Vernunft und Recht. Bausteine zu einem interkulturellen Rechtsdiskurs.* Suhrkamp, Berlin 1996. p. 77.

45   Susan Neiman: Widerstand der Vernunft. Ein Manifest in postfaktischen Zeiten. Ecowin, Salzburg 2017. p. 57.

not relativized by the fact that numerous representatives of the Enlightenment made racist statements. A curative medicine does not become bad because its inventors were ill themselves.

In 2020, a debate broke out in Germany about whether the monuments to Immanuel Kant should be dismantled. The background to this was an increased sensitivity to racist traditions and structures based on American models. Together with many other incidents, the disturbing police violence against George Floyd had once again highlighted how deeply rooted racism is even in societies that are supposedly organized according to Enlightenment principles. The horror heightened awareness of representation in the public sphere. Indeed, heroic depictions of slave traders or southern generals in American squares are just as difficult to understand as Wehrmacht generals giving names to German army barracks. Dismantling or conversion is called for. However, any reform of the public space requires differentiation, criticism and self-criticism. Claus Philipp Maria Schenk Graf von Stauffenberg was a Wehrmacht general and a passionate nationalist[46], but he was also the Hitler assassin of July 20, 1944. Thomas Jefferson was a slave owner, but also the author of the Declaration of Independence, which, in Jefferson's own opinion, exposed slavery as an evil. Anyone who sees no reason for differentiation here is caught up in an iconoclasm that is fed by those dull motives that should actually be overcome.

A debate on racism has also flared up around Immanuel Kant, the icon of the Enlightenment.[47] Therefore, this case is particularly suitable for promoting a differentiated view of the problem.

Three questions need to be clarified: 1. Are parts of Kant's writings to be considered racist? 2. Is Kant as a person and Kantian philosophy as a whole to be regarded as racist? 3. What consequences should be drawn for the preservation of monuments or the shaping of the educational canon?

Let's start with the first set of questions.

The transcripts of Kant's lecture on anthropology are a particularly unpleasant find:

> Humanity is at its greatest perfection in the white race. The yellow Indians have a lesser talent. The Negroes are far lower, and the lowest are a part of the American peoples.[48]

---

46 Wolfgang Venohr: *Stauffenberg: Symbol of resistance*. 3rd edition. Herbig, Munich 2000. p. 278.
47 See: https://www.bbaw.de/mediathek/archiv-2020/kant-ein-rassist-interdisziplinaere-discussion series [last accessed 15.08.2022].
48 Kant: AA IX, p. 312.

If that is not racism, what is? All attempts to defend or relativize are based on feet of clay.

It could be argued that Kant did not claim to present reliable findings in his anthropological explanations, but merely summarized the state of research at the time. In fact, the students were taught all kinds of bizarre absurdities:

"Negroes are born white except for their reproductive organs and a ring around the navel, which are black. From these parts the blackness extends over the whole body in the first month."[49] In addition, many of the statements originate from a lecture given in 1772 and are therefore dated nine years before the first edition of the *Critique of Pure Reason* and the beginning of critical philosophy. The lecture was not published in printed form until 1802 by Friedrich Theodor Rink on the basis of notes and transcripts. Kant died almost two years later and did not publish or edit any more at this point. As early as 1801, Ehregott Andreas Christoph Wasianski had been entrusted with the administration and clearing out of Kant's study.

Unfortunately, these objections are only partially convincing. Kant not only authorized the printing of his alleged quotations, but he also refrained from commenting or clarifying them. Moreover, better documented early works such as *Von den verschiedenen Rassen der Menschen* from 1775 or *Beobachtungen über das Gefühl des Schönen und Erhabenen* from 1764 speak a similar language. In the latter, black Africans are denied any "feeling that rises above the trivial".[50] There is therefore no reason to speak of an isolated intellectual escapade. In 1785, when the Critique of Pure Reason had already been published for four years, Kant served the prestigious Berlinische Monatsschrift with another treatise on human races.[51] The assertion that the beginning of transcendental philosophy immediately put an end to all racist terminology unfortunately does not correspond to the sources. In 1788, not only the *Critique of Practical Reason* was published, but also the essay "On the Use of Teleological Principles in Philosophy", in which the indigenous peoples of America are classified as incapable of any "culture". It is of little help when Kant also explains the biological connection between disposition, isolation and adaptation and, in an astonishing way, anticipates many aspects of the Darwinian doctrine. In these passages, the concept of *race* corresponds to a scientific description of phenotypes and Kant adds that "people do not merely belong to one and the

---

49   Ibid.
50   Kant: AA II, p. 253.
51   Kant: Bestimmung des Begriffs einer Menschenrace. In: *Berlinische Monatsschrift* 06 (November 1785). pp. 390–417.

same species, but also to one family."⁵² However, this does not solve the problem of racism. Anyone who agrees with the premise of common descent and a common telos can still proclaim different values for individuals and groups. Even if a republican family of nations is assumed as the goal of history, this does not necessarily mean that all current human phenomena and forms of life are of equal value. If the different progressions are not defined as cultural or historical epochs, but as an expression of the spiritual and mental abilities of the respective population, racist patterns emerge. The incapacity for culture is attributed to a geographically and phenotypically defined group of people as a collective characteristic. This is exactly what is called racism.

Arguments that excuse Kant as a child of his time are also of little persuasive force. Of course, Kant was a contemporary of James Cook. Appreciative exploration of other peoples and cultures was in short supply. Humboldt did not return to Europe until the year of Kant's death. Heinrich Barth was not born until 17 years later. Even in the port city of Königsberg, Kant could never have met a person with dark skin.

So what? More can certainly be expected from an intellectual titan like Kant. He could have known and taught better. Unscientific reports can be debunked even if they cannot be compared with personal experience. In addition, alternative interpretations were available, alternative points of view were accessible. Rousseau, whose portrait was the only one to hang in Kant's study, is known to have drawn a perhaps naïve but positive picture of the 'noble savage' and did not cultivate any racist distinctions ("The savage lives in himself, the civilized man, always outside himself, lives only in the opinion of others, and it is, to put it thus, exclusively their judgment from which he draws the feeling for his own existence").⁵³ Christian Wolff, whom Kant revered as "the great wolf", had already caused a scandal in 1721 with his *Speech on the practical philosophy of the Chinese*⁵⁴ at the University of Halle. Central to this was the assertion that Chinese society, although pagan, was at least on a par with Christian Europe. Kant could also have heard and perhaps read Anton Wilhelm Amo. Amo was born in 1700 in what is now Ghana and taught as a philosopher of the Enlightenment at the universities of Halle, Wittenberg and

---

52   Kant: AA II, p. 430.
53   "[L]e sauvage vit en lui-même; l'homme sociable, toujours hors de lui, ne sait vivre que dans l'opinion des autres, et c'est, pour ainsi dire, de leur seul jugement qu'il tire le senti- ment de sa propre existence", Jean-Jaques Rousseau: Discours sur l'origine et les fonde- mens de l'inegalité parmi les hommes. 1755. p. 181.
54   Cf. Christian Wolff, Michael Albrecht (transl.): Oratio de sinarum philosophia practica – Rede über die praktische Philosophie der Chinesen. Meiner Verlag, Hamburg 1985.

Jena. At the University of Halle in 1729 he presented his polemic on the *legal status of Moors in Europe*[55]. Yes, Kant should have known better.

However, this does not answer the second question. Should Kant as a person and Kantian philosophy as a whole be regarded as racist? At least two aspects deserve consideration: the first is the need for contextualization. The concept of racism was probably unknown to Kant, and the classification of human species could not be linked to the horrors of the twentieth century. In addition, microanalysis of the writings shows that Kant repeatedly relativizes the truth claims of his problematic statements and emphasizes that only a "tolerable correctness can be demanded" for them.[56] The impression of stereotypical prejudices regarding all representatives of a phenotype is also disturbed. This happens, for example, when Kant describes the First Nations of Canada as Spartans of the New World with a "sublime character of mind."[57]

The second aspect is much more serious and concerns the nature and systematics of Kant's work as a whole.

It should be noted at the outset that Kant's philosophical cosmos revolves around the possibility and meaning of synthetic propositions a priori. Experiential sciences such as ethology or biology, on the other hand, present observations and conclusions a posteriori, which, according to Kant's understanding, must always be falsified and verified. It is also particularly important that the concept of "race" is without any systematic function for Kant's main work. According to Eisler's Kant lexicon, this term is not used once in the three major critiques. However, something else is even more important:

Why do we condemn discrimination, abuse and humiliation of people today? Because people have dignity and not a price.[58]

Every being that is able to distinguish between being and ought by virtue of its reason is the bearer of a potential but absolute freedom to do good. As *causa noumenon*, man is able to rise above the determination of his instincts as well as his imprints and prejudices and to recognize and obey what is morally imperative. This dignity must be respected under all circumstances, which is why it remains categorically forbidden to abuse a person as a mere means to an end. "Act in such a way that you use humanity both in your person and in the person of every other person at all times as an end, never merely as a means."[59]

---

55   This manuscript is considered lost. A contemporary reference to its content can be found in: Wöchentliche Hallische Frage- und Anzeigungs-Nachrichten. November 28, 1729. pp. 271–274.
56   Kant AA II, p. 244.
57   Kant AA II, p. 252.
58   Kant AA IV, pp. 434–441.
59   Kant: AA IV, p. 429.

The last paragraph may sound pathetic, but this derivation forms the most coherent bulwark against racism and oppression of all – and it comes from Immanuel Kant. It is not a matter of beliefs, but of a system that has been rigorously scientifically developed over decades. The inane and racist statements from various small writings are therefore in stark contrast to this categorical defense of human dignity that Kant develops in his major works.

In his important treatise *Kant's Untermenschen*, Charles W. Mills argues that Kant had only regarded whites as persons, which is why the protection of human dignity did not apply to other "races".[60] Alice Hasters was able to add: "Kant's idea of man, who could only reach perfection through knowledge, functioned through demarcation. The whites were clever because the blacks were not. [...] In my opinion, this does not sound so much like philanthropy, peace and progress."[61]

However, Kant's main work does not contain a single corresponding formulation. Rather, moral categories such as dignity, responsibility, civil and world civil rights are explicitly attributed to the whole of humanity as a "species of rational earth beings."[62] Recognizing this is a requirement of analytical and hermeneutical fairness.

> Now I say: man, and every rational being in general, exists as an end in itself, not merely as a means for arbitrary use for this or that will, but must at all times be regarded as an end in all his actions directed both towards himself and towards other rational beings.[63]

At this point, the question of Kant's personal convictions can also be taken into consideration. The consequences that Kant drew from his major works shaped the moral and political demands of his late writings. It is hard to imagine that personal racist prejudices were spared from this rigorism.

However, a blanket absolution cannot and should not be granted. Kant has too often written intolerable and dangerous nonsense. Just think of his assessments of homosexuality.[64] Even racist gradations have not immediately disappeared through ethical universalism. Someone who grants dignity to all people can nevertheless diagnose gradations in talents and virtues. With regard to

---

60 Charles W. Mills: Kant's Untermenschen. In: *Race and Racism in Modern Philosophy*. 2001. pp. 169–193.
61 Alice Hasters: *Was weisse Menschen nicht über Rassismus hören wollen aber Wissen sollten*. hanserblau, Munich 2020. p. 55.
62 Kant: AA VII, p. 331.
63 Kant: AA IV, p. 428.
64 Kant: AA VI, p. 333.

individual character traits, this is an unproblematic determination of realities. However, if group-specific characteristics are constructed, the biological racism that has just been suppressed creeps back in through the back door as cultural chauvinism. However, a rigorous universalism of the Kantian variety leaves little scope for this. All members of the human species have dignity, not a price. Since dignity cannot be measured or weighed up, all gradations of human value are also invalid. Racism, understood as the normative hierarchization of people on the basis of their real or constructed membership of a group, is incompatible with a consistent ethical universalism of Kantian character. The strength of this insight is not relativized by the fact that Kant himself repeatedly fell short of his own theory.

According to Pauline Kleingeld, there was an obvious inconsistency between Kant's ethical universalism and his personal prejudices. Nevertheless, the rigor of ethical universalism gradually gained the victory.[65] Kant continued to use the term "race", as did most of his contemporaries. However, a normative hierarchy can no longer be found from 1790 onwards. In the late treatise *Anthropologie in pragmatischer Hinsicht* from 1798, a work of over 200 pages, only one brief page on races can be found. It states that groups and races are not becoming more and more similar to each other, but that nature has "enough stock in itself"[66] to create ever new individuals. However, both in the preface and in the longer treatise on the species, Kant emphasizes that the whole of humanity is to be understood "as an animal endowed with reason (*animal rationabile*)"[67] with technical, cooperative and moral abilities.

In 1795, nine years before Kant's death, his treatise *On Perpetual Peace* was published. There is nothing more to be read here about deficient races. Rather, Kant formulates harsh criticism of exploitation and colonialism and advocates a republican right to self-determination for all peoples as well as a right of world citizenship.[68] He speaks of a "society of people over whom no one other than himself has the right to command and dispose".[69]

Many a colonialist has tried to evade this ethical universalism with pseudoscientific racial theories, for example by declaring Africans to be unreasonable. Many an inane quote may have helped Kant in this. However, the late Kant leaves no doubt about the inadmissibility of such considerations. This applies

---

65 Kleingeld, Pauline (2007): Kant's Second Thought on Race. In: *The Philosophical Quarterly*, Vol. 57, Issue 229. pp. 573–592.
66 Kant: AA VII, p. 321.
67 Ibid.
68 Cf.: Kant: AA VIII, p. 360.
69 Kant: AA VIII, p. 344.

to racist categorization as well as to exploitation or pseudo-paternalistic dictation.

> I confess that I am not at ease with the expression which even clever men use: a certain people (which is in the process of working out a legal freedom) is not yet ripe for freedom; a landowner's own body is not yet ripe for freedom; and so too, people in general are not yet ripe for freedom of faith. According to such a presupposition, however, freedom will never occur; for one cannot mature to it if one has not first been placed in freedom (one must be free in order to be able to use one's powers in freedom appropriately).[70]

The systematics of his complete works has not only cured Kant himself, it is perhaps the most coherent derivation of ethical universalism. It is a doctrine that has stuck. Culturally sensitive anthropologists such as Alexander von Humboldt and Heinrich Barth referred to Kant simply as "the great spirit"[71] and clearly used Kantian criteria in their judgments on slavery and colonialism.

To describe Kant's philosophical system as racist therefore lacks any coherent justification. On the contrary, there is much to suggest that we can dare to speak of an indispensable basis for anti-racism.

About the third question: What consequences can be drawn for curricula or monument preservation?

Heroizations and idealizations are inappropriate and rarely have a positive effect. In any case, they contradict the Enlightenment appeal for critical thinking, of which Kant himself was the most passionate advocate. There are all kinds of bizarre anecdotes about the historical Kant that may be forgotten. One of these anecdotes, for example, is the belief that you can get rid of moths by not airing the room. The memory that one of the intellectual forefathers of the Enlightenment, ethical universalism, human rights and international law had racist prejudices, on the other hand, must be kept alive. The same applies to the insight that he was able to reduce this dangerous nonsensical power of his mind. It is therefore important to expand the knowledge of Kant without discrediting his achievements. However, removing him from the philosophical canon would be fatal. A curative medicine remains valuable even if its inventor initially fell ill himself. Whoever wants to judge Kant as a person may do so. His personal rejection of racist prejudices remains disappointing in its tenacious protractedness. But it was ultimately successful. Yes, Kant was a racist, but he did not remain one.

---

70   Kant: AA VI, p. 188.
71   Cf.: Eberhard Knobloch: Naturgenuss und Weltgemälde. Gedanken zu Humboldts Kosmos. In: *Internationale Zeitschrift für Humboldtstudien* 5, 09. 2004. pp. 30–43.

Those for whom this is not enough and who therefore demand the dismantling of Kant memorials should also reject memorials in honor of Hans and Sophie Scholl. After all, both were ardent supporters of National Socialism before their heroic commitment to the White Rose. It was their experiences with the totalitarian world, war and war crimes, as well as their studies in philosophy, that brought about a rethink.

If all this is taken into account, monuments to Kant are suitable as a representative of ethical universalism and less as an object than as a rallying point for anti-racist demonstrations. They are a reminder of the creator of one of the most important justifications of universal human rights and of an old white man who, by virtue of his intellect, was able to overcome unscientific and immoral prejudices. A memorial to Anton Wilhelm Amo could be erected right next to it.[72] He would certainly have felt very much at home in the company of the late Kant.

Their common message is: "Racism can be cured!".

2.6 Alternatives: possible, but inhumane

As already made clear, the Enlightenment advocates critical realism. Facts exist. There are things in themselves. Only our perception, the categories of our thinking and the structures of our language can lead to manifold distortions and interpretations. Self-criticism is necessary. Nevertheless, facts are difficult to discover and even more difficult to prove. But they do exist.

Constructivism, postmodernism and cultural relativism emerged from the self-criticism of the Enlightenment and are developing an astonishing dynamic. These are ideas that have emerged from the philosophical thought laboratory and, due to their exoticism, have achieved an attraction and spread that, on sober reflection, they do not deserve. According to these theories, no facts exist; everything is merely the result of an individual or collective construction. There are also no objective standards for more or less objectivity. Everything is only relative to an arbitrarily set reference system. Scientific orientation is just as arbitrary a meta-narrative as religion. Cultures can only be evaluated according to their own standards and criteria. They cannot and must not be compared.

---

[72] In Berlin, the "Mohrengasse" was renamed after Amo. Incidentally, the former owes its name to the black musicians that the "Soldier King" Frederick I settled there. So Kant would only have had to leave Königsberg to have real encounters with black contemporaries.

At first glance, the illusion of exemplary tolerance and full acceptance of others is created. This may also be the reason why these concepts have become so stubbornly entrenched in left-wing intellectual circles. Unfortunately, it usually goes unnoticed that this opens the door to post-factuality, identity mania, culture wars and an absurd understanding of tolerance. As shown above, the premises of the Enlightenment are not self-evident. Alternative interpretations are certainly possible. Those who speak out in favor of constructivism, postmodernism and cultural relativism should, however, realize that their effects are toxic for democratic rule of law, peace and tolerance.[73]

Let's start with the consequences for the democratic rule of law. Constructivism, postmodernism and cultural relativism cultivate a mindset that rejects objectivity and rational justification. Consequently, there can be no objective criteria for assessing power and rule. A central achievement of Enlightenment, namely the distinction between legitimate state power and tyranny on the basis of intercultural justification, thus becomes obsolete. The tradition of contract theory founded by Hobbes, which led via increasingly differentiated separation of powers to the United Nations (cf. Chapter 2), is based on the criterion of rational justification. As mentioned above, this is precisely where Michel Foucault's fundamental critique comes in. In a much-cited interview, every manifestation of power and domination is placed under general suspicion: "Isn't power a form of warlike domination? Shouldn't one therefore conceive of all problems of power in terms of relations of war? Isn't power a sort of generalized war that, at particular moments, assumes the forms of peace and the state? Peace would then be a form of war, and the state a means of waging it."[74]

There is no doubt that dialectical language constructions are very impressive. However, anyone who cheers the general discrediting of all power should be prepared to face a few counter-questions: Cannot even a rhetorically brilliant emperor be argumentatively naked? What is the intellectual value of describing peace as a form of war? Is it not clearer and more productive to ask what criteria a phenomenon must fulfill in order to deserve the term peace? Do we not have good reasons to distinguish between the civilian rule of law, tyranny and war? By what argument does Hannah Arendt's differentiation

---

[73] Cf.: Markus Tiedemann, Constanze Tinawi: *Verzerrtes Normalitätsempfinden und toxische Toleranz*. Bundeszentrale für politische Bildung, 2021: https://www.bpb.de/themen/islamismus/dossier-islamismus/343155/verzerrtes-normalitaetsempfinden-und-toxische-toleranz/ [Last accessed 24.06.2022].

[74] Michel Foucault: Truth and Power. In: Colin Gordon (ed.): *Power/Knowledge: Selected Interviews and Other Writings, 1972–1977*. Pantheon Books, New York 1980. p. 123.

between legitimate empowerment and violence in the sense of overpowering become obsolete?[75] Is there not a danger that criticism of any form of power will ultimately no longer affect or change any of them?

If everything is a construction, then it is only logical to speak of alternative facts. It would be even more consistent to abandon terms such as virtuality, fact, or objectivity. Of course, in this case there is also no longer any compelling need for the better argument either in social interaction, in court or in political debate. For human coexistence and especially for democratic societies, this basic attitude is far more destructive than lying. Lies derive their identity ex negativo from the existence of truth. Lies construct pseudo-truths and can be exposed as such. Lies can be countered with criticism and doubt. Nevertheless, "the game of doubt itself presupposes the [possibility of] certainty."[76] Without reliable criteria, this distinction becomes impossible. Truth is replaced by personal perception. Which interpretation prevails is not a question of evidence, but of power, or rather of force. It is a return to pre-Enlightenment times and to a standard model of humanity (see chapter 4.1.2). The transmission of events, the legitimacy of claims to power or beliefs: none of this is a question of the better argument, but of presentation or sheer force or the manifestation of the irrational.

With regard to Donald Trump's reign, the shock cannot be deep enough. From his inauguration to the results of his removal from office, the 45th President of the United States has refused to acknowledge evidence and attempts at objectification that did not match his inclinations. At the same time, his own proclamations were validated primarily by assertion and emotion. Evidence became superfluous. The problem is not so much that a deficient character ruled the oldest democracy of modern times. Lies and deceit existed in all previous generations. The novelty is that at least 72 million Americans were willing to vote for a man for president who did not even try to disguise his anti-factual claims as truth. They elected a candidate who knew no regulative for his own interpretation of the world. Without the recognition of objectivity, there is neither the necessity nor the possibility of justification. Let's not kid ourselves, it is only thanks to the constitutionally guaranteed authorities in the USA that between 2016 and 2020 the country could still be described as a democratic constitutional state. Both the president and large sections of the population had said goodbye to this model. In their bestseller "How Democracies Die", Steven Levitsky and Daniel Ziblatt point out that it does not take a bloody

---

75   Cf. Hannah Arendt: *Macht und Gewalt*. R. Piper & Co, Munich 1969.
76   Ludwig Wittgenstein: Über Gewissheit. In: G.E.M. Anscombe/g.H. von Wright (eds.): *Werkausgabe*. Volume 8. p. 144.

coup for democracies to fail. Even less spectacular erosions are possible. This process is characterized by a threefold failure. At the first stage, both the critical public and the political parties fail to keep demagogues and populists away from political mandates. Instead of insisting on professional competence and integrity and isolating extremists, they make common cause with dubious promises and irrational hostility. If such a demagogue gains power through democratic elections, the second stage of decay begins with the undermining of constitutional institutions. Judges are replaced, parties are banned, information is restricted or channeled, new laws are pushed through parliaments by majority vote. These processes are exemplary in Hungary and Poland. The institutions of democratic constitutions are only able to withstand this erosion if they are supported by a society with robust democratic norms. The erosion of these norms therefore also represents the final stage of democratic decline. When political rivals begin to regard each other as enemies, when acceptance of parliamentary procedures declines and political opinion-forming becomes associated with a sense of existential threat, respect and appreciation for the institutions of the constitution dwindle.

Levitsky and Ziblatt's analysis is convincing. The developments in countries such as Poland or Hungary follow exactly these patterns. In Turkey or Russia, the dismantling of democratic structures is already complete. Even democratic systems that are taken for granted are showing signs of erosion. Imagine if, following the election of Donald Trump in 2017, Marine Le Pen had become president of France instead of Emmanuel Macron, and if the AfD had gained parliamentary sovereignty in Germany following failed coalition negotiations and new elections.

A vulgar understanding of democracy is also possible without Enlightenment. Despite possible electoral fraud, it can be assumed that Vladimir Putin was elected by the majority of Russian voters. He therefore has a democratic mandate. The same applies to Viktor Mihály Orbán, Jarosław Aleksander Kaczyńsk and Recep Tayyip Erdoğan. Only liberal, constitutional democracy is under threat, as there is a lack of an enlightened basic attitude among the population, particularly at the first and second levels. Citizens and political parties who feel committed to the principles of Enlightenment have a healthy skepticism and aversion to democracy. "The educated in this sense knows how to distinguish between mere rhetorical facades and real thoughts. They can do this because two questions have become second nature to them: "What exactly does that mean?" and: "How do we know that this is the case?".[77] It is the prin-

---

77 Peter Bieri: Wie wäre es, gebildet zu sein? In: Hans-Ulrich Lessing, Volker Steenblock (eds.): *"Was den Menschen eigentlich zum Menschen macht ..."*. *Klassische Texte einer*

ciples of the Enlightenment on which liberal democracies are based, in which it is possible to live humanely. The constitutional bodies of the second level are themselves a product and expression of the Enlightenment. Without an enlightened view of humanity, their legitimacy dwindles. On the third level, the difference between bourgeois and citoyen comes to light. Both capitalist profit individualism and herd democracy are possible without Enlightenment. In a society that is committed to Enlightenment, however, politics is more than an instrument for asserting personal interests. Political vigilance and participation are both a civic duty and a guarantor of freedom. The citizen cultivates the principle of rational justification. He demands that he and others give reasons and feels appreciation for all institutions that guarantee this process.

Anyone who now, and this closes the loop, relativizes factuality and objectivity, removes the ground from the enlightened process of justification. Democracy understood as majority rule or liberalism understood as capitalist individualism are still possible. Democratic constitutional states, however, are beginning to disintegrate. Post-factuality and the rule of law are incompatible. Real democracy needs truth[78]. It is no different with the normative principles of Enlightenment. They are also indispensable for a democratic constitutional state.

> Without an inclusive cultural practice based on equal recognition and equal individual freedom, founded on the idea of the equal dignity of every person, regardless of their respective affiliations, there can be no vital democracy. Without the guiding culture of humanism, there can be no democracy as a way of life.[79]

Another mistake is to regard cultural relativism as a pillar of multicultural tolerance. Let us remember: Enlightenment emphasizes what all people have in common as rational beings. Our cultural background, our skin color, our gender: all of this is secondary. What is important is that, despite all our differences, we share a common reason. We can struggle together for epistemic and moral objectivity.

This process also provides enough arguments to mutually respect or criticize our different life plans. Anything that does not stand up to intersubjective justification has no right to continue to exist. But what can be justified with good reasons is to be accepted. We derive our dignity, our rights as human

---

    Philosophie der Bildung. Verlag Karl Albert, Freiburg im Breisgau 2010. p. 208.
78 Cf.: Julian Nida-Rümelin: Demokratie und *Wahrheit.* Verlag C.H. Beck, Munich 2006.
79 Julian Nida-Rümelin: Demokratie als Lebensform. In: Dieter Birnbacher, Klaus Goergen, Markus Tiedemann (eds.): *Normative Integration. Kulturkampf im Klassenzimmer und netzgeprägte Schülerschaft.* Bill/Schönigh, Paderborn 2021. p. 41.

beings from the process of justification, from the giving and taking of reasons, not from our random cultural, social or biological identity.

The situation is quite different with cultural relativism and identity theory. These collective terms unite ideologies and concepts that not only understand cultures and evolved and constructed concepts of identity as possible reference values, but also declare them to be valuable and worthy of protection in principle. The commonality of human reason is neglected in favor of divisive identity characteristics. The result is an identity mania with an affinity for violence in all directions.

Identity theories construct values on the basis of belonging to groups. In this way, they negate one of the central achievements of the Enlightenment: the primacy of the individual. They are profoundly inhumane because they reduce the individual to belonging to a community of some kind. Respecting a person means granting them the right to define and create their own identity. Racism disregards this dignity by ascribing an identity tainted with prejudice. But in an anti-racism that classifies people as discriminated against, oppressed and disadvantaged in principle, similar mechanisms are at work. "Basically, we deprive them of the very privilege that we fundamentally grant to other beings by regarding them as persons."[80] Concepts of identity usually go hand in hand with peer pressure and exclusion. In Dresden, I got to know people who were accused of not living their homosexuality openly enough and thus disregarding the identity of their group. A Scandinavian student of mine was the target of massive hostility in Berlin because he wore earrings that were originally worn by Polynesian ethnic groups. The accusation: cultural appropriation.[81] Above all, however, concepts of identity are directed against the idea of fundamental equality.

A world view that elevates the contrast between natives and immigrants, between Muslims and non-Muslims, between white and black to the central explanatory vehicle cements this. "As global as its claim may be, this thinking must be resolutely opposed to the idea of humanity as an equal community."[82]

Anyone who uses culture, gender or other identities as a yardstick for our ethical or political orientation should know who they are in the same boat with. It is no coincidence that one of the most successful extreme right-wing

---

80 Ursula Renz: Was den bitte ist kulturelle Identität? Eine Orientierung in Zeiten des Populismus. Schwabe Verlag, Basel 2019. p. 45.
81 Cf: Hengameh Yaghoobifarah: Fusion Revisited: Karneval der Kulturlosen – Bis in zwei Jahren. Vielleicht auch bis nie. In: Missy Magazine, 2016 https://missy-magazine.de/blog/2016/07/05/fusion-revisited-karneval-der-kulturlosen/ [Last accessed 15.08.2022].
82 Thomas E. Schmidt: Ist der Rassismus etwa unüberwindbar? In: *DIE ZEIT* from July 22, 2021. p. 47.

movements of our time is called *the Identitarian Movement*. It would be an interesting experiment to have Carl Schmidt's theses discussed in left-wing intellectual circles without naming the author. The common conviction is that cultures and identities are evolved structures that must first be accepted. The difference lies in the consequences that are drawn from this. Right-wing extremist ideas traditionally advocate organization into culturally homogeneous territories. Left-wing cultural relativists, on the other hand, hope for a coexistence of a priori acceptable identities, lifestyles and cultures. The fact that racism, misogyny, nationalism or fascism also represent cultural identities and should also be accepted is suppressed. It is just as steadfastly ignored that the emphasis on cultural imprints or even biological endowments are the core substance of racism. The cultural relativism of right-wing extremist and left-wing circles differs here in one respect: the former group has taken the approach to its logical conclusion.

> A comparably great threat is identity politics from the right in the form of unilateralism and nationalism, but also identity politics from the left in the form of multiculturalism, which understands democracy as a modus vivendi of cultural identities. In both cases, the political community and republican practice in democracy eroded.[83]

To further debunk the myth of tolerant cultural relativism, it is worth taking a closer look at the concept of tolerance. The concept of tolerance is one of the most valuable achievements of the Enlightenment. The root of the word (Latin tolerare: to suffer, to endure) already indicates that in this case an unloved phenomenon is to be accepted on the basis of higher-order arguments. That these higher-order arguments exist is a necessary premise. Intellectually, tolerance stems from the distinction between faith and knowledge achieved through the Enlightenment (cf. chapter 2.3), the necessity of which was made clear by the inhuman European confessional wars, among other things. Beliefs elude objective justification. However, what cannot be legitimized as necessary vis-à-vis others must not be forced upon them. A practice that is rejected due to one's own inclinations, influences or interests, but without good reasons, must be tolerated. Step by step, it became clear that this principle can be extended to religions, cults, lifestyles, sexual preferences and much more. Nevertheless, this acceptance cannot and must not be unlimited. If good reasons are put forward against the acceptance of religions, lifestyles, sexual preferences, cults,

---

83 Julian Nida-Rümelin: Demokratie als Lebensform. In: Dieter Birnbacher, Klaus Goergen, Markus Tiedemann (eds.): *Normative Integration. Kulturkampf im Klassenzimmer und netzgeprägte Schülerschaft*. Bill/Schönigh, Paderborn 2021. p. 40.

etc., these can and may very well be sanctioned. Otherwise, tolerance degenerates into a synonym for indifference or nihilism. A claim to tolerance also requires good reasons. Rainer Forst speaks of the duty of general and reciprocal justification.[84] Tolerance therefore has three necessary components. The objection component may arise as it will. It is fed by our personal preferences. The acceptance component does not undo the perceived objection, but submits to arguments of a higher order. However, acceptance is by no means unlimited. Otherwise, tolerance would dissolve into indifference. Acceptance only extends as far as intersubjective reasons underpin the claim of the unpopular practice. However, there is also a rejection component. This always takes effect when the practice in question cannot be justified intersubjectively and higher-order arguments justify an objection.

It quickly becomes clear how demanding genuine tolerance is. It does not consist of blind acceptance of others. Rational criticism is not an insult, but demonstrates recognition as a rational being. Genuine tolerance is more than coexistence. Its core is the commitment to reciprocal and general justification. The recognition of arguments of a higher order is existential for this. This is precisely why constructivism and cultural relativism are not sources of tolerance, but its gravediggers.

There are currently more and more examples of any rejection, indeed any criticism of other cultures or concepts of identity, being placed under general suspicion in the name of a degenerate understanding of tolerance. The owner of a boutique is labeled Islamophobic because she refuses to hire a saleswoman wearing a headscarf. Critics of boy circumcision are accused of anti-Semitism.[85]

However, arguments are rarely listened to. One reason for this is that cultural relativism limits the validity of arguments to the context of their cultural and historical genesis. Not accepting these boundaries and insisting on intersubjective and intercultural mediation is seen as overwhelming, as Eurocentrism or cultural chauvinism. Other ways of life, customs and traditions can only be understood and evaluated from an internal perspective and on the basis of criteria generated there. Time and again, I have discussions with students about whether Europeans are entitled to make normative judgments about cultural

---

84 Cf. Rainer Forst: *Toleranz im Konflikt*, 4th edition, Suhrkamp, Frankfurt am Main 2003. §1 p. 31ff, §30 p. 588ff.

85 Cf. Roger Collier: Ugly, messy and nasty debate surrounds circumcision. In: *CMAJ: Canadian Medical Association Journal = journal de l'Association medicale Canadienne*. Vol. 184/1, 2012. pp. 25–26.

practices in other parts of the world. In these debates, for example, the term genital mutilation is declared inadmissible as a term for cutting off and sewing up the female genitalia, as it already implies a Eurocentric assessment. Only the neutral term *female cutting*[86] is appropriate. The situation is very similar with the sale of children or workers, which are deeply rooted in the respective culture. The fact that the mistreatment of women, wars of conquest or slave trade are deeply rooted in all cultures and therefore triangular trade, colonialism and chauvinism should not be condemned is generally ignored. The point that even UNESCO does not want tolerance to be understood as unlimited rarely catches on.

The Declaration of Principles of Tolerance of November 16, 1995 reads:

> 1.2 Tolerance is not synonymous with yielding, condescension or indulgence. Above all, tolerance is an active attitude based on the recognition of the universally valid human rights and fundamental freedoms of others. Under no circumstances should it be misused to justify any restrictions on these fundamental values. Tolerance must be practiced by individuals, groups and states.[87]

The counter-argument is that UNESCO, as part of the United Nations, is characterized by the dominance of individual nations and cultural groups. Consequently, UNESCO has no moral authority. The hope that not only national interests but also universal values are negotiated within the framework of the United Nations is also rejected, as universal values do not exist from the perspective of cultural relativism.

The consequence is a moral *anything goes*.[88] You might call this consistent. But it has nothing to do with tolerance. Tolerance without limits loses all moral value, indeed it turns into its opposite.

Few have debunked the negative dialectic of unlimited alleged tolerance with a sharper pen than Pascale Bruckner. Bruckner speaks of "paradox of multiculturalism". This consists of granting equal treatment to all communities, but not to the people who make them up, as they are denied the

---

[86] There are also contributions at university conferences that at least accept the social status of circumcisers and the danger of Western medicine dominating as an argument. https://www.gender.hu-berlin.de/de/publikationen/gender-bulletin-broschueren/bulletin-texte/texte-28/bulletin-texte-28 [last accessed 15.08.2022].

[87] UNESCO: Declaration of Principles of Tolerance, drawn up by the participating member states of the 28th UNESCO General Conference, Paris 28.10.-16.11.1995.

[88] It should only be mentioned in passing that Feyerabend's credo calls for a methodological scientific anarchism and does not refer to social or ethical issues.

opportunity to renounce their own traditions".[89] A basic ethical principle of the Enlightenment is that only individuals are the bearers of primary rights. Communities are only valuable if they contribute to the well-being of the individuals who make them up. This applies to states, sports associations, cultural groups and families. None of these institutions are sacrosanct. Individuals have the right to break away from them and must be protected from them in cases of hardship. Anyone who believes that this principle must be abandoned in the name of cultural relativism becomes a victim of negative dialectics. Bruckner calls this the "racism of the anti-racists "[90].

Like all discrimination, racism essentially consists of the normatively devaluing reduction of the individual to their membership of a group. Occasionally, human history appears to be a single horrific sequence of these crimes. Recent German history has produced the most horrific example in the form of the Holocaust.

The human rights of millions were trampled underfoot without consideration of individuality solely on the basis of actual or alleged membership of designated enemy groups. The rule of thumb of this persecutory racism is: *We violate your human rights because you belong to a certain group!* In order to prevent this barbarism from ever happening again, scrupulous care must be taken not to discriminate against ethnic or cultural groups. However, it is a dramatic mistake to declare cultural communities, religions or concepts of identity a priori valuable and worthy of protection. It overlooks the fact that racism by omission is also possible alongside racism by persecution. The rule of thumb of racism by omission is: *We do not protect your human dignity because you belong to a certain group!* In this case too, an individual is reduced to their membership of a group.

Let's imagine three young people. A boy has a part of his body removed against his will and without medical indication. An underage girl is married off to an unknown man without being asked and another child is kept away from important educational content such as sex education or biology lessons.

And now let's continue to imagine that the names of those affected are Max, Susanne and Luisa.

Be honest: did you expect different-sounding names? Is the degree of your moral indignation different now? Do you think that if the names sound

---

89 Pascal Bruckner: Fundamentalismus der Aufklärung oder Rassismus der Antirassisten? In: Thierry Chervel, Anja Seeliger (eds.): *Islam in Europa. Eine internationale Debatte.* Suhrkamp, Frankfurt a. M. 2007. pp. 55–74.
90 Ibid.

different, the matter is regrettable but cannot be changed? Are you perhaps even of the opinion that you are not entitled to judgment in this case? If so, the racism of the anti-racists has already taken root in your mind. A society that does not afford people equal protection on the basis of their cultural affiliation is not tolerant, but intrinsically racist.

It remains to be mentioned that constructivism, post-factuality and cultural relativism do not have a positive effect on peace and international understanding.

Samuel P. Huntington was a staunch cultural relativist. According to one of his core theses, the culture of the West should be seen as "unique", but not as "universal".[91] The instruction or even colonization of other cultural circles would therefore lack any justification and should to be rejected as "immoral imperialism".[92]

Insofar as we are talking about the cultural sphere of the West, we can agree with these statements in their entirety.

The Western-style capitalist consumer society is in fact neither without alternative nor universally valid. Violent expansion lacks any moral basis. However, Huntington does not differentiate between ways of life, economic systems, religious traditions and ethical justification discourses. Therefore, the achievements of the Enlightenment are also subsumed under the relative cultural assets of the West. The fact that the essence of Enlightenment consisted precisely in breaking away from cultural influences and striving for objectivity is ignored. According to Huntington, people rally around the symbols, religions and traditions of their cultures. Internationally, the world is divided into eight cultural groups, with conflicts and wars arising at their borders. Above all, the lack of a world language and a world religion stand in the way of a universalization of the world community.[93] For Huntington, ethical universalism is at best the illusion of an educated elite referred to as the "Davos culture"[94] in reference to the World Economic Forum.

Kant's idea of an epistemic and ethical cosmopolitanism, a league of nations and non-violent conflict resolution is summarily laid to rest.

---

91   Samuel P. Huntington: *Kampf der Kulturen – The Clash of Civilizations. Die Neugestaltung der Weltpolitik im 21. Jahrhundert.* Siedler, Munich 1996. p. 513.
92   Ibid. p. 511.
93   Ibid. p. 76.
94   Ibid. p. 78.

Anyone who goes along with this is caught in the Huntington trap. What remains when the pursuit of cosmopolitan reason is thrown overboard? The clash of civilizations!

> Those who believe that truth is only power, that ideals only conceal interests, will quickly come to the conclusion that only the interests of their own tribe count.[95]

2.7 Take it or leave it

In his famous lectures on ethics, Ernst Tugendhat addresses the problem of ultimate justification. According to Tugendhat, all morality presupposes the willingness to "want to be a cooperative being". This basic decision is the necessary prerequisite for all ethics. On the other hand, anyone who does not value understanding and justification is inaccessible to moral argumentation. It is, one could say, about the *Walking Dead* of morality.

"Take it or leave it" is Tugendhat's succinct summary.[96]

The situation is quite similar with the Enlightenment. The premises and ideals of Enlightenment have not necessarily been proven, but they have been sufficiently substantiated. The coherence of its justification is far superior to that of all other conceptions. Of course, it can be argued at this point that a system is declaring itself the winner according to its own rules. The Enlightenment itself has produced the insights that coherence is valuable, that there are arguments of a higher order and that these are characterized by intersubjectivity, reciprocity and generality.

The only way to avoid circular reasoning is to understand rationality and the giving of reasons as an anthropological constant and to trust reason to develop criteria for the quality of its own arguments and to derive its own normative primacy from them. Rather, we find ourselves at the point where, according to Kant, pure reason becomes practical by virtue of its insight into objective morality.

However, this does not have to be accepted either. Even if the existence of a general human reason is conceded, no normative claim follows from this. The fact of a disposition does not imply its normative superiority. Those who argue

---

[95] Susan Neiman: *Widerstand der Vernunft. Ein Manifest in postfaktischen Zeiten*. Ecowin, Salzburg. 2017. pp. 57–58.
[96] Ernst Tugendhat: *Vorlesungen über Ethik*, Suhrkamp, Frankfurt am Main 1993. p. 89.

that we owe each other reasons and that rational justification is better than orientation towards feelings, traditions or religions fall back on the rationality that they want to justify.

Here, in fact, the moment is reached at which, according to Wittgenstein "the spade bends back".[97] We cannot dig any deeper in our search for intersubjective justification.

What remains is the reference to empiricism. Are the natural sciences, the game of chess or mathematics not evidence enough of a rationality that transcends genres? Why should beings who can argue together about scientific principles not also do so in moral contexts? The ideal of the neutral observer may have been an idea of the Enlightenment philosopher Adam Smith. A neutral referee is known and recognized in sports and competitions in almost all cultures. Do institutions such as the United Nations not prove that rational justification is already practiced globally? Is there a single society that is not guided by the principles of the Enlightenment and does even come close to being regarded as just, free and low in violence? Does it not speak for itself that the majority of people would like to live in countries that were shaped by Enlightenment?

These rhetorical questions do not necessarily work either. Someone who is guided by emotions or religious traditions will prefer societies that satisfy their needs and despise rational criticism. The fact that his choice cannot be made comprehensible to us, while we are able to justify our choice to him, is a difference in his eyes, but not a sign of quality.

However, experience teaches us that our newly constructed, irrational traditionalist does indeed demand justification from others. But those who demand reasons from others can hardly ignore their value. According to Hans Otto Apel, those who deny the discourse have already confirmed it through their argumentation. The wheel of rationality begins to turn.

The summary of this chapter is therefore quite simple. Neither the epistemic nor the normative assumptions of the Enlightenment are beyond doubt. Nevertheless, a dense "fabric of motives and reasons" can be invoked to justify them[98] and their achievements are as impressive as they are desirable. Inhuman developments are not the result of a striving for objectivity and Enlightenment, but arise from their neglect. Rather, Enlightenment is needed in order to be able to criticize these evils at all. It therefore seems only fair to reverse the compulsion to justify. Alternative models of an epistemic and

---

97   Ludwig Wittgenstein: *Philosophische Untersuchungen*, §217.
98   Ernst Tugendhat: *Vorlesungen über Ethik*, Suhrkamp, Frankfurt am Main 1993. p. 28.

normative explanation of the world cannot be refuted as necessarily false. Nevertheless, their basic assumptions achieve a significantly lower degree of coherence and intersubjective communicability. Above all, however, they are unable to show how a humane coexistence has ever existed or could ever exist on their basis.

The final verdict on the Enlightenment could be summarized with Ernst Tugendhat and Tina Turner:

Take it or leave it. It's not perfect, but it is simply the best.

CHAPTER 3

Transience

If Enlightenment is, as claimed above, the best thing that humanity has ever produced, the question naturally arises as to why it is coming to an end again. The reasons for this are both human nature and the internal structure of the Enlightenment as well as the historical framework conditions. In order to make the process easier to understand, the permanent and current stress factors that are driving the decline of the Enlightenment will be presented below.

3.1 The eternal competition

Anyone who thinks that the Enlightenment, with its liberal understanding of freedom, has an irresistible attraction on its side is mistaken. Freedom is a breathtaking beauty, but it is strict and demanding. For those who put happiness and pleasure first, freedom is best avoided.

At first glance, the competition between happiness and freedom is often overlooked. Do we not all want both? Is not one a necessary condition of the other? Are they perhaps synonyms? However, a closer look reveals astonishing frictional losses, and under certain conditions even a dichotomy.

In his 1974 work *Anarchy, State and Utopia*, Robert Nozick designed a famous thought experiment. Imagine an experience machine that is able to simulate all desired experiences through neuronal stimulation of the brain. A connection is possible for months and years. Beforehand, the desired experiences can be selected from catalogs. During the simulation, there is no awareness of the original identity. Everything seems one hundred percent real. You can be who you want to be and experience what you want. Meanwhile, your real body suffers no damage. At the end of the simulation, you can leave or start a new simulation.[1]

The construction of the thought experiment has two essential aspects. Firstly, an important difference between freedom and happiness is made clear. Happiness, understood as pleasure, can only exist on the basis of illusion or doxa. Freedom understood as autonomy requires authenticity, truth, episteme.

---

1 Robert Nozick: *Anarchy, State, and Utopia*. Basic Books, New York 1974. pp. 42–45.

Secondly, the thought experiment forces us to clarify our personal priorities. If you a) understand happiness as the greatest possible value and b) define it through feelings of pleasure, everything speaks in favor of allowing yourself to be connected. You can be a heroine, a great lover, a revered musician and a famous doctor all at the same time. What does the reality of your personal life have to offer that could not be surpassed many times over by the experience machine? The answer is: freedom. If you value freedom more than happiness, do not let yourself be connected. What a shame, you simply cannot have both! The grandiose happiness experiences of the machine require you to give up freedom. Choosing freedom means giving up happiness. You may decide in favor of autonomy and self-determination with a chest full of conviction, but let's be honest: the temptation of the machine cannot be denied.

No futuristic scenario is needed to understand that happiness and freedom are often competitors. Happiness is the highest good of human endeavor. No one has made this clearer than Aristotle. For him, the significance of happiness is derived both from empirical surveys and from a metaphysical system. If you ask people what they long to achieve and what they strive for, the final answer is always happiness. If one also assumes that all movement, all striving and endeavor is aimed at achieving an ideal state, then bliss appears to be the best description of this state. As a rule, we do not strive for most goods for their own sake. We desire beauty and wisdom in order to be admired and wealth in order to be able to do or acquire desirable things. We can only think of an end to this pursuit if we achieve a supreme good that leaves nothing more to be desired. The only candidate for this highest good is bliss. Those who are blissful want nothing other than what they are currently experiencing. There is no impulse to change anything or to strive for something new. This is a state that we only achieve very rarely and only in orgasmic brevity, but which we all desire in the long term. We may argue about what happiness consists of, but not about the fact that we all want it.

The value of freedom, on the other hand, is by no means so self-evident. Most people would probably initially regard freedom as a necessary component of happiness: without freedom, there is no happiness. However, the question quickly arises as to whether a feeling of freedom or substantial autonomy is meant. Sailing, for example, can convey a colossal feeling of freedom. Strictly speaking, however, this experience has very little to do with the absence of determination. Rather, it is a feeling of pleasure that is evoked by a special kind of movement. Freedom in the essential sense means experiencing oneself as the cause of one's own decisions and actions. The concept of freedom is only appropriate if our decisions and actions are not determined by drives, instincts and psychological or social indoctrination. Access to this freedom is not provided by a sailing boat, but only by reason striving for objectivity. Only through it is it possible to behave not only in the world, but also towards the world and thus also towards oneself. If it succeeds, man rises above physical and social determination. A truly dignified event, but it is a pity that this act contributes so little to euphoric states of happiness. Nowhere is this clearer than in Kant's moral philosophy. According to Kant, true morality is characterized by the absence or even the overcoming of personal inclinations. An approach that convinced Friedrich Schiller in theory, but drove him to despair in his rigorism. "I would gladly serve my friends, but unfortunately I do so with reluctance. And so it often troubles me that I am not virtuous."[2] According to Kant, man is able to recognize moral duty a priori through pure rational activity, i.e. without recourse to experience. Compliance with the duty identified by reason is freedom. Only this elevates man above the forces of nature and society. Happiness plays no role in this. What is moral duty takes no account of needs or desires. We are all familiar with situations in which our desires and the morally good are at odds with each other. According to Kant, moral behavior makes us worthy of happiness at best, but it has little to do with real happiness. When we learn of morally exemplary behavior, we are quick to believe that those responsible deserve to be happy. However, experience teaches us that at least a pleasurable life is far more accessible to the moral scoundrel than to those who try to fulfill their moral duties.

This is precisely where the individual human psyche and the organization of societies are at risk of being overwhelmed. *Sapere aude* is known to be the motto of the Enlightenment. It calls for judgment, maturity and autonomy. There is no mention of happiness or pleasure. The Enlightenment is not hostile to happiness or pleasure. In case of doubt, however, it always demands a decision in favor of reason and freedom.

Kant diagnosed a self-inflicted immaturity for the vast majority of humanity. The cause is not a lack of intellect, "but of resolution and courage."[3] It is much more comfortable and carefree to leave decisions to authorities and traditions than to take full responsibility for one's own life and for social development. Erich Fromm wrote of the "flight from freedom"[4], as this is by no means

---

2   Friedrich Schiller: Xenien – 388. Gewissensskrupel. In: *Sämtliche Werke*, Volume 1, Hanser Verlag, Munich 1962. p. 299.
3   Kant: AA VIII, p. 35.
4   Erich Fromm: Die Flucht vor der Freiheit. In: Rainer Funke (ed.): *Gesamtausgabe in zwölf Bänden*, vol. I: Social Psychology. DVA, Stuttgart. pp. 299–314.

always exhilarating, but can also be stressful and frightening. From birth to the grave, we are constantly confronted with the intimidating experience that the world is huge and uncontrollable, while we remain comparatively small and powerless. Nevertheless, it is possible to establish a positive relationship with the world through love and work. Certainly, the world is big and scary, but a part of the world loves me and is loved by me. So I welcome both my existence and the existence of the world. Yes, the river is wild and intimidating, but I am able to build a bridge. Yes, the foreign culture is unsettling, but I am able to learn the language and gain understanding. Yes, abuse of power is a real problem, but we can organize the separation of powers. These processes of love and work enable the "mature person"[5] who does not fear freedom, but values it. However, this is a great emotional and intellectual achievement that, even according to Fromm, is only accomplished by a few. The majority of people strive unabatedly to satisfy their needs for pleasure and to compensate for their fear of freedom.

Viktor Emil Frankl never tired of emphasizing the political dangers that result from an escape from freedom:

> Unlike animals, no instinct tells man what he must do, and unlike man in earlier times, no tradition tells him what he should do – and now he no longer seems to know quite what he actually wants. So it happens that he either only wants what the others do – and there we have conformism – or he only does what the others want him to do – and there we have totalitarianism.[6]

The political theory of the Enlightenment always endeavored not to lose sight of the pursuit of happiness. According to Hobbes, leaving the state of nature and concluding the social contract are the result of a rational insight, but they pursue the strategic interest of enabling a more peaceful and happier life. As is well known, the preamble to the American Declaration of Independence includes the *Pursuit of Happiness* alongside *Life* and *Liberty* among the *unalienable rights*. However, the Enlightenment project goes far beyond the reciprocal facilitation of different ways of life and views of happiness. The enlightened society is more than the peaceful competition of happiness aspirations. It demands the citoyen, the mature, responsible and informed citizen. Only with him can a resilient system of *checks and balances* guaranteeing freedom be kept

---

5 Erich Fromm: The authoritarian personality. In: *German University Journal.* 12th vol. no.9/1957. p. 3.
6 Viktor E. Frankl: The Will to Meaning. Selected lectures on logotherapy. Piper, Munich 1997. p. 24.

alive. However, the practice of the responsible citizen is by no means a pleasurable business. It requires self-discipline, energy, perseverance and moderation. This is precisely where the concept loses its integrative power. It only remains attractive if personal and political autonomy are seen as a necessary part of a desirable existence or, in case of doubt, take precedence. History teaches us that poverty and oppression can inspire the ideas of the Enlightenment and the urge for freedom. This does not apply to the lasting appreciation of these principles. The French Revolution might have remained true to its ideals if food shortages had also disappeared with the adoption of the Declaration of the Rights of Man and of the Citizen in 1789. Instead, hunger and war immediately called the newly won freedom into question. In times of existential threats, people have repeatedly sacrificed their freedom for greater security and prosperity. However, this problem also arises in less dramatic times. Too much prosperity and security can also jeopardize freedom. In this respect, the Enlightenment shares the fate of all achievements that are perceived as natural. If this state of affairs occurs, the emotional attachment forces decline. The advantages of freedom are understood as a natural right, while the associated duties are perceived as an imposition (see chapter 4.3.2). It quickly becomes clear that the long-term preservation of Enlightenment requires economic and political security with a simultaneous awareness of the preciousness of freedom rights. This state is difficult to achieve and at least as difficult to maintain. As soon as a critical mass values its personal, usually economic, well-being more highly than freedom, the Enlightenment way of life is lost.

The economic success of the so-called liberal West was able to conceal this problem for many decades. Another factor was the deterrent character of the political alternatives that actually existed. Compared to the totalitarian regimes of the twentieth century, which insisted on a dominant narrative of salvation and enabled a low standard of living, liberal societies appeared to be a haven of freedom and happiness.

Currently, however, the ambivalence of happiness and freedom is becoming increasingly apparent. Capitalism, which has enabled liberal societies to achieve considerable economic success, only values the free forces of the market. Civil or even moral liberties are of secondary importance at best. The lifeblood of capitalism, on the other hand, is the ever-growing satisfaction of real or fictitious needs for happiness through consumption. For a long time, the political concept of Enlightenment protected this mechanism as a *pursuit of happiness*. Now, however, confrontation is unavoidable. Freedom manifests itself through the use of reason and its message is scientifically and morally clear: we must massively restrict our pleasure-oriented consumer behavior if the "permanence of genuine human life on earth"[7] is to be preserved. If this imperative of reason is undisputed, the exciting question arises as to whether society has the strength to realize the primacy of freedom. There are reasons for hope. The *Fridays for Future* movement may unite many motives. Nevertheless, it is clear that a generation is fighting on the basis of scientific findings as their economic future could be of a lesser quality than that of their parents. An impressive moral achievement that clearly breaks with the narrative of constant economic progression. However, the opposite spectrum of society ranges from the yellow vests in France and the "environmental policy" of the AfD in Germany to libertarian economists at numerous international universities.[8] These forces also put forward a concept of freedom, albeit a vulgar one. What is meant is the right to consume cheaply. A compromise between the two wings of society is only possible to a limited extent. In essence, freedom in the sense of a rationally oriented sense of responsibility and the consumer-oriented pursuit of happiness are irreconcilable. This confrontation is new in liberal societies. Until now, the unbound forces of individual creative possibilities had fulfilled the need for moral and political freedom as well as for an increasing quality of life. The joint venture principle between ethical, political and economic liberalism is reaching its limits, and it will become clear what the much-invoked commitments to freedom are really worth (cf. Chapter 4.3).

Meanwhile, authoritarian states are working to present themselves as an alternative worth living in and to relativize the normative guiding function of liberal civil rights. According to Clive Hamilton and Mareike Ohlberg, China has been striving for decades to propagate "human rights with Chinese characteristics". With success: in 1991, the Information Office of the State Council of the People's Republic of China published its first declaration on human rights. This focused on the importance of "social and economic rights", while individual and political freedom rights were, as expected, neglected.[9] What seemed like sheer cynicism two years after the massacre in Tiananmen Square has since been disseminated through clever public relations work. The XXIV World Congress of Philosophy took place in Beijing from August 13 to 20, 2018.

---

7 Hans Jonas: Das Prinzip Verantwortung – Versuch einer Ethik für die technologische Zivilisation. Suhrkamp, Frankfurt 1984. p. 36.
8 Cf: Nils Markwardt: *Pappkameraden des Ökopaternalismus*. In: Zeit Online https://www.zeit.de/kultur/2019-01/umweltpolitik-klimawandel-klasse-sozialpolitik-vereinbarkeit?page=5 [last accessed 05.10.2022].
9 Information Office of the State Council of the People's Republic of China: *Human rights in China*, Beijing 1991. https://www.china.org.cn/e-white/7/index.htm [Last accessed 05.10.2022].

Thousands of philosophers were attracted by the good organization, the dignified hotels and the successful congress center. The opening ceremony took place in the Great Hall of the People on Tiananmen Square. Chinese media reported truthfully that philosophers from all over the world had traveled to Beijing under the title "Learning to be Human". There were no reports of a controversial plenary debate on the topic of human rights. How could there, when there where none.

In a personal conversation, two Chinese colleagues candidly expressed the following position: "Western liberalism has failed. It demands too much from its citizens. What people really want is personal happiness and economic advancement. As long as this is guaranteed, political self-determination is more of a nuisance."[10]

The expansion of these views is already well advanced. The years 2018–2021 witnessed a heroic struggle by the people of Hong Kong against the loss of their civil liberties. People from all walks of life put their personal happiness on the line in order to defend their right to participation, debate, search for information – in short, to strenuous self-determination. The leadership in Beijing was not very impressed. On the one hand, because the so-called "free world" articulated very little protest and thus indirectly confirmed the primacy of the economy. Secondly, because there was little danger of the spark of freedom spreading. In mainland China, the quest for political freedom seems to have largely died out.

For the eternal competition between freedom and happiness, this gives rise to an uncomfortable consideration: perhaps the Chinese model is closer to human nature than the sophisticated idea of the Enlightenment. Perhaps the orientation towards reason and responsibility to the detriment of pleasure and satisfaction is possible as an individual brilliant achievement, but for societies it is an excessive demand. Perhaps the development of freedom simply takes a back seat to the pursuit of happiness.

3.2   The reproduction problem

It is one of the tragic elements of human history that the noblest of all forms of society has low productivity.

The classical philosophers of the eighteenth century believed that humanity was on an arduous but steadily ascending path to reason, self-determination

---

10   The quote is reproduced solely from the author's memory.

and freedom. The idea of a history of global civilization[11] was based on the notion of a worldwide expansion of the principles of freedom through the ever-growing power of reason. Doubts were justified from the outset. Historical evidence of the failure of Enlightenment movements ranges from ancient Greece to the French Jacobins and the Weimar Republic to contemporary Europe. At the same time, colonialism and totalitarianism have demonstrated how quickly irrationality and inhumanity can dominate.

The hopes that an Enlightenment-oriented way of life would develop an irresistible attraction have not yet been confirmed. Even where the principles of the Enlightenment have been counted among the foundations of society for generations, their existence remains constantly under threat.

The problem begins with biological reproduction. Societies that are oriented towards the ideals of the Enlightenment have very low fertility rates.[12] Of course, this is primarily due to the economic success of these societies, which makes children superfluous as old-age insurance, among other things. But the overcoming of fixed gender roles, family concepts and lifestyles has also made its contribution. There are good reasons to celebrate all of this. However, it is also a fact that a society with a reproduction rate of less than 2.1 will disappear in purely mathematical terms.[13]

None of this would actually be a problem, as our planet is suffering from overpopulation. Immigration can fill the resulting gaps and at the same time relieve the pressure on other regions of the world. However, immigration into a generally enlightened society is not the same as its reproduction. If it is true that the struggle for objectivity and responsibility arises from a demanding educational process, then this must begin early. The majority of immigrants are adults. Of course, they too can be won over to the ideals and practice of Enlightenment, but the effort involved is incomparably greater than with children, whose learning ability is more pronounced and whose previous world view is less established.

But even if enough children go through an appropriate education program in good time, the continuation of education cannot be guaranteed.

---

11 Kant: AA VIII, p. 15.
12 The birth rates of all EU member states, without exception, are below both the global average of 2.4 and the threshold value of 2.1 required to stabilize a population (see: United Nations, Department of Economic and Social Affairs, Population Division: *World Population Prospects 2022*).
13 *"The reproduction of a population is guaranteed if the birth rate is permanently 2.1."*, Federal Bundeszentrale für politische Bildung: *Geburten* https://www.bpb.de/kurz-knapp/zahlen-und-fakten/soziale-situation-in-deutschland/61550/geburten/ [last accessed 15.08.2022].

One reason for this is that the ideals of the Enlightenment have little mass psychological inertia. In his major work *Psychology of the Masses* from 1895[14], Gustave Le Bon illustrates the extent to which shared, irrational beliefs shape collective identity and are therefore unconsciously defended by the masses. Ideologies often shape the thinking of several generations. Religions even survive for millennia without any rational justification. Enlightenment, however, is suitable neither as a religion nor as an ideology and is therefore difficult to anchor in the collective consciousness.

According to Le Bon, the pictorial, simple and dogmatic repetition finds its way into the "mass soul."[15] The pursuit of freedom and the struggle for objectivity do not fulfill these criteria. They are suitable neither for euphoria nor for hysteria. They are virtues that are bound to the laborious process of rational justification. In addition, the primacy of the individual over the collective is constitutive of the ideal of maturity. Norbert Elias therefore understood the entire process of civilization as an overcoming of collective identities in favor of individual identity.[16] Enlightenment can therefore not hope for an emotional rooting in the "mass soul".

The continued existence of enlightened ways of life can only be guaranteed through the maturity of as many individuals as possible. Activating, maintaining and preserving these principles is time-consuming and costly. Educational systems need to be financed. Educational subjects not only need care and time to learn reading, arithmetic and writing, but also leisure to develop creativity and judgment. It is therefore no exaggeration when Ekkehard Martens speaks of the fourth cultural technique for shaping human life.[17]

Even too much prosperity and security can jeopardize freedom. In this respect, the Enlightenment shares the fate of all achievements that are taken for granted. If this situation arises, the emotional attachment forces decline (see chapter 3.3.3). It quickly becomes clear that the long-term preservation of Enlightenment requires economic and political security and a simultaneous awareness of the preciousness of freedom rights. A state that is difficult to achieve and at least as difficult to maintain.

---

14 Gustave Le Bon, Rudolf Eisler (transl.): *Psychologie der Massen*. 2nd edition, Dr. Werner Klinkhardt Verlag, Leipzig 1912.
15 Ibid. p. 10ff.
16 Norbert Elias: *Über den Prozess der Zivilisation*. Published by Haus zum Falken, Basel 1939.
17 Cf.: Ekkehard Martens: Philosophie als Kulturtechnik humaner Lebensgestaltung. In: Julian Nida-Rümelin, Irina Spiegel, Markus Tiedemann (eds.): *Handbuch der Philosophie und Ethik. Volume I: Didaktik und Methodik*. 2nd edition. Schöningh, Paderborn 2017. pp. 41–47.

The fragile productivity of enlightened societies is condensed in the dictum first formulated in 1964 by the constitutional lawyer and legal philosopher Ernst-Wolfgang Böckenförde:

> The liberal, secularized state lives on preconditions that it cannot guarantee itself. That is the great risk it has taken for the sake of freedom. On the one hand, it can only exist as a liberal state if the freedom it grants its citizens is regulated from within, from the moral substance of the individual and the homogeneity of society. On the other hand, it cannot seek to guarantee these internal regulatory forces of its own accord, that is, by means of legal coercion and authoritative command, without giving up its freedom and – on a secularized level – falling back into the claim to totality from which it led in the confessional civil wars.[18]

Two pillars support liberal societies. A constitution characterized by the separation of powers and an active, critical and self-critical citizenry. The epochs of the Enlightenment have produced grandiose constitutions. Nevertheless, all of them offer scope for abuse of power. This was true of the combination of paragraphs 25, 48 and 53 of the Weimar Constitution and it is true of the drawing of electoral districts in the United States of America. But even if design flaws are avoided or rectified, constitutions alone cannot guarantee the continued existence of a free, rational and responsible society.

One reason for this is the lack of authority that all secular forms of government have. The political order is not able to invoke a transcendent "higher law"[19], but derives its legitimacy from the civil freedom that it itself attempts to establish and maintain. According to Hannah Arendt, republics endeavor to compensate for this deficit with an almost sacred founding myth. This is as true for ancient Rome as it is for the United States of America.[20]

However, even these emotional charges cannot guarantee respect and appreciation. On January 6, 2021, a violent mob stormed the United States Capitol in Washington D.C. to prevent the formal confirmation of the 2020 presidential election. Five people died and 56 were injured. Members of parliament had to be evacuated to safety and the parliamentary session was interrupted. All of this happened not despite, but because the constitutional bodies had prevented a massive erosion of democracy between 2016 and 2020.

---

18   Ernst Wolfgang Böckenförde: Die Entstehung des Staates als Vorgang der Säkularisation. In: *Recht, Staat, Freiheit. Studien zur Rechtsphilosophie, Staatstheorie und Verfassungsgeschichte*. Suhrkamp, Frankfurt 1991. pp. 92–114.
19   Hannah Arendt: *Über die Revolution*. Piper, Munich 1963. p. 238.
20   Ibid. p. 236.

"An [enlightened] democracy lives not only from the functioning of constitutional procedures and institutions, but it also needs a democratic attitude among its population, a life-world anchoring of its normative principles, if it is not to become an empty shell, which can be effortlessly blown away by anti-democratic forces."[21] What is needed is a "sense of citizenship" through which "actors who see themselves as 'individuals' consciously and with 'value-rationally' thought-out good reasons stand up for the 'constitution' of the respective society and support it in their thoughts, feelings and actions."[22]

This civic attitude forms the substantial basis of enlightened, liberal societies, without being able to be guaranteed by them. In the final instance, all hope is based on education. But it is precisely here that the frightening fragility of the Enlightenment project is revealed. Precisely because the craft of freedom has to be learned again and again, it is enough to neglect, unsettle or manipulate a single generation. At the same time, education to maturity is incomparably more difficult and costly than indoctrination and manipulation. Human beings are endowed with reason, not with an affinity for reason. Even when reason and autonomous judgment have developed and provide a reliable immunity against prejudice, fanaticism and dogmatism, it is all too easy to silence their bearers. Thomas Rentsch illustrated this idea in a breathtakingly impressive way during a Christmas party in 2016. The train of thought is as follows: consider how many resources, love, effort and care have gone into the care, upbringing and education of a responsible person and yet it only takes a brief moment of unscrupulousness to twist their throats.

3.3 The self-destructive tendencies of freedom

The use of reason is a necessary prerequisite for freedom. Without reason it is not possible to be guided by causes, struggle for justice or behave autonomously towards the world. Unfortunately, however, reason alone is not a sufficient guarantee for these virtues. There are many ways to use reason and not all of them cultivate freedom, responsibility and humanity. Moreover, freedom always carries the seeds of self-destruction within it.

---

21   Klaus Goergen: Einleitung. In: Dieter Birnbacher, Klaus Goergen, Markus Tiedemann (eds.): *Normative Integration. Kulturkampf im Klassenzimmer und netzgeprägte Schülerschaft*. Schöningh, Paderborn 2021. p. VII.
22   Hartmut Esser: Integration und ethnische Schichtung. In: *Arbeitspapiere – Mannheimer Zentrum für Europäische Sozialforschung*, 40/2001. p. 3.

3.3.1 The instrumental shortening

Fritz Haber was an impressively clever and educated man. In 1918, he was awarded the Nobel Prize for Chemistry. The recognition of his invention, which was patented in 1911, seems extremely justified. It seems impossible to feed the world's population today without the catalytic synthesis of ammonia developed together with Carl Bosch. Millions of biographies owe their existence to Fritz Haber, at least indirectly. Unfortunately, Fritz Haber is not only the man who "turned air into bread "[23] but also the scientific father of German poison gas operations during the First World War. In clear disregard of the Hague Convention of 1899, Haber developed and directed the use of chlorine gas and phosgene as the first "weapons of mass destruction in world history."[24] For his efforts, Fritz Haber was made a captain. This was the highest rank possible for a Jewish citizen outside the fighting forces. Hermann Haber took his own life in 1946 when he realized that his father's developments had also laid the foundation for Zyklon B and the millions of murders in German concentration camps. His mother Clara Immerwahr castigated her husband's activities as a "perversion of science" as early as 1915, before taking her own life with his service weapon.[25]

Clara Immerwahr's formulation castigates the essence of a purely instructive use of reason. Science and rationality are not perverse in themselves, but they can be perverted. Science necessarily asks two questions: "What is it?" and "What is possible?". Only ethics and Enlightenment also insist on the questions: "How should it be?" and "What should I do?". Kant elevated the distinction between hypothetical and categorical thinking to the essence of morality.[26] Ignoring the ethical perspective reduces science to mechanical and functional feasibility.

To deny the immense dangers of purely instrumentalized reason borders on historical and social ignorance. As shown in chapter 2.3, normative achievements of the Attic Enlightenment continued to have an impact in the Roman world. This applies, among other things, to republicanism and the legal system. The perfection of instrumental reason, however, was much more durable and successful. It found its expression in organizational units, logistics and military technology. One of the reasons why the crimes of the twentieth century are

---

23 A. Hermann: Haber and Bosch: Brot aus Luft – Die Ammoniaksynthese. In: Physikalische Blätter 21, 1965. pp. 168–171.
24 Margit Szöllösi-Janze: *Fritz Haber 1868–1934. Eine Biographie*. Verlag C.H. Beck, Munich 1998. p. 317.
25 Ibid. p. 397.
26 Kant: AA III. p. 522.

so shocking is that they were also driven by rational calculation and scientific precision. According to Horkheimer and Adorno, the "collapse of bourgeois civilization" is the rule of the factual over the normative, the primacy of power over the individual, inherent in the dialectic of Enlightenment.[27] A danger that also comes to bear outside totalitarian forms of rule. According to Carl Friedrich von Weizsäcker, we live in a scientific-technical age[28]. Its dynamics tend to be detached from the awareness of responsibility and ethical implications. This applies to the use of weapons technology as well as to shopping behavior in the supermarket. Added to this is the unprecedented quality and quantity of what is possible. Few ideas have described the scientific and technological age more precisely than Günther Anders' thesis of the end of hypothetical questions. Plato and Aristotle could also have had an interesting argument about whether humanity should be. However, their dispute would have been purely hypothetical. For us, it is a very practical question. We are living in the "end times". Not because the end must be imminent, but because we can bring it about at any time.[29] For Hans Jonas, this was the reason to look for a new categorical imperative, an "imperative that fits the new type of human action and is addressed to the new type of subject of action [...]: "Act in such a way that the effects of your action are compatible with the permanence of genuine human life on earth".[30]

Technical development cannot be ignored. We need technology in order to control the problems that we have caused through technology with technology. This applies to the ruins of Chernobyl and Fukushima as well as to climate change. At the same time, there is a lack of both unquestionable evidence and undisputed moral categories that would enable us to fully comprehend the consequences of our decisions and actions. According to Ulrich Beck, humanity is inevitably faced with risk assessments without sufficient scientific and moral knowledge.[31] The coronavirus pandemic has once again highlighted the nature of a global scientific and technological risk society. The invention of technical and logistical solutions is part of the existential question of humanity.

---

27   Max Horkheimer, Theodor W. Adorno: Dialektik der Aufklärung. In: Max Horkheimer: *Gesammelte Schriften*. Vol. 5, Fischer, Frankfurt am Main 1987, pp. 16, 25.
28   Carl Friedrich von Weizsäcker: Der Mensch im wissenschaftlich-technischen Zeitalter. In: *Ausgewählte Texte*. Goldmann, Munich 1987.
29   Günther Anders: *The nuclear threat*. Published by C.H. Beck, Munich 1981.
30   Hans Jonas: *Das Prinzip Verantwortung – Versuch einer Ethik für die technologische Zivilisation*. Suhrkamp, Frankfurt 1989. p. 36.
31   Ulrich Beck: Risikogesellschaft. Überlebensfragen, Sozialstruktur und ökologische Aufklärung. In: *Aus Politik und Zeitgeschichte*. Supplement to the weekly newspaper Das Parlament, 1989. pp. 4–7.

At the same time, there is an urgent need for fundamental reflection on which problems should and may be solved and how.

Reason reduced to instrumental feasibility is threatening. It threatens the whole of humanity. For example, when people possess nuclear weapons, for whom a fictitious afterlife seems more desirable than the continued existence of this world, or when unchecked mass consumption destroys the livelihoods of future generations with their eyes wide open. The gateways for an instrumental reduction of reason are numerous. For religions and political totalitarianism, only a reason that strives for the best possible implementation of predetermined goals and truths is acceptable. Reason as a fundamental criticism, on the other hand, is toxic for these ideologies. But economic dynamics also exhibit corresponding patterns. The God of capitalism is profit maximization. Impressive sacrifices are made to it: the livelihoods of one's own children, personal lifetime, natural resources, social relationships. Instrumental reason proves to be a diligent servant of this deity. It devises increases in efficiency and products to satisfy needs, which for their part must first be invented.

Resisting the instrumental reduction remains breathtakingly demanding and laborious. Argumentation, ideology, social and self-criticism are required. So far, only the self-understanding of the Enlightenment has produced such virtues. The fact that the evils described above could not be prevented does not prove that Enlightenment and the pursuit of objectivity are wrong. It only proves how fragile the project is and how easily it can be perverted.

3.3.2 *Uprising of the masses*
It should already be clear that Enlightenment is an ambitious, rare and elitist project in the best sense of the word.

The aim of the Enlightenment is to elevate as many people as possible politically to citoyens, communicatively to competent speakers and morally to autonomous rational beings. Imagine a world population made up exclusively of responsible citizens who are guided in political and moral questions by the unconstrained compulsion of the better argument. A wonderful utopia! Nevertheless, the Enlightenment thinkers of all times were not naïve. According to Kant, the history of mankind can only be thought of as an infinite process of approaching the cosmopolitan state. A quick or even final success was not to be expected. The "crooked wood" of human nature, to use Kantian imagery, is too sluggish to be won over quickly and comprehensively to the efforts of maturity. A mature, enlightened existence is at best reserved for a steadily growing elite. For numerous authors from Aristotle to José Ortega y Gasset, elite is a normative and not a social or even an economic category.

"Nobility can be recognized by its demands on itself, by its obligations, not by its rights. – Noblesse oblige."[32] These are characters for whom the common good is more important than personal gain, and who cultivate virtues such as self-discipline, perseverance and a willingness to take responsibility. This concept of the elite differs significantly from a frequently observed understanding of the term, which refers to economically or politically privileged classes.[33] "Contrary to popular belief, it is not the masses, but the great individual who lives in servitude by nature. His life is stale if he does not spend it in the service of something higher."[34]

Certainly, these statements can be accused of naïve Platonic idealism. However, categorical distinctions are not invalid just because no flawless empirical examples can be found. What is also striking is the proximity to Kant's ethics of duty, a product of the Enlightenment, which also cannot be identified beyond doubt in social reality.

> The exquisite or outstanding person, on the other hand, is characterized by the inner necessity to look up from himself to a higher, objective norm, in the service of which he voluntarily places himself.[35]

The work of the elite understood in this way is noble because it aims to overcome its own special status by spreading Enlightenment.

Every person won over to these ideals reduces the number of minors and the specificity of the elite.

Unfortunately, humanity is not passively waiting to finally be enlightened. It is not a dormant quarry from which more and more mature jewels can be gradually extracted. A more suitable metaphor is that of an ocean, which can lie there peacefully, but can also pile up into huge and violent wave crests. Crowds that gather behind a common idea, goal or leadership are among the most powerful factors in world history. Political science, psychology and philosophy all speak of the phenomenon of the crowd.

Gustav Le Bon, the father of mass psychology, was convinced that the development of a self-determined personality is set back several stages by joining a

---

32   José Ortega Y Gasset: *Der Aufstand der Massen*. Rowohlt Taschenbuch Verlag, Hamburg 1970. p. 66f.
33   For a precise differentiation, see: Rainer Paris: Autorität- Führung- Eliten: A differentiation. In: Stefan Hradil, Peter Imbusch (eds.) *Oberschichten- Eliten- Herrschende Klassen*. Opladen: Leske + Budrich (Series Sozialstrukturanalyse; Vol. 17) 2003. pp. 55–72.
34   Gasset: p. 66.
35   Ibid.

crowd. Freud speaks of the "descend into the mass individual"[36]. Other authors, such as Erich Fromm or Theodor W. Adorno, understand the union with the masses primarily as compensation for character deficits. Almost all authors agree that masses have numerous characteristics that counteract the ideals of the Enlightenment. Le Bon mentions, among other things, "impulsiveness, irritability, inability to think logically, lack of judgment and critical spirit [and] exuberance of emotion".[37] He describes the emergence of a kind of mass soul as the part in which the individual loses all capacity for self-determined judgment. Unfortunately, history is rich in examples of hysterical or ideological mass delusion.

Masses do not always have to have a destructive effect. Heroic and humane deeds are also possible. Everything depends on the direction in which the masses are steered. For this reason, the enlightened elite cannot withdraw from the masses. On the one hand, this would be a betrayal of its own convictions, which ascribe the potential for maturity to every human being, and on the other, the destructive power of the masses would be left to its own devices. In the process, the educational work ends up in paradoxes. A guide to self-determination inevitably contains a residual element of heteronomy (see chapter 4.3.3). As long as the masses have to be motivated and guided towards Enlightenment, their status is not overcome. At best, they act in accordance with the ideals of Enlightenment, but not enlightened.

To refrain from exerting influence, however, would mean allowing irrationality and immaturity to develop freely. Just like education for maturity, not only the spread but also the continued existence of Enlightenment is always tainted with elements of incapacitating precepts. As long as the masses are masses, but should not remain so, elitist authorities are needed. Desirable authorities, according to Erich Fromm[38], have a tendency to dissolve themselves. A good teacher strives to gradually reduce the difference in knowledge between her pupils and herself. The situation is similar with the elites of the Enlightenment. Their work is also aimed at overcoming their own special status. Every person won over to the ideals of the Enlightenment causes the masses to dwindle and reduces the special status of the elite.

The Enlightenment-oriented societies of the modern era were extraordinarily successful in winning over large proportions of the population to an at

---

36   Sigmund Freud: *Massenpsychologie und Ich-Analyse*. Internationaler Psychoanalytischer Verlag GmbH, Leipzig, Vienna, Zurich 1921. p. 89.
37   Gustave Le Bon, Rudolf Eisler (transl.): *Psychologie der Massen*. Alfred Kröner Verlag, Stuttgart 1982. p. 19.
38   Erich Fromm: *Escape from Freedom*. 18th edition. Avon Books, New York 1965. p. 187.

least partially elitist way of life. The construction used to achieve this can be described *as asymmetrical symmetry*. This is a fragile construction of equality of rights and access with simultaneous inequality of expertise and argumentative justification. In his theory of justice, John Rawls formulated principles according to which inequalities are acceptable. These include "equal rights to the most extensive system of equal basic freedoms [...] that is compatible with the same system for all others" as well as "positions and offices [...] that are open to everyone."[39] In the asymmetrical symmetry of modernity, this applies not only to social and economic inequalities, which Rawls was particularly concerned with, but also to political and social rights. Those who bear political responsibility are no better before the law than those who shy away from this burden. All those who are prepared to face up to these demands must also have the opportunity to qualify themselves and seek approval. However, the following also applies: expertise is better than amateurism, knowledge is more valuable than opinion and well-founded justification is more important than mere proclamation. Our knowledge of history, politics and psychology provides good reason to believe that democracy is the best of all possible forms of government. But knowledge itself is not democratic.[40] The asymmetrical symmetry of modern, Enlightenment-oriented society is based on equality, permeability, the need for justification and the appreciation of good causes. Equality before the law, the abolition of class privileges and free access to education, qualification instances and participation forums are among the most important achievements of modernity and a guarantee of political and social permeability. Everyone who wants it should be given the opportunity to achieve qualifications and take on responsibility through discipline and effort. In any case, the ability to distinguish genuine qualification and well thought-out justification from ignorance and speculation should be acquired. The obligation to justify makes claims and desires subject to a general and reciprocal deliberation. The appreciation of good reasons guarantees the rational character of deliberation. The same applies to the recognition of expertise justified by good reasons. This applies both to the assumption of political functions and to responsibility as a voter. In representative democracies, the parties have the task of presenting voters with elaborated alternatives. Voters, in turn, are called upon to critically examine and qualitatively evaluate the alternatives. There

---

39 John Rawls: *Eine Theorie der Gerechtigkeit*. Suhrkamp Verlag, Frankfurt am Main 1979. p. 81.
40 See: Mai Thi Nguyen-Kim, Linda Tutmann: Wissenschaft ist keine Demokratie. In: *Zeit.de*. Online: https://www.zeit.de/gesellschaft/zeitgeschehen/2021-05/mai-thi-nguyen-kim-hass-internet-wissenschaftsjournalismus-pressefreiheit [Last accessed 15.08.2022].

is also the option of switching roles and presenting a political program themselves if none of the offered alternatives appear acceptable. A certain amount of gratitude can at least be expected from all those who are not prepared to make any of these efforts. Gratitude for a growing ecological and political quality of life, which they owe to the innovations and self-discipline of their fellow citizens.

The revolt of the masses now consists in the refusal of civic virtues and in the denunciation of the asymmetrical symmetry of the Enlightenment process. It undermines and denies the intellectual asymmetry between better and worse justifications as well as the connection between the claim to organization and qualification. According to Ortega y Gasset, the masses are all those who make no or at most average demands on themselves and their individual achievements, but at the same time make maximum demands regarding the fulfillment of personal wishes and needs. Particularly in times of economic and political stability, the masses forget the great achievements that made their prosperity possible in the first place. Gratitude, recognition and respect for high achievers are lost on the masses. This applies just as much to drinking water from the tap and waste disposal as it does to vaccinations or free elections. Instead, the masses are absorbed in the illusion that everything is at their disposal without being tied to any obligations.[41] The uprising of the masses describes a process that was declared by Plato as a transition to mob rule and by Ortega y Gasset as "hyperdemocracy"[42].

In a healthy democracy, according to Ortega y Gasset, the masses accept that

> Finally, despite all their mistakes and shortcomings, politicians understand a little more about public issues than they do. Now, on the other hand, they believe it is their right to push through their regulars' wisdom and endow it with the force of law. [...] It is characteristic of the present moment, however, that [sic!] the ordinary soul is aware of its ordinariness, but has the impudence to stand up for the right of ordinariness and to enforce it everywhere.[43]

Dissatisfaction does not lead to effort and the development of alternatives, but only to accusation and protest. In addition, there is an increasing demand for symmetry with a simultaneous discrediting of asymmetrical quality criteria.

---

41   Cf. Gasset: p. 41.
42   Ibid. p. 15.
43   Ibid.

According to y Gasset, the masses mistrust or hate "everything that is different, excellent, personal, gifted and exquisite".⁴⁴

This is a basic attitude that the Enlightenment itself contributed massively to developing. For y Gasset, it was a kind of hubris to familiarize the average person with liberal ideas and to trust that they would then also behave in an elitist manner.⁴⁵ "Everyone is equal." "Your voice counts as much as any other." "You have a right to be heard!". The masses heard all of this from the Enlighteners wooing them. They were happy to believe it without internalizing the elitist elements of the construction. But without striving for objectivity, without self-criticism, without distinguishing between personal preference and intersubjective justification, the hour of populism has come. A term that itself illustrates the fragility of asymmetrical symmetry. On the one hand, the involvement and active participation of the people (lat. populus) is highly desirable. This is the only way to legitimize power and the only way to counteract the formation of political and economic cartels. On the other hand, the needs of the community must not override the principle of rational justification. This is a balancing act that must be carried out on a daily basis in democratic societies.⁴⁶ "One man's populism is another person's democracy," commented Ralf Dahrendorf.⁴⁷ A loss of balance is both an expression and cause of a loss of maturity. At this point, the desirable activation of the broader population turns into destructive populism. Significant is a rhetoric that is as aggressive as it is undifferentiated, constructing a contrast between a diffuse understanding of "the people" on the one hand and the "elite" or "establishment" on the other. This leads to absurd cognitive dissonances. In the USA, a multimillionaire elected president can refuse to disclose his tax returns or push through tax relief for top earners and still be celebrated as a representative of the "little man" and a liberator from the establishment. In Germany, supporters of the AfD speak of the "lying press" and lament "ideological influence on the part of the state"⁴⁸ while at the same time articulating sympathy for Valdimir Putin's leadership. Populism constructs an emotional we-identity in contrast to a non-we and thus comes

---

44   Ibid. p. 12.
45   Ibid. p. 16.
46   Cf: Bernd Stegemann: *Das Gespenst des Populismus*. Verlag Theater der Zeit, Berlin 2017. p. 16.
47   Ralf Dahrendorf: Über Populismus. Acht Anmerkungen zum Populismus. In: *Transit. Europäische Revue* 25, 2003. pp. 156–163.
48   Election program of the 'Alternative für Deutschland' for the election to the German Bundestag on September 24, 2017. p. 47.

into conflict with the liberal view of humanity, which focuses on the free and rational choice of the individual.

This is exactly what is happening during the uprising of the masses. According to Le Bon, the masses are not interested in analysis and argumentation. They rally behind those who make them feel and believe. We remember: an awareness of the epistemic and normative differences in quality between opinion, belief and knowledge is part of the core substance of Enlightenment. If it is lost, not only personal maturity erodes, but also the collective organization as a liberal constitutional state. Of course, it would be naïve to believe that all members of a society will ever actively support the asymmetrical symmetry of Enlightenment. Nevertheless, a critical number must not be undercut. Unfortunately, this tendency is not only to be observed on the periphery of the Enlightenment-oriented world. In almost all liberal democracies, populists have taken power for at least a few election periods or form a major opposition party. With France, England and the USA, the core countries of democracy are also affected. The horror at the behavior of the 45th President of the United States of America has obscured the identification of the real problem: electorally decisive sections of American society have turned their backs on the principles of the Enlightenment. It is not about Donald Trump exhibiting unacceptable social behavior or deliberately lying. These offenses have been deplored many times long before him. What is new is that a person elected to the most important office in the land does not even try to give the impression of being interested in objectivity. If an electorate accepts this, it relieves its government of the need to justify itself with arguments.

It is little consolation that rational politicians can once again take responsibility. The fall from grace is perfect. The oldest and most influential democracy of modern times must once again be expected to be overwhelmed by the masses.

The uprising of the masses means breaking with the asymmetrical symmetry of the Enlightenment. The masses demand dominance and release both themselves and their leaders from the claim to rational justification. If this is successful, not only the ideals of the Enlightenment but also the democratic rule of law will be lost. The institutional bodies of liberal democracy may continue to resist for a while, but they cannot compensate for the loss of a majority committed to the Enlightenment. This development is currently omnipresent.

3.3.3 *Education without Humanism*
Humanism and Enlightenment are like siblings. They are not identical and can have different emphases. Nevertheless, they remain connected and know how

to complement and promote each other. Both emerged from ancient philosophy and fell into oblivion along with it. During the Renaissance, the idea of humanism was initially revived. In Pico della Mirandola, we can read how he painstakingly extracts freedom from the Christian genesis and defines man as the being who is capable of being the "sculptor of himself". "You are free to degenerate into the underworld of cattle. You are equally free to elevate yourself to the higher world of the divine by the decision of your own spirit."[49] This idea of education not only defines the heart of the humanist self-image, it also helped to bring the Enlightenment of the modern age onto the scene.

Setbacks, but also mutual tensions, had to be endured. Luther degraded Pico's free (self-)creator back to a servant of the divine plan of creation.[50] A humanism that reduced itself to pure philology needed the biting criticism of Friedrich Nietzsche. A philosophy that, with Descartes for example, retreated to pure formal science needed the cultural criticism of Rousseau. It was also necessary to remind the humanities shaped by Hegel that "the idea of complete education remains a necessary ideal"[51] and cannot be brought to a final conclusion.

Nevertheless, education, understood as a service to and process of the self-creating being, remained the central link and mutual reinforcement of humanism and Enlightenment. "Freedom is the first and indispensable condition for this education."[52] It is about cultivating the disposition that elevates people to the author of their own lives and thus generates freedom and dignity. General education was therefore always one of the core demands of the Enlightenment.

"It can be read as a continuation of Pico's anthropology when, following on from Rousseau, Kant gives his pedagogy the guiding principle that "Providence" has "not already laid" the "disposition to goodness" in man, but wants him to

---

49 Giovanni Pico della Mirandola: Über die Würde des Menschen. In: Hans-Ulrich Lessing, Volker Steenblock (eds.): *"Was den Menschen zum Menschen macht ...". Klassische Texte der Philosophie der Bildung*. Verlag Karl Alber, Freiburg im Breisgau 2010. p. 50.

50 Cf.: Jörg Ruhloff: Vom Gottesknecht zum Selbstliebhaber. Ausblicke auf Individualität, Subjektivität und Autonomie in Interpretationen des Menschen in Renaissance und Aufklärung. In: *Bildung und Erziehung 46*, 1993. pp. 167–182.

51 Hans-Georg Gadamer: *Wahrheit und Methode – Grundzüge einer Philosophischen Hermeneutik*. 7th edition. Mohr Siebeck, Tübingen 2010 [1st edition 1960]. p. 20.

52 Wilhelm von Humboldt: Ideen zu einem Versuch, die Gränzen der Wirksamkeit des Staates zu bestimmen. (1792) In: *Humboldt-Werke*, vol. I. WBG [Abt. Verlag], Darmstadt 1966, p. 64.

bring everything in the development of the species "out of himself" through the gradual development of reason and the cultivation of education.[53]

At the same time, education is the only hope for the reproduction of emancipation, maturity and autonomy. Education without humanism is therefore always an indication of the decline of the Enlightenment. It is therefore all the more regrettable that humanistic education rarely receives the attention and admiration it deserves. When I ask students about their understanding of humanistic education, they regularly refer to grammar schools that teach classical languages. A sad reduction. Although the idea of humanism is rooted in the philosophical schools of antiquity, it has little to do with cramming Latin vocabulary. Rather, it is about the ability to philosophize in a broader sense. In this context, Ekkehard Martens speaks of the fourth cultural technique for shaping human life.[54] Accordingly, humanistic education was then and is now a school of emancipation understood as rational empowerment over traditions, authorities and emotions as well as a practice of mutual respect on the basis of a rationally generated sense of responsibility.

> The ability to form reasonable, well-founded convictions (1), the ability to shape one's life autonomously (2) and the ability to assume responsibility (3) are the central educational goals of a renewed humanism.[55]

The program is as noble as it is demanding and failure is possible at any time, not only at the level of individual biographies, but also at the level of entire collectives. The problems begin with the fact that humanistic education contains two unavoidable paradoxes. The first is that education for maturity can never be organized without a moment of incapacitation. This moment is already abundantly clear in the original narrative of pedagogy, Plato's allegory of the cave. The shadow worshipper has to be taken up the steep, stony path to the cave exit against his will. Once there, he wishes for some time to pass and suffers from the many overwhelming pressures. Only gradually does he recognize the quality of his new existence and see through the connection

---

53   Jörg Ruhloff: Die Tradition der humanistischen Bildung seit der Renaissance und die gegenwärtige Neudefinition der "Bildung". In: Hans-Ulrich Lessing, Volker Steenblock (eds.): *"Was den Menschen zum Menschen macht ...". Klassische Texte der Philosophie der Bildung*. Verlag Karl Alber, Freiburg im Breisgau 2010, p. 194.

54   Ekkehard Martens: Philosophie als Kulturtechnik humaner Lebensgestaltung. In: Julian Nida-Rümelin, Irina Spiegel, Markus Tiedemann (eds.): *Handbuch der Philosophie und Ethik. Volume I: Didaktik und Methodologie*. 2nd edition. Schöningh, Paderborn 2017. pp. 41–47.

55   Julian Nida-Rümelin: *Philosophie einer humanen Bildung*. Edition Körber-Stiftung, Hamburg 2013. p. 83.

between cause and image of being and appearance. Once he has reached this insight, he would rather "till the field as a day laborer to a poor man and let everything pass him by than to have such ideas again as there and to live like that."[56] Numerous dramatic examples can be found for Platon's parable. In their early years, Hans and Sophie Scholl were enthusiastic supporters of national socialist youth organizations. Only the bitter impressions of the war and the intellectual stimuli of their studies allowed them to see through the shadowy game of Nazi propaganda. But even seemingly mundane things such as compulsory schooling illustrate the moment of incapacitation on the path to maturity. The power of judgment enables freedom, but its development requires instruction, practice and a minimum of guidelines. The advantages of acquired skills, the explanatory power of basic theories and historical knowledge, the beauty of literary works or the empowering effect of logical thinking can only be explained a priori to a limited extent and only become apparent once they have been acquired. The central problem is that indoctrination and systematic incapacitation also follow a similar pattern. "Everything still feels wrong, but just wait and see. When we have worked on you long enough, you will think for yourself that everything was for your own good!" The only difference between Enlightenment and indoctrination, the all-important *game changer*, is education in criticism. Only humanism and Enlightenment also make themselves the object of criticism by their educated subjects and rely solely on the unconstrained compulsion of the better argument. A certain degree of paradox cannot be avoided on the way to this goal. The development of judgment and autonomy cannot be realized without moments of guidance and authority. Understanding this also means realizing the difficult balancing act that has to be performed day after day in a humanistic education system.

The second unavoidable burden of any educational system striving for Enlightenment is the paradox of freedom. In an act of freedom, we can choose unfreedom. Any humanistically educated person capable of an enlightened life can decide to lead a life of immaturity out of convenience, fear or indifference. Precisely because an appropriate education places free choice at the center and at the same time maturity and Enlightenment promise freedom and dignity, but not happiness, it is always possible that all efforts were in vain and the freedom made possible remains unused. Once again: man is only endowed with reason, he is not rational. For Kant, man has a natural inclination towards good and a tendency towards evil. The gift of reason

---

56 Cf.: Plato: Politeia 516 e-d. In: Friedrich Schleiermacher (ed.): Platons Werke: Dritten Theiles erster Band. Reimer, Berlin 1862. p. 234.

makes it possible to recognize and acknowledge what is ethically imperative. This creates the potential to rise above one's inclinations in an act of freedom. However, if there is a lack of willpower, then despite insight into the moral law, a primacy of inclinations, egoism and comfortable incapacitation can be decided. In these moments, education for maturity has failed. In order to resist this tendency, the strength and determination must be gained from a humanistic self-education process.

Enlightenment is therefore dependent on a minimum of humanistic educational success. The educational goals described above are indispensable for the existence of enlightened ways of life. Unfortunately, it does not follow that their success could be guaranteed. Education without Enlightenment, without humanism, is possible at any time. Authoritarian societies deliberately avoid emancipatory elements and use their education systems as an instrument of externally controlled formation. But even societies that have already undergone processes of Enlightenment can lose the level of education they have achieved. This does not require a dramatic political upheaval. A creeping dehumanization of the education system can currently be observed. One of the driving forces behind this is another facet of institutional shortening. This is a lack of appreciation and a moment of constructivist self-destruction.

Let's start with the economic reduction of the concept of education. This is expressed in the increasing equation of education and training. But education "is actually quite different from being educated. We undergo training with the aim of being able to do something. When we educate ourselves, on the other hand, we work on becoming something – we strive to be in the world in a certain way."[57] Pure education can be pursued in any social system. Bricklayers, doctors, architects or train drivers are trained almost everywhere according to very similar subject-specific curricula. Only the general education components indicate whether overarching virtues such as critical faculties or judgment are desired in addition to pure skills. The reduction to the mere teaching of skills can be the result of an ideological calculation. Dictators want train drivers, but not autonomously judging citizens. However, reducing education to training can also result from an economically narrow perspective.

When school leaving exams are reduced in order to get young people into the job market more quickly and the dramatic decline in school theater groups, music clubs, debating clubs or sports events is not heard as a counter-argument, this tendency becomes abundantly clear.

---

57   Peter Bieri: Wie wäre es, gebildet zu sein? In: Hans-Ulrich Lessing, Volker Steenblock (eds.): *"Was den Menschen eigentlich zum Menschen macht ...". Klassische Texte einer Philosophie der Bildung.* Verlag Karl Albert, Freiburg im Breisgau 2010. p. 208.

"In countries without natural resources, education is the only resource!" – Put this phrase to the test and enter it into a search engine such as Ecosia. You will find that the corresponding titles are part of the standard repertoire of the media landscape. There is actually nothing wrong with this. On the contrary: on the one hand, the statement is fact-based and, on the other, it results in pleasing calls for increased investments in daycare centers, schools and universities. Nevertheless, it should be noted that once again the economic perspective alone sets the tone. The statement is not "If we want to continue living in a liberal democracy, we need people who are able and willing to engage in critical deliberation". Rather, the decisive factor is what generates added value. A dramatic shortening of the understanding of education.

> The return on 'investment' in 'human capital' becomes the central criterion of educational quality. As a consequence, however, this means 'dumbing down'. For the interpretation of the content of learning and education, it fosters a tendency to favor topics or thematic accentuations of meaning that are behaviorally relevant in the sense of educating a higher personal market price. Philosophy and the teaching of philosophy are not completely sidelined as a result, but they do come under specific pressure to legitimize themselves [...].[58]

Of course, education is also a key driver of our value chains, but above all it is a necessary condition for the continuation of our collective freedom.

"Without education, our free social order cannot be saved!". The usual search engines find headlines like these in much smaller numbers.

The lack of appreciation that humanistic education suffers from is also partly due to the instrumental reduction. Those who see education solely as preparation for working life primarily see their own economic opportunities and not the importance for a free social system. Arts and humanities subjects, political education and the training of judgment are quickly degraded to an incidental 'nice to have'. But even when the necessity of these educational goods has been realized, their production can be dismissed as an incidental side effect. An attitude that can express snobbery or trivialization in equal measure. While some formulate expectations that are utopian under the given framework conditions, others ignore any obligation to deliver. In public discourse, too, the school, which was originally conceived as an educational institution was

---

58   Jörg Ruhloff: Die Tradition der humanistischen Bildung seit der Renaissance und die gegenwärtige Neudefinition der "Bildung". In: Hans-Ulrich Lessing, Volker Steenblock (eds.): *"Was den Menschen zum Menschen macht ...". Klassische Texte der Philosophie der Bildung.* Verlag Karl Alber, Freiburg im Breisgau 2010. p. 199.

increasingly understood as a pedagogical compensation instance.[59] It is often forgotten that it is the task of parents and caregivers to ensure that children start school ready for education. The creation of elementary educational skills is a task of education and not of the institution of school. In conversations with teachers, educators and school administrators, I am increasingly told that a steadily increasing number of children do not have the social and emotional prerequisites to be educated. In many places, gratitude for a free education seems to be giving way to mindless expectations.

If the workload increases and social esteem decreases at the same time, there is a risk of a downward spiral. Fewer and fewer mentally and intellectually suitable individuals see teaching as an attractive profession. At the same time, a massive increase in demand is making it possible for less qualified people to enter the teaching profession. They will set lower standards and have a corresponding influence on the student body. The standard of schools is falling and a growing number of school leavers will have poor teachers as role models when they decide to study to become teachers themselves. No one can say when the threshold will be reached at which the many excellent teachers still available will be outnumbered. Norbert Seibert, Professor of Education at the University of Passau and initiator of the "Parcours" aptitude test, currently considers 40% of students studying to become teachers to be unsuitable.[60] However, it would not be difficult to organize a cure. All universities that offer teacher training would only have to offer an exclusive teacher training course in addition to the well-known course. Applicants for this course would have to qualify not only through good school grades, but also through a separate selection process. Extended technical and pedagogical requirements would then also have to be integrated during the course of study. Graduates of the exclusive course would not only be rewarded with a higher starting salary, but should also be given preferential access to multiplier functions such as specialist seminar or school management. All of this could be achieved at a manageable cost. Obviously, however, there is a lack of awareness of the emerging problem and the value of good humanistic education.

The third factor to be discussed here is the self-deconstruction of humanistic education. The low intellectual persuasive power of radical constructivism has already been addressed in this book, as have its dangerous social and

---

59 Peter Gathen, Martin Mönikes: Eltern überlassen Erziehung der Schule. In: *Rheinische Post* 22.01.2022.
60 Cf. https://www.sueddeutsche.de/bildung/bildung-paedagogik-professor-ueber-40-prozent-der-lehrer-uneeignet-dpa.urn-newsml-dpa-com-20090101-210924-99-339532 [last accessed 31.08.2022].

political dynamics. Education is not spared from this either. Decades in which deconstructivism and postmodern thinking dominated universities and were taught to prospective teachers have left serious traces. Without the obligation to justify, without an increasing quality of good reasons, there is no humanistic education.

Humanism and the Enlightenment attempt to promote emancipation through the training of judgment. Educational subjects should be enabled to relate to X in a critical and category-led way. Constructivism and relativism take away the ground from this project when they neglect or even seek to overcome categories such as "true or false, justified or not justified, real or illusory, scientific or ideological, legitimate or abusive"[61].

Of course, the principles and the program of Enlightenment must also become the object of criticism. The Enlightenment itself demands this. However, it is quite a different matter to proclaim the fundamental equality of all interpretations of the world, to negate the existence of better arguments and to place every universal claim to truth under general suspicion.

Strictly speaking, this makes any transfer of knowledge impossible. The natural sciences, which are characterized by data collection, still show a fairly high resistance to relativistic tendencies. The situation is different in the humanities, where man-made facts, values and norms are negotiated. This tendency can be observed quite clearly among prospective teachers. In my seminars, the Big Bang theory and the creation myth have been compared several times. Two very different positions often clash here. The scientific faction claims certainty for the Big Bang theory, while the constructivist faction speaks of a multitude of equally valid narratives. Neither position corresponds to the principle of enlightened criticism.

Of course, the Big Bang theory also works with unproven premises. The assumption that something exploded out of nothing is beyond our imagination, which is why the mystery of the beginning in time and space remains unresolved. However, this does not mean that the Big Bang theory and creationism are epistemically equal and that the dominance of the physical explanation of the world is solely the result of domination. The physical explanation of the world has prevailed against the dominance of myth because it has rationality and evidence on its side. A free society must not prohibit parents from taking their children to the "Ark Encounter" amusement park in Kentucky to be told that the earth was created by an old man within seven days around 6000 years ago. However, there is neither a normative nor an epistemic

---

61   Michel Foucault: Was ist Kritik? (translated by Walter Seitter). Merve Verlag, Berlin 1992, p. 31.

necessity to recognize this myth as an equal educational asset. It is not discriminatory to point out that although the physical theory of the creation of the world is not ultimately justified, it is supported by empirical, intersubjectively verifiable evidence as well as by coherent calculations. The same applies to the network of neighboring sciences which confirm the physical explanation of the world. Likewise, it is neither disrespectful nor discriminatory to point out that religious explanations of the world do not fulfill any of these criteria. Anyone who disagrees with this is turning away from the principle of general, reciprocal and intersubjective justification. In short: they throw Enlightenment and humanism overboard.

In educational work, the fallacy quickly arises that the purely additive naming of different opinions already embodies a significant added value or even the final learning objective. This may be true in individual socially highly problematic learning groups. As a general rule, however, it means nothing less than elevating indifference to an educational goal. Enlightenment demands more than that. Enlightenment demands the willingness not only to name one's own and others' convictions, but also to subject them to critical scrutiny. Everyone has the right to their own opinion, but not to recognition of it. While opinions exist in the plural, truth does not. In particular at school and in teacher training, other tones are increasingly being heard instead. "Everyone has their own truth!" – "I am allowed to have my opinion!" – "Criticizing our traditions is intolerant!". Pupils' statements of this kind reflect a growing part of the public discourse.

If, at the same time, teachers at universities are taught that Enlightenment and the pursuit of objectivity are only a narrative dominated by prejudice and that the aim must now be to accept everyone as the "inventor of his reality"[62], the claim to reciprocal and intersubjective justification will disappear.

Unfortunately, in numerous academic discourses, but also in teacher training, deconstructionism and relativism have mutated into a crude ideology with a paradoxical claim to universality.

In spring 2021, I took part in a conference on racism-sensitive teaching. The paradigm of constructivism was omnipresent. An opening contribution, with a brilliant knowledge of Derrida and Foucault, was able to demonstrate the extent to which our everyday language is permeated by racism and power structures. A reflection that should be shared with all prospective teachers. The same applies to the thesis that education must contribute to exposing and deconstructing these structures. What was irritating, however, was the

---

62 Kersten Reich: Systemisch-konstruktivistische Pädagogik. Beltz, Weinheim 2010. p. 193.

absoluteness with which this perspective was presented as the only correct one for assessing teaching material and social situations. The youth novel "Our Wild Blood" by Nur Öneren and Wolfgang Schnellbächer served as an example. It is about the secret love between Alexander and Aysel as well as Aysel's brother Ilhan, who on the one hand tries to preserve the family honor by harassing his sister and on the other hand is himself attracted by the promises of a liberal lifestyle. An identification of the stereotypes contained in the text was presented as an appropriate teaching unit in German. An approach that was entirely convincing. In fact, the protagonists of the novel serve not only stereotypes but also prejudices: the good German boy, the oppressed, clever Muslim girl, the chauvinistic brother. All of this deserves to be reflected upon. However, the thesis that this is the only didactically legitimate way to treat the novel in class was shocking. Indeed, it was even said that a book like "Our Wild Blood" should not have been printed, especially as the play "Wild Blood" had long since deconstructed the prevailing clichés. When I asked whether there were not also real chauvinistic brothers, real oppression of Muslim girls and real desperate lovers, I was accused of constructing discriminatory prejudices without reflection.

In February 2022, a grotesque production of a similar kind unfolded in Germany. It was triggered by a task in the textbook "Zugänge zur Philosophie" (Approaches to Philosophy) published by the renowned Cornelsen publishing house.

In the volume for the introductory phase, the following case study can be found in the topic area "An ethic for all cultures" (cultural relativism vs. universalism):

> A Turkish father in Germany marries his daughter to his brother's son without her consent in order to secure him a residence permit for Germany and thus a livelihood.[63]

According to one of the editors, the case was constructed in this way,

> "because the Turkish father mentioned there has a thoroughly recognizable and understandable moral motive: concern for the well-being of the family, especially that of the fatherless nephew. It should become clear to the students that two well-founded moral principles – with different cultural values – are in conflict here: concern for the well-being of the family as a whole and

---

63   Lothar Aßmann, Reiner Bergmann, Roland W. Henke, Matthias Schulz, Eva-Maria Sewing: *Zugänge zur Philosophie – Grundband für die Oberstufe*, Cornelsen Verlag, Berlin 2002. p. 36.

the autonomy of the girl as an individual. And this chapter is about such conflicts between conflicting moral principles of different cultures. The textbook explicitly calls for respect towards other cultures, precisely because – and this is also explicitly stated – European civilization has oppressed these cultures for centuries, and appeals to people to distance themselves from their own prejudices."[64]

In a philosophy class at a grammar school in Siegburg near Bonn, a teacher had put the case in question up for discussion in his class. The corresponding worksheet found its way to Fatih Zingal, a social media activist with close ties to the Turkish AKP.[65] The suspicion spread via Facebook that teachers were using the material to discriminate against students of Turkish origin. Shortly afterwards, the Turkish state broadcaster TRT took up the case and the school was hit by what is known as a 'shitstorm'. The deputy state chairman of the Federation of Turkish Parents' Associations in North Rhine-Westphalia accused the exercise of "racism" and a "vocabulary of right-wing extremist populists" and wrote an open letter to the Minister of Education.

This initial situation would actually have been a great opportunity to practice an enlightened way of life. The following arguments would have been absolutely compelling in order to rightly reject the teaching practice or the textbook as racist and in need of reform. Firstly, it would be racist if the teaching and the textbook were to portray the fictional father's behavior as representative of all Turks in Germany. Secondly, it would be racist to only thematize people of Turkish origin in negative contexts. Thirdly, it would be racist if only conflict-ridden issues of the Turkish-Muslim cultural area were discussed, but other problems such as right-wing radicalism and xenophobia were concealed. Fourthly, the accusation of racism would be justified if the problem of forced marriages were fictitious and did not exist in reality. But none of this is the case.

The textbook "Zugänge zur Philosophie" has been in use since 1995 and has been confirmed as balanced and suitable by the accreditation commissions of numerous federal states. The same applies to the curriculum of North Rhine-Westphalia and the school in question, which participates in the "School without Racism" program. All of them address numerous social problems, including right-wing radicalism and xenophobia. Above all, however, forced

---

64   Cf. Klaus Draken and Matthias Schulze: Im Gespräch: Über den Umgang mit kontroversen Beispielen im Philosophie- und Ethikunterricht. In: ZDPE. Issue 4/2022.
65   Claudia Hauser: Schulaufgabe sorgt für Entrüstung. In: Bonner Generalanzeiger, 14.02.2022. p. 22.

marriages are real and not a rare fate. To remain silent about them would be to deny reality.

It should be added in passing that academic subject didactics attaches great importance to the so-called "life-world reference" for philosophy and ethics lessons.[66] When the Georg Eckert Institute – Leibniz Institute for International Textbook Research awarded the philosophy book "philo" in 2016 the "Textbook of the Year", the jury praised the illustration of the "classic questions of philosophy based on current controversies."[67]

It would therefore have been appropriate to protect the textbook, the school and, above all, the colleague concerned. Only the opposite was practiced. Although the school management rejected the accusation of racism, it apologized to anyone "who might feel hurt".[68] The Ministry of Education of North Rhine-Westphalia announced "that the specific task [...] violated the criterion of non-discrimination" and that it would "also intensively examine the textbook in question and ask the publisher to revise the textbook."[69] The obligation to justification is abandoned. It is enough for someone to feel offended. A fatal signal effect. A post-Enlightenment structure is beginning to dominate education.

When asked, the German office of the organization TERRE DES FEMMES emphasized that they were not aware of the relevant materials and could not assess them. With regard to the context, however, permission was granted to quote the following statement.

> "Girls and young women are oppressed for various reasons. In Germany, too, girls and young women are controlled by their brothers or male relatives; they are not allowed to shape their lives freely and independently; they are betrothed/(forcibly) married at an early age in traditional/religious ceremonies (and sometimes deported abroad) and are threatened with concrete violence in the name of

---

66 Cf.: Tilo Klaiber: Die Macht des Beispiels beim Philosophieren (Lehren und Lernen). In: ZDPE 4/2018: Klima und Umwelt. pp. 80–94; Hubertus Stelzer: Lebensweltbezug. In: Julian Nida-Rümelin, Irina Spiegel, Markus Tiedemann (eds.): Handbuch der Philosophie und Ethik. Volume I: Didaktik und Methodik. 2nd edition. Schöningh, Paderborn 2017.
67 Cf: Bundeszentrale für Politische Bildung (ed.): *Sieger des Preises "Schulbuch des Jahres 2016" stehen fest.* https://www.bpb.de/die-bpb/presse/223256/sieger-des-preises-schulbuch-des-jahres-2016-stehen-fest/ [Last accessed 31.08.2022].
68 Claudia Hauser: Schulaufgabe sorgt für Entrüstung. In: Bonner Generalanzeiger, 14.02.2022. p. 22.
69 Cf. https://www1.wdr.de/nachrichten/landespolitik/siegburg-schulbuch-ethik-diskussion-100.html [last accessed 23.04.2022]; Klaus Draken and Matthias Schulze: Im Gespräch:
    Über den Umgang mit kontroversen Beispielen im Philosophie- und Ethikunterricht. In: ZDPE. Issue 4/2022.

honor if they do not comply with the will of their family/their (future) husband. There are no current figures or statistics on forced marriages or 'honor' killings in Germany. The latest nationwide study by the Federal Ministry for Family Affairs (2011) states that 3,443 people per year in Germany were threatened or affected by a forced marriage, 93% of whom were girls and women who often suffered massive violence from their family members beforehand; the number of unreported cases is estimated to be much higher. This human rights violation must be openly addressed in order to conceive and implement tailored prevention measures and offers of help."[70]

Ignoring the facts described here stems from the pedagogical and conceptual error that it is only possible to carry out either anti-racist educational work or criticism of identity-forming traditions.

For a genuine humanistic, enlightened education, however, there is no either-or, but only a both-and. Prejudices and stereotypes must be criticized just as much as the oppression of women and the idealization of patriarchal traditions. In any case, it is necessary to differentiate between better and worse arguments. The principle of equal rights for all narratives leads to merely methodically prepared school lessons and a long-term erosion of liberal society.

> When students openly express racist, chauvinist and sexist views, when they invoke religious commandments to speak out against freedom and equality, in favor of oppression, dictatorship and violence, when they consider the state monopoly on the use of force and the democratic constitutional order as a whole to be non-binding and void with religious fervor, because God alone tells them what is valid[71], when they declare creationism to be irrefutable and climate change to be a deception, then it is not a good idea to declare a safe theory of Enlightenment, of emancipation, which knows how to proclaim who is to be emancipated and with what content'[72], as obsolete, to warn against 'victor theories' and to rely on the creation of 'open learning environments', 'observer diversity'[73] and the 'movable wall technique'[74].[75]

---

70   Statement of the organization TERRE DES FEMMES from 16.09.2021, archive of the author.
71   Marcus C. Schulte von Drach: Muslime und Migranten: Gibt es Parallelgesellschaften in Deutschland? In: *Süddeutsche Zeitung*, 10. 8. 2016.
72   Kersten Reich: Systemisch-konstruktivistische Didaktik. In: Rudolf Voß (ed.): *Schule neu erfinden*. Luchterhand, Neuwied 1996. pp. 70–91, here p. 70.
73   Ibid. p. 74.
74   Kersten Reich: Konstruktivistische Unterrichtsmethoden. Lehrtheoretische Voraussetzungen und ausgewählte Beispiele. In: *System Schule*, 2/1998. pp. 20–26, here p. 22.
75   Klaus Goergen: Wider den grassierenden Konstruktivismus unter Lehrkräften. In: Hans- Ulrich Lessing, Markus Tiedemann, Joachim Siebert (eds.): *Kultur der*

No less destructive is the fundamental protection of minority opinions.

> Yet schools – and philosophy and ethics lessons in particular – are precisely the place where such controversies can be conducted in a rational manner. If this no longer takes place because teachers have to fear campaigns from outside and a lack of support from their superiors, we will lose one of the most important places for rational social discourse.[76]

Victor Hugo is credited with the quote "In every village there is a torch, the teacher, and someone who extinguishes this light, the priest." The problematic role of religion and its growing influence will not be discussed here. Rather, the aim is to identify secular, humanistic education as the elixir of life in enlightened societies and to realize that its effectiveness cannot be taken for granted. Those who no longer see education as the torch of Enlightenment should not complain about the rapidly increasing darkness.

3.3.4 *Wrong use for the right thing. Cancel Culture and language loss*
In recent years, I have read more and more term papers in which students only write 'N-word' or 'Z-word' in their texts. It is even more noticeable when the corresponding passages in historical sources are interspersed with placeholders. This political correctness, also known as cancel culture, can be attributed to many sympathetic intentions, but it harbors a dangerous dialectic. Racism is not only a sad reality, but also one of the most fundamental threats to enlightened ways of life, which must also be countered through linguistic criticism. However, the challenge is to push back discrimination without becoming dogmatic.

Language is an instrument that is as dangerous as it is necessary and liberating. Language can construct opposites, establish enemy stereotypes and legitimize violence. However, language is just as indispensable for naming injustice, analyzing structures and developing self-understandings. Restricting language always means limiting these possibilities. A genuine emancipation process is about "sounding out sensations and questioning meanings, testing the scope of ideas and attitudes, examining arguments, attitudes, truth claims and courses of action, and to a certain extent also going astray."[77]

---

philosophischen Bildung. Volker Steenblock zum 60. Geburtstag. Siebert-Verlag, Hanover 2018. p. 233.

76 Klaus Draken, Matthias Schulze: Im Gespräch: Über den Umgang mit kontroversen Beispielen im Philosophie- und Ethikunterricht. In: *ZDPE*. Issue 4/2022, in print.

77 Jörg Ruhloff: Die Tradition der humanistischen Bildung seit der Renaissance und die gegenwärtige Neudefinition der "Bildung". In: Hans-Ulrich Lessing, Volker Steenblock

"Language alone protects us from the horror of nameless things." This impressive formulation from Toni Morrison's Nobel Prize speech can be used to recall a central aspect of Enlightenment: empowerment. Every trauma therapy strives to enable the patient to name and evaluate what they have experienced. Education and emancipation are also acts of linguistic empowerment. In the opposite direction, mastery and incapacitation structures have been and continue to be reinforced through speechlessness. That which cannot be named or can only be named imprecisely cannot be analyzed and evaluated. Those who do not even understand the language in which their religion is preached must bow to the interpretations of the priests. Those who have no access to information and terminology cannot participate in central discourses. Those for whom phenomena and terms are stigmatized find it difficult to even formulate some questions and thoughts. In the spring of 2022, Russian state media were banned from using the term 'war' in connection with the invasion of Ukraine. This made it impossible to discuss whether it was a war or whether it was justified. The events took on completely absurd, Orwellian proportions when even supporters of the attack were arrested because they spoke of war and not of a special military operation.[78] Religions have a particularly strong tradition of language stigmatization. As long as the use of terms such as 'Satan' or 'devil' arouse fear and horror, the likelihood of anyone questioning their existence decreases. How convenient for all those whose power is based on this very fear. Important liberation processes in human history have always been linked to the oppressed and disenfranchised overcoming their speechlessness. 'Exploitation', 'capital accumulation', 'equality', 'instrumentalization', 'racism', 'chauvinism', 'structural violence': terms like these represent important additions to our language that make it possible to identify injustice and combat it in a targeted manner. No humane progress has yet been made by banning language.

Nevertheless, current language criticism relies at least as much on prohibition and stigmatization as on empowerment.

Racism-sensitive language is an imperative of fairness and respectful cooperation. However, neither the awareness of the different levels of language nor of claims to validity that can be rationally justified should be overlooked. At least three levels of our language and their potential for discrimination must be distinguished.

(eds.): *"Was den Menschen zum Menschen macht ..."*. *Klassische Texte der Philosophie der Bildung*. Verlag Karl Alber, Freiburg im Breisgau 2010. p. 202.

78 See: https://www.nzz.ch/international/ukraine-russlands-luftwaffe-erleidet-bisher-schwerste-verluste-ld.1674908 [last accessed 23.07.2022].

At the level of direct communication or even personal designation, the use of such terms is simply a racist vulgarity. Why is that? Because it is impolite and unappealing? Certainly, the real problem lies deeper and consists in the manifestation of a vertical distribution of power. Fair communication always strives for a horizontal balance of power and the possibility of reciprocity. During negotiations, it is unfair to temporarily switch to a language that the other party does not understand without the excluded party being able to do the same. Examples can be found at various levels. English-speaking people without foreign language skills in particular are familiar with the situation of switching to a foreign language during a discussion. They are unable to follow without being able to open up an exclusive linguistic space. It is not uncommon for supposed intellectuals to use technical terms only to unsettle less educated interlocutors. Even with insults it is similar. These become particularly vicious when derogatory terms are used that cannot be returned. A situation that can arise not only due to language barriers or educational differences. Until the 1980s, it was a common experience for many young Germans to be called a 'Nazi' in England or the Netherlands. A painful insult on many levels, which could not be reciprocated and thus established a vertical distribution of power. Racist vocabulary often has a similar structure. In his podcast with Bruce Springsteen, Barack Obama talks about an argument with a childhood friend. A normal, emotionally charged argument between adolescents that resulted in mutual insults. But when the insult became racist, an unfair vertical power shift was added. The 'white' friend may not have been a racist in the ideological sense, but he used a way to hurt without having to run the risk of being hurt in the same way. So it is far more than just the rules of politeness that underpin a corresponding vocabulary. It is about the general rules of fairness and reciprocity.

Of course, this also applies if no offense is intended. In 2021, show host Thomas Gottschalk expressed his incomprehension of what he perceived as "hypocritical" linguistic oversensitivity. He justified his lack of understanding regarding racism-sensitive language by stating that he did not intend any disparagement by using certain vocabulary: "[…] it doesn't matter if I call a black person a Moor. That has nothing to do with me disrespecting them in the slightest."[79] Thomas Gottschalk's egalitarian and philanthropic attitude is certainly credible. However, this justification of his use of language only has a very limited scope. If you unintentionally step on my foot, I will not hold this against you. It is different, however, if you remain standing on my foot after I

---

79   WDR 2020 https://www.youtube.com/watch?v=vazgNVl_3jA&t=1120s [Last accessed 23.08.2022].

have pointed it out to you. Making the speaker's intentions the sole yardstick for judging communication not only re-establishes a vertical distribution of power, but also falls short of the most elementary principles of communication theory. Between the intention of the sender and the understanding of the receiver lies a context-bound hermeneutic process that should be reflected upon and taken into account.

Exceptions are acceptable if the vocabulary used is both necessary and without alternative. An emergency doctor may call out loudly for a vascular clamp even if she knows that some bystanders associate the term with traumatic experiences. However, it is almost impossible to construct such a situation in the dispute over racism-sensitive language. Endless debates are possible as to whether the term 'people of color' is an ideal solution; after all, the South African apartheid regime also has a burdened tradition here. However, it is undisputed that there are alternatives to the N-word. Thomas Gottschalk and many others can therefore be expected to rethink their use of language. His communication options are in no way restricted and his intention is insufficient as the sole yardstick for normative assessment.

The situation is very similar at the level of administrative language, such as official announcements or legal texts. It is completely incomprehensible why administrations and legislators should use terms that offend a section of the population. Alternatives are available. Of course, there are limits here too and sensitivity must not be taken to absurd extremes. The progressive Saxon Integration and Participation Act (SITG)[80] was massively delayed because there was no agreement on how the people for whose benefit the law was intended should be named. A linguist who was consulted advised that each group should decide for itself what it wanted to be called. However, as the law was intended to support a large number of groups at the same time and there was no clarity about the desired name either between the groups or within the individual groups, the legislators' despair was quite understandable.[81]

It is of central importance to clearly distinguish the level of meta-language from that of direct communication and administrative language. Talking about discriminatory language is not itself discrimination. *Mentioning* racist terms is not the same as their normative *use*. Much research has been done on the intended and unintended consequences of derogatory vocabulary. Anglo-Saxon literature in particular analyzes the different effects of 'slurs' (disparagement, denigration). These are not only used to directly insult individual

---

80   https://www.zik.sachsen.de/integrationsgesetz.html [Last accessed 15.08.2022].
81   As a member of the Saxon Integration Council, the author took part in the relevant meetings.

target groups, but also for the general spread and hardening of negative attitudes. There is also a psychological aspect. Even the mere mention of vocabulary in a purely factual context can remind people of injuries they have already suffered. Authors such as Luvell Anderson and Ernie Lepore therefore tend to declare both use and mention as inadmissible.[82]

However, this linguistic prohibitionism has been contradicted for good reasons. For example, Stefan Rinner and Alexander Hieke were able to show that the factual mention and citation of discriminatory vocabulary makes an important contribution to the processing of racist phenomena in terms of content.[83] Therefore, an undifferentiated ban is neither justified nor desirable. Of course, the rejection of language prohibition does not mean a blanket absolution for unreflected vocabulary. Psychological insults may not be intended, but they do exist. Of course, language can both reflect and reinforce power structures. However, if language is only reduced to power this presents a sad reduction. It should be mentioned in passing that this simply ignores central findings of the philosophy of language. According to Wittgenstein, the meaning of a word is its use in language which can be very diverse. An example for this is: "Negro is coming tomorrow to repair the roof." Most of us will feel both grammatical regret due to the lack of an article and moral indignation at this utterance. However, when we learn that it is the surname of a real-life tradesman's business, the need for grammatical correction diminishes and moral outrage would be absurd.

In all the previous sentences, I could have written 'Negro' instead of 'N-word' without being racist. The debate about the nature and limits of racism consists of the giving and taking of reasons. There is also no vertical distribution of power. In the dispute over the correct interpretation, origin or skin color are irrelevant. However, psychological factors remain. I will therefore have to ask myself what added value the mention has and whether potential offenses were unavoidable. Nevertheless, the following differentiation remains: quoting and mentioning disparaging vocabulary can have very different causes. These include hidden racism as well as a lack of sensitivity or scientific honesty. Racists are always scientifically dishonest and insensitive, but insensitive people can be just as anti-racist as people who feel committed to scientific accuracy.

---

82 Cf.: Luvell Anderson, Ernie Lepore: Did you call me? Slurs as prohibited words: Setting things up. In: *Analytic Philosophy, 54(3)*, 2013. pp. 350–63; Luvell Anderson, Ernie Lepore: Slurring words. In: Noûs, 47(1), 2013. pp. 25–48.
83 Stefan Rinner, Alexander Hieke: Slurs under quotation. In: Philosophical Studies – An International Journal for Philosophy in the Analytic Tradition, 21.08.2021.

Denying this differentiation means opening the door to numerous forms of irrationality. Some of these problematic developments have already been discussed. Unfortunately, many more can be named.

Let's start with the confusion between role reversal and equality.

During an interview in 2013, a journalist wanted to talk to actor Samuel L Jackson about the use of the N-word in the film "Django Unchained" and was heckled by the actor.[84] In a loud voice, Jackson repeatedly and vehemently demanded that the journalist say the N-word. As oppressive as the situation was, it highlighted an important aspect that will be discussed later. First, however, it should be emphasized that the moral imperatives of fairness and reciprocity were once again disregarded. Equality does not materialize. The vertical distribution of power is not overcome, it merely changes sides. While the use of a vocabulary by one individual is interpreted as an act of empowerment, the other participant in the conversation is suspected of racism. Jackson forces his counterpart into a position that he is unable to force him into. Either the journalist avoids a vocabulary, a sequence of sounds, out of childlike fear, or he has to take the risk of being condemned as a racist. Equality should not be confused with role reversal. It is psychologically understandable and pedagogically and politically productive to a certain extent to grant special linguistic rights to discriminated groups. Nevertheless, there is a danger of losing sight of the goal of a horizontal distribution of power.

At the same time, Jackson's intervention also points to an important aspect: the 'Voldemort effect'. On a meta-linguistic level, in a conversation about a phenomenon, it is infantile not to call it by its name. Through stigmatization, vocabulary is ascribed an almost magical meaning. It is like the name of the evil wizard, which cannot be named without the protagonists of the Harry Potter universe going into either shock, hysteria or falling into an apocalyptic mood. A power that is generated in the novel, as in the real world, by the lack of differentiation between speech acts. Talking about evil does not mean conjuring it up. It makes a difference whether a word is used as a form of address, a designation or as an object of contemplation itself. Talking about racism is not the same as racism, even if terms are used that should be avoided for good reasons in other contexts. It is therefore only logical for Jackson to refuse any discussion of the word 'Nigger' afterwards. Sensitization to language must not lead to a lack of language. There are very good reasons *for* replacing the word '*nigger king*' with '*South Sea king*' in Astrid Lindgren's Pippi Longstocking. This

---

84   See: https://www.spiegel.de/panorama/django-unchained-samuel-l-jackson-diskutiert-das-n-wort-a-875552.html [last accessed 15.08.2022].

avoids the danger of children adopting hurtful vocabulary without reflection. At the same time, the essence of the story is not damaged. However, there is no reason to write 'N-word king' instead of 'nigger king' in this essay. The same applies when linguists argue about whether Astrid Lindgren's or Max Frisch's use of the word 'Neger' should be regarded as an expression of a racist conviction. Regardless of whether Thomas Gottschalk should rethink his vocabulary in everyday language, he is of course allowed to say what he understands by a Moor in a conversation about the phenomenon.

No less irrational is the interpretative sovereignty of those affected. Those who feel discriminated against are ascribed the right to decide on the appropriate terminology.[85] Very often, criticism of vocabulary and terminology can be justified with good reasons. However, the feeling of offense alone is not one of these good reasons. The act of verbal offense very rarely constitutes a criminal offense in a free society and we would do well not to change this. Above all, however, it is not only the mood of the person concerned that determines whether a term is inadmissible or admissible. Otherwise, there is a danger that anyone who feels offended will be allowed to tyrannize their environment with the threat of punishment. Referring to Crimea as Ukrainian territory was an insult to Russia's President Putin. However, this does not mean that this term should be avoided from now on. Criticism of religion can also be easily silenced in this way. It is enough that the followers of the religious community feel offended for the criticism to be declared illegitimate. Just as the intention of the speaker should not be the sole criterion, the expectations of the person being criticized should not represent the sole yardstick for the assessment of appropriate speech acts. Both establish irrational and vertical distributions of power. Unfortunately, there are still population groups in Germany that see themselves as citizens of the German Reich or even as Aryan master race and want to be labeled in this sense. Nevertheless, there is no reason to take these needs into account. On the contrary, there are often good reasons for using designations that are not acceptable to the person being addressed. In summary proceedings, the Meiningen Administrative Court considered it "sufficiently credible" that the Thuringian AfD leader Björn Höcke may be referred to as a fascist.[86] The fact that this may not correspond to the self-image of the person addressed and would then be defamatory can be disregarded.

Virtue actionism is another problem that arises from the lack of differentiation. "Racism is not an opinion, it is a crime." Few slogans are simultaneously

---

85 Cf: Svenja Flaßpöhler: *Sensibel. Über modern Empfindlichkeit und die Grenzen des Zumutbaren*. Klett-Cotta, Stuttgart 2021.
86 Decision of the Meiningen Administrative Court: 2 E 1194/19 Me.

so widespread, sympathetically intended and yet false. Racism as a conviction is not itself a crime, but a scientifically unfounded and morally reprehensible ideology that has motivated numerous criminal acts. Healing has so far only come from the commandment to think and not from the prohibition to think. For this reason, the oppressive systems of human history have always worked with dogmas, disinformation and language bans, while representatives of the Enlightenment rely on inquiry, criticism and the claim to justification. Anyone who is prepared and has learned to think objectively and critically cannot be a racist without cognitive dissonance. Racism is stupid. Anyone who stands up for human rights at demonstrations with the above slogan is not doing any harm. However, the lack of differentiation makes destructiveness easily possible. This is the case when anyone who is accused of racism or who uses stigmatized words is immediately condemned as a criminal. A conviction that makes it possible to reject any discussion with groups that think differently as appeasement and to pursue accusations without argumentation.

According to John McWhorter, the third phase of anti-racism has produced a seemingly religious irrationality under the heading of *Critical Whiteness*. The first phase of anti-racism fought slavery and racial segregation with enormous bravery. In the 1970s and 1980s, the second phase achieved almost worldwide moral ostracism and a deepened awareness of the causes and structures of racism. According to McWhorter, the third wave, on the other hand, loses itself in unsubstantiated theses according to which whites are necessarily involved in complicity with racist structures, while the existence of black people is completely dominated by racist oppression. Both theses are not only questionable, but completely unproven in their totality. They are religious beliefs that, in addition to a kind of revivalist movement, have also produced a priestly caste and an inquisition.[87]

One may counter that progressive aspects can also be associated with the *Critical Whiteness* movement. These include the identification of previously unreflected privileges of whiteness and the associated facilitation of greater equality.

Nevertheless, a negative dialectic is also at work here.

"I do not care about the color of my friends' skin!", "A black Mozart interpreter and a white reggae musician are a valuable expression of multiculturalism and individual freedom."

Sentences like these were still widely accepted a few years ago. Currently, however, it is part of the zeitgeist to criticize such statements or even condemn

---

87   John McWhorter: *Die Erwählten. Wie der neue Antirassismus die Gesellschaft spaltet* (translation by Kirsten Riesselmann). Hoffmann and Campe, Hamburg 2021. p. 21.

them as racist. Anyone who does not care about the skin color of their acquaintances is ignorant of their experiences of discrimination. Celebrating a black Mozart interpreter means practising cultural colonialization. White reggae musicians, on the other hand, are condemned as an expression of exploitative cultural appropriation. Certainly, it is possible to think of situations in which the above statements are insensitive. However, the general suspicion is frightening. Firstly, the achievements of the past are negated. An attitude towards people in which skin color, cultural origin, sexual orientation, etc. are irrelevant is desirable! Martin Luther King formulated nothing else in his speech "I have a Dream". Secondly, we lose sight of the individual as a bearer of human dignity. When I applaud a musician, it is for her performance as an individual artist and not as a representative of any cultural group or even a race. Incidentally, it is irrelevant whether she played Mozart or reggae. Thirdly, the criticism itself implies the darkest, racist ideas. Is it inconceivable that a black musician loves Mozart of her own accord and that a pale boy from Hamburg plays wonderful reggae? Why is this inconceivable? Because there is inviolable ethnic property? Or even because their genetic disposition as black or white exclude them? In short, they conjure up the spirits that should be banished.

It is equally absurd to deny privileged people the moral right to stand up for the underprivileged. Certainly, there are always people who are more concerned with self-profiling than with the social issue. Similarly, privileged white men will certainly not be able to empathize with the everyday experiences of an underprivileged black woman. But does that mean they should not stand up for their living conditions? Was Martin Luther King being overbearing when he spoke out in favor of improving the working conditions of white workers? Is commitment not particularly valuable when it does not arise from a subjective perspective, but is based on general principles of justice? To deny this is to conjure up a sinister form of identity. An inescapable imprint defined by culture and skin color that declares solidarity between ethnic groups constructed in this way impractical or immoral. In 2019, after a lecture at the *Dialog macht Schule* organization, I was told by a prospective democracy trainer that I had no right to criticize Muslim circumcision of boys, as I had not experienced the discrimination of a Muslim. Just a few days later, I was accused of "pro-Muslim propaganda" by representatives of the PEGIDA movement in Dresden of "betraying the legitimate needs of the people" as a representative of the "left-liberal educational aristocracy". Both statements stem from the same standard of evaluation: *you are not one of us and you do not confirm our sentiments. Ergo, you are wrong. Your arguments are irrelevant.*

In addition, all irrational world views create a dynamic of anticipatory moral self-affirmation. It is not about being able to rationally assess an issue, but about being among those who pronounce a moral judgment with the ductus of superiority as early as possible. Unfortunately, this inquisitorial zeal of parts of the *Critical Whiteness* movement differs little from the representatives of far-right conspiracy theories.

In 2020, both the president and the chairman of the American Poetry Foundation had to resign. The reason was not that they had compared police violence to genocide in their declaration of solidarity with the Black Lives Matter movement ("equate to no less than genocide against Black people"), but that their letter was deemed too short.[88]

In the same year, Gary Garrels, the curator of the Museum of Modern Art in San Francisco, was forced to resign. The reason for this was his refusal to exclude more works of art from acquisition if they were made by white men. Such behavior, according to Garrels, would not be a sign of anti-racism, but reverse discrimination.[89]

A year later, the New York Times, previously a flagship of press freedom, forced journalist Donald McNeil Jr, who had been writing for the paper since 1976, to resign. This was triggered by a discussion about racism in which students had asked McNeil whether expulsion was appropriate for using the N-word. McNeil had replied that it made a difference whether the word was used as a quotation or as a form of address. He therefore referred to the difference between active use and mention. Consequently, he himself pronounced the word "nigger".[90] This was followed by a letter from 150 colleagues who demanded and brought about his dismissal.

It can be assumed that most of the signatories would describe the harassment of the press and cultural workers during the so-called McCarthy era of 1950–55 as a historical and moral mistake. However, they do not seem to notice the analogy to their own behavior. A group of doctoral students at Princeton University has called on the president to establish a committee to "lead the investigation and prosecution of racist behavior, racist incidents and publications, and racist research by the faculty."[91] There is actually nothing wrong

---

88 https://www.nytimes.com/2020/06/09/books/poetry-foundation-black-lives-matter.html [Last accessed 08/15/2022].

89 https://www.newsweek.com/sfmoma-curator-gary-garrels-san-francisco-museum-modern-art-reverse-discrimination-racism-1517984 [Last accessed 05.10.2022].

90 Peter Mücke, Eckhard Roelcke: Debatte um "New York Times" – Political Correctness or "Gesinnungsterror"? In: Deutschlandfunk Kultur. February 15, 2021. https://ondemand-mp3.dradio.de/file/dradio/2021/02/15/rassismus_oder_gesinnungsterror_debatte_um_new_york_drk_20210215_2308_4cbc6c02.mp3 [Last accessed 15.08.2022].

91 John McWhorter, Kirsten Riesselmann (transl.): *Die Erwählten. Wie der neue Antirassismus die Gesellschaft spaltet*. Hoffmann and Campe, Hamburg 2021. p. 74.

with this. Only the question of urgency should be allowed. Is Princeton, the place where Albert Einstein, Toni Morrison, Elena Kagan, Michelle Obama and Jhumpa Lahiri worked and studied, a place that urgently needs such a committee? Senator McCarthy also thought he was on the morally right side. But he chased ghosts and did a lot of damage.

"Fear and terror are not suddenly good, even if they are spread by the left or by black people. Reason should have the upper hand. That is the core of Enlightenment."[92]

It is also highly regrettable that an all-encompassing anti-racist paradigm obscures the view of other causes of social ills. A first example is the confusion between fighting ideology and sophism.

Reflecting on language makes an important contribution on the way to a society with a low level of racism. Language and symbolism provide a breeding ground for the construction and reproduction of resentment. In addition, words and symbols can be gateways for conscious and unconscious discrimination. They enable massive cruelty as well as subtle micro-aggressions.[93] Language criticism is urgently needed. Nevertheless, vocabulary and ideology must not be confused. Words alone are not racism itself. Neither is everyone who speaks insensitively necessarily a racist, nor is it to be expected that the stigmatization of vocabulary is sufficient to eliminate misanthropic ideologies. In Germany, there is a steadily growing number of legally banned phrases and symbols. This is more than justified in view of German history. Unfortunately, this has done little to push back neo-national socialist milieus. The ideologies in question represent unreflected world views and suffer little damage if individual words or symbols are taken away from them. It is all too easy to find alternatives. It is common knowledge that the number combinations 18 or 88 stand for "Heil Hitler" and "Adolf Hitler" in certain milieus. However, numbers cannot be banned. A constitutional state cannot prohibit combinations of numbers. Many of us live in houses with the number 18 or 88.

The helplessness in the face of a linguistic development that has found its way into European schoolyards is particularly shameful. The phrase "you Jew"

---

92   John McWhorter, Katja Ridderbusch: Schattenseite des Antirassismus – Ein unorthodoxer Blick auf die identitätspolitische Debatte. In: *Deutschlandfunk*. 31.01.2022 https://www.deutschlandfunk.de/john-mcwhorter-die-erwaehlten-100.html [Last accessed 15.08.2022].

93   Cf: Azadê Peşmen: Wie Tausende kleine Mückenstiche – Rassismus macht den Körper krank, In: *Deutschlandfunk Kultur*. 05.07.2018. Online: https://www.deutschlandfunk-kultur.de/rassismus-macht-den-koerper-krank-wie-tausende-kleine-100.html [Last accessed 15.08.2022].

is often used there as a swear word, insult or exclusion.[94] In view of German history, this is almost unbearable. The causes range from youthful irreverence and a lack of historical education to religious and ethnic anti-Semitism and an undifferentiated understanding of international politics. Education and Enlightenment can and must counteract this. However, the term "Jew" must not be banned under any circumstances. The latter would mean ceding sovereignty of interpretation to those who promote discriminatory abuse. Of course, there are many psychological, sociological and political aspects to consider, but the goal remains a society in which a term like "black person" is a casual attribute description like "blonde" or "wearer of glasses". For this, however, there must be a corresponding linguistic practice.

The second example is perhaps even more serious and could be summarized under the heading "race instead of class".

This refers to the reduction of all social, economic and political grievances to racial discrimination. The identification of racist structures is absolutely necessary. However, it must not replace the equally necessary criticism of social, economic and political grievances. For Marx and Engels, racism and chauvinism were so-called secondary contradictions that can only be eliminated once the main contradiction between capital accumulation and exploitation has been overcome. However, you do not have to be a Marxist to diagnose a causality between social classes and the emergence and reinforcement of racist prejudices. It is well known that there is a vicious circle between social status, susceptibility to crime, prejudice and low chances of advancement. Those who focus solely on the aspect of racist or chauvinist prejudice are falling short, and those who focus solely on linguistic correctness may have settled on a convenient sideshow in order to avoid the core of structural violence. John McWhorter has countered this tendency with several courageous publications.

> I do not deny that racism exists, that systemic racism exists. And we will probably never be able to eradicate it completely. But these psychologizing, self-centered teachings about white guilt do not help us to overcome the real problems of black people in this country.[95]

---

[94] Roland Willareth: Diskriminierung durch Sprache. Antisemitismus an Schulen. In: Tiedemann, Markus (ed.): *Migration, Rassismus, Menschenrechte. Herausforderung ethischer Bilung*. Brill/Ferdinand Schöningh, Paderborn 2020. pp. 91–124.

[95] John McWhorter: *Die Erwählten. Wie der neue Antirassismus die Gesellschaft spaltet* (translation by Kirsten Riesselmann). Hoffmann and Campe, Hamburg 2021. p. 86.

According to McWhorter, it is a fact that racist police violence is an unacceptable problem in the USA. But it is also a fact that the risk of being killed by one's own neighbors is many times higher for an African American than falling victim to a racist police officer.[96] Furthermore, there is by no means a homogeneity of victimization in the so-called black community. Several studies show a divergence between the experience of discrimination and the perception of discrimination. Surprisingly, studies show that "when minorities have a high level of participation opportunities, perceived discrimination within these groups is also high – and, interestingly, vice versa."[97] African Americans with a university degree and higher income feel racially discriminated against more often than those with a basic education and low income.[98] A finding that allows for at least two interpretations. A) A higher level of education and social status enables the perception and identification of subtle and comprehensive discrimination. B) As a result of social advancement, the more massive discrimination of other social classes has fallen out of sight. The pure case statistics speak for themselves: black people who are victims of violence in general and racist violence in particular rarely come from the so-called upper class. Social class, not race, has the greatest influence on their fate.

The fight against racism remains a central task of enlightened ways of life. However, critical reason demands that we distrust monocausal explanations. Moreover, it would be tragic to confuse the struggle for social justice with language education or even replace it with the latter.

Helen Pluckrose and James Lindsay also emphasize that "racism is still a social problem that needs to be addressed today." At the same time, however, they deny that "*critical* race theory and the concept of intersectionality provide the best tools to do this because [...] problems with racism are best solved by analyzing them as rigorously as possible." In addition, Pluckrose and Lindsay emphasize the freedom of the individual to decide against discriminatory or racist behavior. At the same time, they deny that racism is "unavoidable and present in every interaction and can therefore be discovered and denounced [in every context] and that this is part of a ubiquitous systemic problem that permeates everything, always and everywhere." Rather, it is counterproductive to combat racism by "giving categories such as race a social meaning again

---

96   Ibid. p. 48.
97   Aladin El-Mafaalani, Julian Waleciak, Gerrit Weitzel: Tatsächliche, messbare und subjektiv wahrgenommene Diskriminierung. In: Scherr, El-Mafaalani, Yüksel (eds.): *Handbuch Diskriminierung*. Springer Fachmedien Wiesbaden GmbH, Wiesbaden 2017. p. 175.
98   Ibid.

and radically increasing their visibility."[99] The last worrying development is the anti-racist modeling of history.

Let's start with a rather harmless example: after Mohrenstrasse in Berlin was renamed Anton-Wilhelm-Amo-Strasse, a corresponding discussion is also being held in Dresden-Radebeul. The representative of an organization of young migrants told me that it was almost impossible to understand a debate because many participants only said the M-word street. This is initially just a funny anecdote, but there was also a certain amount of virtue-signaling. There are good reasons for changing the street name. However, there is no justifiable reason to accuse all those of racism who point out that the name "Mohr" had very different connotations. This is precisely where anti-racist historical modeling comes in. It was simply claimed that discrimination had always been involved. The spectrum ranges from neutral designations of origin as inhabitants of Mauritania to reverence, for example for Saint Mauritius, the patron saint of Magdeburg, to romantic glorifications, infantilization, degradation and racist discrimination. Denying this means not wanting to differentiate and cultivating blanket judgments. In short, it means practicing what you want to fight against.

The ideological modeling of history is an old acquaintance. It was not enough for the Romans to be a very successful Mediterranean community. They traced their ancestry back to either two Demigods or the last survivors of the legendary Troy. In the Eisenach "Institute for the Research and Elimination of Jewish Influence on German Church Life", German theologians spent a lot of energy between 1939 and 1945 trying to prove that Christ was an Aryan.

Stalin made sure that Trotsky was retouched out of photos showing him together with Lenin. In Poland, the school subject "History and the Present" was recently introduced along with a textbook that propagates the world view and moral concepts of the ruling PiS party.

In comparison, the intention of anti-racist historical modeling is of course much more sympathetic. Nevertheless, a fatal problem remains: the falsification of history.

If Enlightenment is the way of life that strives for objectivity, then it must endeavor to deal with the past and present with as little ideology as possible. This is the only way to avoid the sad realization that both are strongly permeated by racism, discrimination and other evils and that massive social and educational efforts are needed to counteract them.

---

99   Pluckrose, Helen / Lindsay, James: *Zynische Theorien. Wie aktivistische Wissenschaft Race, Gender und Identität über alles stellt – und warum das niemandem nützt*. C.H. Beck, Munich 2022, pp. 311–312.

However, the analysis itself must not be ideological or pedagogical. If you want to learn from the past, you have to understand what it was like. Unfortunately, this principle of Enlightenment also seems to be increasingly being suppressed. In his 2019 book *Wahnsinn der Massen – Wie Meinungsmache und Hysterie unsere Gesellschaft vergiften* (*Madness of the Masses – How Opinion-Mongering and Hysteria Poison Our Society*)[100], Douglas Murray has worked out how Google algorithms, for example, create an ideologically distorted representation of history. Anyone who enters "European art" in the image search, says Murray,

> would like to think that the paintings shown first include the Mona Lisa or Van Gogh's Sunflowers or another equally well-known work. But the first picture is by Diego Velázquez. The artist himself is not really a surprise, but the selection of his works is. Neither *The Court Maidens* nor the portrait of Pope Innocent X are shown, but the portrait of his assistant, Juan de Pareja, a man of color.

The search process described here could be repeated today with comparable results.[101] However, the results vary depending on the language used. Anyone who begins to deal with European art for the first time must gain the impression that it has essentially been shaped by people with dark skin color as artists or motifs. This is actually a very sympathetic idea, but it does not correspond to the facts.

It is hard to believe that these search results stem from an effort at objectivity. How many non-white artists were involved in European art in purely percentage terms? Are all previous introductions to the art history wrong if, for example, you see Michelangelo, Van Gogh or Salvador Dali as classic representatives of European art?

It might also have been desirable if Michelangelo had painted either God or Adam with dark skin on the ceiling of the Sistine Chapel. But that is not what happened.

Of course, it is an injustice that the many women who have most probably gained great scientific insights over the centuries have not been passed down. However, it is epistemically dishonest to want to correct this injustice retrospectively. This happens, for example, when pupils or students learn that the influence of Hypatia of Alexandria was just as important for ancient philosophy as that of Aristotle or Cicero. I have repeatedly experienced in framework

---

100　Douglas Murray: *Wahnsinn der Massen – Wie Meinungsmache und Hysterie unsere Gesellschaft vergiften* (translation: Birgit Schöbitz). FinanzBuch Verlag, Munich 2019. p. 152.
101　https://archive.ph/nxyN7 [Last accessed 08/15/2022].

commissions that equality was demanded because women would otherwise be underrepresented in the canon. However, women were underrepresented in antiquity and the great systems were created by men. Those who do not want to reproduce this situation should take care to change the present and not the writing of history. In order to achieve this, a good education still seems to be the means of choice, especially for the previously underrepresented sections of the population. A good education implies factual knowledge. However, an ideologically distorted view of history is counterproductive. It would be a great relief if Luther had not made anti-Semitic remarks, but he did. It would be good if the icons of the Enlightenment had been fifty percent female and had already used racism-sensitive language, but that was not the case. To ignore or model this would be to create half-knowledge in Adorno's sense.

The increasingly one-sided portrayal of slavery is another prominent example. If white, male capitalists had been the only racial exploiters in history, there would be hope of eliminating this evil as a minority phenomenon. Unfortunately, historical sources speak a different language.

The enslavement of millions of Africans and their deportation to the two American continents is one of the greatest crimes against humanity. Unfortunately, however, it is a singularity only in terms of the economic organization and the quantities achieved. Slavery existed before and still exists today. Racist delusions of superiority with regard to one's own tribe, religion and nation have unfortunately been handed down from numerous cultures and have led to the oppression and exploitation of people on all continents just as much as pure self-interest. Unfortunately, we are a species prone to injustice and irrationality.

The culture of remembrance can be shaped in such a way that the delivery corresponds to one's own wishes, is easier to bear or suggests easy solutions to problems. Only the opportunities to learn from history are, thus, obstructed. Slavery is one of the great crimes against humanity and reached a sad climax in the triangular trade of the 17th, 18th and 19th centuries. But slavery is neither white nor black. It is necessarily inhumane, but not always racist. Slavery always affected people of all skin colors. The ancient world did not have a racist concept of slavery, but forms of rule in the Orient did. Slavery existed in Africa before the Europeans exorbitantly increased its extent. The buyers were Europeans, but also Arabs. For centuries, Muslim pirates captured Portuguese, Spanish, French and Italians and sold them in North Africa. In the labor and extermination camps of National Socialism, the gulags of the Soviet Union and the mass operations of the Cultural Revolution, people were enslaved who did not look any different from their peers. Slavery was and is a scourge of all humanity. It can therefore only be overcome or at least contained if anthropologically universal criteria apply to its condemnation.

> Those Critical Whiteness activists who make an opposition between whites and people of color a major contradiction distort the picture of lived life. They minimize oppression – not only the oppression of whites by whites, but also the oppression of non-whites by non-whites [...][102]

If there is any chance at all of learning from history, it is ruined by ideological narrowing. Gerald Horne's nuanced work has helped to broaden our understanding of the American Revolution and to point out that, alongside liberal ideas, an interest in the continuation of slavery also played a role.[103] Nevertheless, the assertion that racism and slavery were the dominant causes of the American Revolution would hide entire bibliographies of research and collections of sources.

The Nigerian writer Chimamanda Ngozi Adichie coined the term *"single story"* and thus identified the danger that one-sided understandings of the world created by colonial supremacy persist as historical tradition.[104] It is very convincing that previously neglected voices should intervene to correct the collective understanding of history. However, the danger of a *single story*, a closed and narrow paradigm of interpretation, is at work from various directions.

It seems as if a powerful category error is spreading. Belonging to minorities or majorities has many social consequences, including injustice, discrimination and marginalization. In the context of universalist ethics, however, nothing at all follows from belonging to minorities or majorities! This distinction is of the utmost importance, especially in order to protect people from discrimination. Let us take the example of the "Heteronormativity" identified by Judith Butler. Anyone who sees heterosexuality as the average behavior of the majority of people is certainly right, at least at present. On the other hand, anyone who derives a normative claim, a demand for conformity or even hostility towards people with a different orientation is very much mistaken. Nothing follows normatively from empirical majority ratios. It is not necessary to refer

---

102   Former Federal President Joachim Gauck: "People who love freedom, democracy and human rights don't ask whether someone is black or white". In: *Die ZEIT*. 31.03.2021. p. 56.
103   See: Gerald Horne: The Counter-Revolution of 1776: Slave Resistance and the Origins of the United States of America. New York University Press, New York 2014.
104   Chimamanda Ngozi Adichie: Die Gefahr einer einzigen Geschichte. In: *TEDGlobal* 2009. https://www.ted.com/talks/chimamanda_ngozi_adichie_the_danger_of_a_single_story [Last accessed 15.08.2022].

to George Edward Moore to point out a naturalistic fallacy. No norm follows from a description. Just because I am short-sighted, it does not follow that I should be. Just because the majority of European politicians are male, it does not follow that this should be the case or even remain so. It is not logically possible to infer from being to ought. These are separate categories. Ergo, belonging to a minority is only a sociological argument, not an ethical one. It neither permits discrimination nor does it give rise to rights. If, for example, people with a non-heterosexual disposition demonstrate for equal rights and against discrimination, they are in the right. This right can be derived from their status as a human being, as a person or as a citizen. However, nothing follows ethically from belonging to the so-called LGBTQI community.

On the other hand, anyone who elevates membership of a group, the fact of a social identity, to an ethical norm, opens the Pandora's box from which countless discriminations escape and which could only just be provisionally closed by the Enlightenment's orientation towards reason.

On July 10, 2021, the Haus der Kulturen der Welt in Berlin hosted an international conference on "The White West IV: Whose Universal?". In addition to the intelligent and worthwhile lectures and the magnificent weather, it was striking that not one speaker was invited to argue in favor of universalism and the principles of Enlightenment. Instead of cultivating diversity, only one interpretation of the world was served. According to this, the history of the modern era is not to be explained by the main Marxist contradiction between capital and labor or various emancipation movements, but by the ideological construction of white superiority, which manifests itself in narratives of objectivity, rationality and state contract. The practice of (self)critique and universal ethical norms have not changed the immanent white racism. Rather, they are instruments of obfuscation. There is no logical or empirical evidence for this thesis.

In his lecture, Dirk Moses from the University of North Carolina explored "the FRG's commitment to equating 'civilization' and "West" in the post-war period and the "rose-tinted" understanding of Enlightenment and colonialism as a vehicle of "human progress."[105] This interpretation is by no means self-evident. After all, it could be argued that the Frankfurt School and its critique of the Enlightenment must also be counted among the formative factors of the Federal Republic. It is also worth taking a look at the empirical facts. No German school has a history book in use that conveys a "rosy" picture of colonialism. Unfortunately, there has been no corresponding debate. The same applies to the interpretation that the German culture of remembrance, together with the

---

105 Announcement text for the lecture. See: https://www.hkw.de/en/programm/beitragende_ hkw/m/dirk_moses.php [last accessed 15.08.2022].

Western need for state-guaranteed security, contributes to the legitimization of Israel and thus to a white, capitalist colonization of the Palestinians.[106]

Theses of this kind would have received thunderous applause at events organized by the Identitarians or the NPD. The latter alone is of course only an indication, not an argument. Nevertheless, it should be reason enough to listen to other voices that see the existence of Israel as part of Germany's raison d'être as a complicated web of historical guilt, moral responsibility, international law, ideology and pragmatism. Voices that do not understand the right to exist as a right to unconditional support. Voices whose "level of consciousness and unconsciousness [has] penetrated deep enough into the monstrous "[107] to understand that criticism of Israel is always necessary, but in German language it reaches the limits of what can be said. Voices for whom white racist colonization simply falls short as an explanation.

A society striving for Enlightenment must not go down this path. Societies committed to Enlightenment must struggle to formulate and differentiate as precisely as possible what was, what is and what should be. They require a linguistically differentiated discourse. Claims to interpretation must be justified rationally and cannot be based solely on concern or good intentions. It is also necessary to distinguish between the different levels of language. If this is not done, there is a risk of losing the third level, the forum for critical and self-critical reflection, altogether. Nothing good can therefore be expected from over-regulation of language.

> But by 2050 – probably even earlier – there will no longer be any real knowledge of the old language. All the literature of the past will have been destroyed. Chaucer, Shakespeare, Milton, Byron will only exist in new versions, not just in a transformed form, but as the opposite of what they once were. Even the writings of the party will change. Even the slogans will change. How could a slogan like 'freedom is slavery' exist if the concept of freedom has been abolished? The whole climate of thought will be different. There will be no more thinking at all, at least not in our current sense. Orthodoxy means: not thinking, not having to think. Orthodoxy is unconsciousness.[108]

As we know, this passage from Orwell's 1984 does not describe an enlightened society.

---

106 Cf: A. Dirk Moses: The Problems of Genocide: Permanent Security and the Language of Transgression. Cambridge University Press, Cambridge 2021.
107 Adorno, Theodor W.: Erziehung nach Auschwitz (1966) In: Gerd Kadelbach (ed.): Erziehung zur Mündigkeit. Vorträge und Gespräche mit Hellmut Becker 1959–1969, 25th edition. Suhrkamp, Frankfurt am Main 1970. p. 88.
108 George Orwell: 1984. 23rd edition, first edition 1984. Ullstein, Munich 2002. pp. 67–68.

3.4 Current stress factors

History shows that Enlightenment movements have repeatedly emerged from experiences of crisis. Unfortunately, however, this does not mean that the principles are themselves resistant to crises. Their dominance was just as short-lived in Ancient Greece as it was after the French Revolution. Only in the USA were Enlightenment principles able to have a lasting effect on the constitution and public life immediately after the first political revolution. Nevertheless, the project remained incomplete. The principles of the Enlightenment were not able to overcome crimes against the indigenous population, slavery, wars that violated international law and racism that still persists today. At least they succeeded in establishing a liberal legal system and gradually extending basic rights to previously oppressed population groups. In addition, a community of liberal states succeeded in resisting the fascist and totalitarian threats of the twentieth century and overcoming unprecedented regimes of injustice. A process that was not realized without contradicting its own ethical principles. Ships carrying refugees were sent back to the ports of their persecutors, colonies were instrumentalized, major civilian cities were bombed and much more. Nevertheless, the outcome of this phase can be considered a success. A fascist Europe and a fascist Asia were prevented, the Holocaust was ended, the United Nations was founded, the Universal Declaration of Human Rights was adopted and instances of international law were established from Nuremberg to The Hague. However, it should by no means be concluded from these successes that the Enlightenment process is now firmly in the international or even just the national saddle. The project remains fragile and susceptible to crises.

Enlightened societies are currently facing at least three existential challenges and it is not certain whether this stress test can be overcome. These are the destruction of natural resources, extremism and migration.

3.4.1 *Destruction of natural resources*
Apart from nuclear war, the destruction of natural resources is by far the most serious threat to humanity and therefore also to societies striving for Enlightenment. The climate change caused by mankind results in crop losses, drinking water shortages, species extinction, extreme weather events and much more. All of this is already leading to war, migration, famine, corruption, authoritarianism and much more. These are conditions that are anything but conducive to the pursuit of Enlightenment.

At the same time, an enlightened scientific use of reason is absolutely necessary in order to realize the dimensions of the problem and the required interventions. The questions "What is the case?" and "How would we like it?" must be clearly separated from each other. Reality is not constructed according to personal, national or religious needs. Presbyterian televangelists like Kevin Swanson or Rick Joyner may see Hurricanes Katrina or Florence as God's punishment for legalizing abortion and same-sex marriage.[109] Enlightened people know that hurricanes are aided by rising ocean temperatures. They also know that prayers do not cool oceans. They pay more attention to climatology because its findings are based on empirical surveys and natural laws, allow reliable forecasts and are reproducible under laboratory conditions. Eccentric presidents such as Donald Trump or Jair Messias Bolsonaro may deny climate change and claim to know more than "the scientists".[110] People who strive for Enlightenment value scientific honesty and know that, depending on the survey, between 95 and 99% of all climate scientists speak of a threatening and man-made phenomenon.[111]

---

109 Kevin Swanson described Hurricane Harvey as "God-sent" in the August 31, 2017 edition of his podcast *"Generations with Kevin Swanson"*. The state of Texas, where the hurricane struck, was primarily to blame for Houston's "aggressively pro-homosexual" political leadership in previous years and the recent failure of a bill that would have prohibited trans people in Texas from using public restrooms according to their gender identity. (Podcast archive: https://www.generations.org/ programs/743 [last accessed 08/15/2022]).

   In a video uploaded to his Facebook page on September 12, 2018, Rick Joyner named "sin" in general and the "shedding of innocent blood [of unborn life]" in particular as the cause of Hurricane Florence (archive of the video and partial transcript: https://www.rightwingwatch.org/post/rick-joyner-sin-not-climate-change-is-responsible-for-hurricane-florence [last accessed 08/15/2022]).

110 On September 14, 2020, in the wake of the severe California wildfires, Donald Trump responded to a request from the California Secretary of Natural Resources to trust the scientific explanatory models by saying, "I don't think the science knows." See: https://www.cbsnews.com/news/trump-western-wildfires-science-climate-change/ [last accessed 15.08.2022].

   Cf: Herton Escobar: 'A hostile environment. Brazilian scientists face rising attacks from Bolsonaro's regime. In: *Science.org* https://www.science.org/content/article/hostile-environment-brazilian-scientists-face-rising-attacks-bolsonaro-s-regime [last accessed 15.08.2022].

111 See: John Cook, Naomi Oreskes, Peter T. Doran, William R.L. Anderegg, Bart Verheggen, Ed W. Maibach, J. Stuart Carlton, Stephan Lewandowsky, Andrew G. Skuce, Sarah A. Green, Dana Nuccitelli, Peter Jacobs, Mark Richardson, Bärbel Winkler, Rob Painting, Ken Rice: Consensus on consensus: a synthesis of consensus estimates on human-caused global warming. In: *Environmental Research Letters* 11, No. 4, 2016;

   Mark Lynas, Benjamin Z. Houlton, Simon Perry: Greater than 99% consensus on human caused climate change in the peer-reviewed scientific literature. In: *Environmental Research Letters* 16, 2021;

   James Powell: Scientists Reach 100% Consensus on Anthropogenic Global Warming. In: *Bulletin of Science, Technology & Society*, 37(4), 2019. pp. 183–184.

The same applies to the question of what needs to be done. This applies to simple causal chains such as the reduction of CO_2 emissions and technical innovations as well as to moral responsibility. Ethics based on standards of rationality leave little doubt as to what our moral duty consists of. We may argue about whether the complex structure we call nature has value in itself or only for humans. The fact is that without it, humanity will perish. It is also possible to deny responsibility for future generations. Those who do not yet exist do not yet have any rights, so the theory goes. If humanity were to decide to stop reproducing from now on, it could be allowed to destroy itself and its planet in a final consumption frenzy. But even if the first premise (the unborn have no rights) is accepted, all the other premises do not correspond to the facts. Firstly, there is no global decision to stop procreation and secondly, real people are already suffering massively from the consequences of environmental destruction. So anyone who shares the premise that existential human suffering must be avoided and cannot be offset by more luxury for others, logically comes to the conclusion that the protection of natural resources and the reduction of greenhouse gases must be seen as an ethical duty.

Unfortunately, this results in a tragic constellation: on the one hand, the most global, rational and enlightened attitude possible is required to counter the destruction of the natural foundations of life. On the other hand, the consequences of climate change trigger stress factors that make it increasingly difficult to remain true to the principle of rationality. Even those societies in which the Enlightenment had a formative influence are reacting with shocking slowness to the existential threat of climate change. The reason for this is that the Enlightenment had a formative influence here and there, but never a dominant one on humanity. This is also or especially true for the so-called West, as its identity-forming factors include capitalism.

The genesis of the Enlightenment and capitalism are closely linked. The Enlightenment calls for maturity and a sense of responsibility, while capitalism demands independent participation in market activities. The one can be understood as a partial aspect of the other. Under certain conditions, ethical, political and economic liberalism can cooperate excellently and merge into a single thought structure. However, the Enlightenment's concept of responsibility encompasses far more than economic autonomy and profit maximization and can come into massive conflict with these.

So far, the resulting tensions have been defused by principles of distributive justice. A prime example of this is John Rawls' so-called difference principle, according to which economic differences are permitted as long as they enable the worst-off members of society to enjoy a higher quality of life than equal distribution.¹¹² Nevertheless, all classic economic theories from John Locke to Adam Smith and Karl Marx failed to take one aspect sufficiently into account: the finite nature of resources! While for John Locke, the supposedly unowned expanses of America offered enough land for everyone, Marx believed that rising productivity could one day enable virtually unlimited consumption for all. Today we know that both were wrong. Our resources are limited and will be used up in the near future. Moreover, humans are not only consuming their environment, they are reshaping it. The result is an increasingly dangerous and hostile place. Taking this into account is both a requirement of scientific honesty and an ethical duty. It also implies breaking with the traditional principles of capitalism and redefining concepts such as value creation or profit. If Enlightenment is to continue to exist as a social force, it must contribute to overcoming the false equivalence of money and value. An act that has already been successful in the past. At that time, the aim was to detach human beings as dignitaries from the economic understanding of commodities. This development found its most substantial justification in Kant's statement that every human being has dignity but no price, as their moral value has no economic exchange value. Politically, this Enlightenment rebellion against the market led to the end of slavery.

Today, values such as unpolluted air, clean drinking water and intact ecosystems must be removed from economic control. Instead, these values must become the benchmark for legitimizing economic activity.

> We need to renegotiate what makes people prosperous the day after tomorrow. To do this, we need new terms and concepts that express what we consider important in the future. Destroying the planet must no longer mean growth. Pure monetary increase should no longer mean value creation. Limits to growth should mean overcoming the creation of ecological and social damage.¹¹³

The associated ideological and economic paradigm shifts will not be able to be organized without resistance, and it remains questionable whether the voices of Enlightenment will be able to assert themselves against the influence of economic interests. Pessimists point to powerful interest groups and egocentric consumer behavior. Or to paraphrase Brecht: "First comes profit or consumption, then comes reason!" Optimists can point to phenomena such as Fridays for Future. According to various estimates, at least 4 million mostly

---

112   John Rawls: *Eine Theorie der Gerechtigkeit.* Suhrkamp Verlag, Frankfurt am Main 1979. p. 81.
113   Maja Göpel: *Unsere Welt neu denken: Eine Einladung.* Ullstein, Berlin 2021. p. 96.

young people from 150 countries took part in the *Global Climate Strike* on 20 September 2019 alone.[114] The largest demonstrations took place in societies shaped by both the Enlightenment and capitalism. The fact that a young generation is going on strike here for wanting a lower economic standard of living than their parents is an ethically impressive achievement and historically unique.

The demonstrators can justifiably claim to represent the tradition of Enlightenment. Whether they can develop sufficient creative power despite consumer-oriented social structures and a crisis mood that tends towards irrationality is a question of fate for humanity in general and enlightened societies in particular.

3.4.2 *Extremism*

Liberal societies will always produce extreme and opposing positions and must tolerate these as best they can due to their liberal self-image. Tolerance reaches its limits, however, when the open society is actively attacked or infiltrated. There is always a double threat here. On the one hand, it is the duty of constitutional states to protect their citizens to the best of their ability and, on the other, it is important not to reduce their own principles to absurdity when taking countermeasures.

Two extremist groups in particular are currently putting a strain on enlightened societies: right-wing radicalism and Islamism.

Let's start with right-wing extremism, a diffuse mixed culture of neo-Nazis, racists, anti-Semites and conspiracy theorists. The spectrum ranges from right-wing populist parties to militant terrorism. Whether in Oslo, on the island of Utøya, in Halle or in Christchurch, fanatics of this type of terrorism have committed horrific crimes by attacking perceived foreigners and representatives of democracy. Nevertheless, measured against their own goals, they were anything but successful. They did not succeed in shaking democracy, dividing the multicultural society or even unleashing a civil war anywhere. On the contrary! Fortunately, the majority of liberal societies have reacted to such experiences by strengthening cohesion and holding large demonstrations against racism and in favor of solidarity. For example, after the attacks in Christchurch, the opposite of what the attacker wanted to achieve happened in New Zealand society. The various population groups expressed their mutual solidarity and the imam of the community in Christchurch called for the continuation of

---

114 Frankfurter Allgemeine Zeitung (ed.): *Proteste für mehr Klimaschutz: Globaler Klimastreik geht in die zweite Runde.* September 27, 2019, ISSN 0174-4909.

the previous social tolerance[115]. The rule of law was not shaken either. Norway, which was one of the first countries to be affected, provided the model for an exemplary criminal procedure. The decisive factor is not justifiable joy at the maximum sentence of life imprisonment. Of central importance is the professionalism and adherence to principle that the Norwegian constitutional state maintained even in the face of fanatical terror. Defense lawyers, independent experts, the replacement of lay assessors, the examination of sanity, even the customary handshake in Norway – all of this was granted to the despiser of the rule of law and humanity.

The technical implementation of the attacks may have been horribly successful, but they did not succeed in shaking democracy. On the contrary: society and the rule of law emerged stronger.

Unfortunately, this resilience against political right-wing extremism is far less pronounced. On the contrary, worrying erosions can be observed. In many democracies that are considered established, right-wing populist movements have entered parliaments, which at least enable a conceptual proximity to right-wing terrorism. In countries such as Hungary and Poland, these movements even use their government responsibility to devalue the right to asylum, freedom of the press and the separation of powers. When Catholic priests also preach against the acceptance of Muslim refugees or equal rights for homosexuals[116], we can speak of a misanthropic infiltration of broad sections of society. Donald Trump has openly practiced his closeness to right-wing extremist and violent groups. During his first six months in office, the 45th President of the United States appointed Steve Bannon, a prominent member of the Breitbart Network, which is classified as right-wing populist to far-right[117], as chief strat-

---

115 Global Campaign for Peaceducation (ed.): "Liebe exportieren" – Imam im Zentrum des Terroranschlags von Christchurch verbreitet weiterhin Friedensbotschaft https://www.peace-ed-campaign.org/en/export-love-imam-at-centre-of-christchurch-terrorist-attack-continues-to-spread-message-of-peace/ [Last accessed 15.09.2022].

116 Cf: Florian Hassel: Wie Geistliche in Polen Ängste vor Flüchtlingen schüren. In: Süddeutsche.de. https://www.sueddeutsche.de/politik/polen-angst-und-kalkuel-1.2640725 [Last accessed 15.08.2022].

   On August 1, 2019, on the anniversary of the Warsaw Uprising, Archbishop Marek Jędraszewski of Krakow gave a speech in which he said that Poland had overcome the "red plague" but was now struggling with a "rainbow epidemic" (cf: Federal Agency for Civic Education (ed.): Chronicle: July 2, 2019-September 2, 2019 https://www.bpb.de/themen/europa/polen-analysen/296127/chronik-2-juli-2019-2-september-2019) [Last accessed 15.08.2022].

117 See: Southern Poverty Law Center (ed.): Is Breitbart.com Becoming the Media Arm of the 'Alt-Right'? https://www.splcenter.org/hatewatch/2016/04/28/breitbartcom-becoming-media-arm-alt-right;

egist in the White House. On August 12, 2017, right-wing extremists, including supporters of the Ku Klux Klan, demonstrated in Charlottesville not far from the University of Virginia, which was founded by Thomas Jefferson. A member of the march drove his car into a group of counter-demonstrators, killing one person and injuring 19 others. Although the President condemned neo-Nazis, he spoke of "very fine people on both sides. "[118] On September 20, 2020, the incumbent addressed the Proud Boys, a far-right group classified as terrorist in Canada, with the words "stand back and stand by!"[119] in view of the outcome of the presidential election.

On January 6, 2021, militant Trump supporters stormed the Capitol in Washington and attempted to prevent the formal confirmation of office of Joe Biden. Trump, who did not recognize the election, had previously at least indirectly encouraged this step at a demonstration.

> So we're going to, we're going to walk down Pennsylvania Avenue, I love Pennsylvania Avenue, and we're going to the Capitol and we're going to try and give ... The Democrats are hopeless. They're never voting for anything, not even one vote. But we're going to try and give our Republicans, the weak ones, because the strong ones don't need any of our help, we're going to try and give them the kind of pride and boldness that they need to take back our country.[120]

During the coronavirus pandemic, far-right movements in numerous democratic countries succeeded in infiltrating and instrumentalizing protests against the epidemic control measures. They were helped by the widespread irrationality among conspiracy theorists and so-called "Querdenker" (lateral thinkers). The majority of those demonstrating against the coronavirus measures would hardly describe themselves as neo-Nazis. Instead, they repeatedly use the narrative that they are defenders of democracy and the rule of law. For example, self-proclaimed lateral thinkers marched in front of the district court in Bochum on the first of May 2021, "in memory of the constitutional

---

Ders: *Breitbart exposé confirms: far-right news site a platform for the white nationalist "alt-right"* https://www.splcenter.org/hatewatch/2017/10/06/breitbart-exposé-confirms-far-right-news-site-platform-white-nationalist-alt-right [Last accessed 08/15/2022].

118 Archive link of the original quote: https://web.archive.org/web/20180113052441/ https://www.whitehouse.gov/briefings-statements/remarks-president-trump-infrastructure/–08/15/2017, archived 01/13/2018, [last accessed 08/25/2022].

119 Jason Wilson: *Who are the Proud Boys, 'western chauvinists' involved in political violence?* In: The Guardian Online https://www.theguardian.com/world/2018/jul/14/proud-boys-far-right-portland-oregon [Last accessed 15.08.2022]

120 Donald Trump: *The Ellipse*. Speech by the US President at the White House, January 6, 2021. See: https://edition.cnn.com/2021/02/08/politics/trump-january-6-speech-transcript/index.html [last accessed 15.08.2022].

state."[121] The fact that self-confessed neo-Nazis are active at lateral thinker demonstrations and that police officers have been repeatedly injured does not seem to detract from this self-image. Comparable situations were reported from Holland, Belgium and Austria. On both sides of the Atlantic, an infantile understanding of the rule of law is spreading, according to which every situation, every result that does not correspond to one's own wishes calls the political system into question in its entirety. One of the decisive achievements of the Enlightenment was the ability to distinguish between personal interest and systemic justice. Enlightened citizenship is not demonstrated by protesting against political decisions that one does not personally like – this can have many motives – but by accepting them, provided that the procedures that led to this decision comply with the social contract. The political right-wing populism, on the other hand, valorizes the feelings of the dissatisfied and elevates them to a legitimate criterion for right and wrong. The narrative of the betrayed majority is nourished in defense mode. The fact that such a threat cannot be rationally substantiated becomes unimportant. The perceived threat suffices as confirmation and justification of violence against the political system, material assets and people.

So while numerous right-wing extremist acts of terror failed to achieve their goals and rather led to a revitalization of the rule of law and enlightened civility, in other parts of society there was a dramatic rise in right-wing populism and infantile anti-democratic sentiment. The dramatic nature of this development cannot be overestimated. Anyone who doubts this should bear in mind that just a few years ago, the following scenario would have only been imaginable in a disaster movie: the outgoing president of the United States of America refuses to hand over power peacefully, the basic principle of democracy. His supporters storm the Capitol and bring down the oldest democracy of modern times, if only for a few hours. The fateful year 2017 is also often pushed out of the public consciousness. Let's assume that this year's run-off election for the French presidency had not been won by Emmanuel Macron, but by Marine Le Pen. At the same time, the SPD in Germany would have once again reluctantly refused to enter into a grand coalition following the failed coalition negotiations between the CDU, FDP and Greens. In the subsequent new elections, the AfD would have become the strongest party in the German Bundestag. In the USA, Donald Trump would have already governed, and just

---

121 Cf: Bernd Kiesewetter: 1. Mai Bochum: "Querdenker" stellen Grablichter vors Gericht. In: *Westdeutsche Allgemeine Zeitung* from 01.05.2021. Online version: https://www.waz.de/staedte/bochum/1-mai-bochum-querdenker-stellen-grablichter-vors-gericht-id232186527.html [last accessed 15.08.2022].

under two years later Boris Johnson would have moved into No. 10 Downing Street. Where would it have been then, the so-called free West? Comparable constellations could arise again as early as 2026.

The second variant of the extremist threat stems from fundamentalist Islam.

2021 marked the twentieth anniversary of the attacks on the World Trade Center in New York. This shows a parallel to right-wing terrorism. The execution of the attacks was successful, but the resilience of free society remained unbroken. Life in New York today is as vibrant and colorful as it was before 9/11, and the World Trade Center was replaced in record time by a taller and at least as impressive landmark. The United States is still one of the world's most important economies and the most sought-after country for immigration. If it had stayed that way, the global culture of remembrance would have been dominated by images of morbid assassins, innocent victims, a proud nation and overwhelming international solidarity. Even the invasion of Afghanistan and the pursuit and destruction of al-Qaeda could and can be based on international understanding and a possible interpretation of international law.

Just like right-wing terrorism, Islamist terrorism is not able to substantially endanger the ideas of Enlightenment and the practice of liberal societies. The hated liberal lifestyle continues unabated today in Paris and many other places of horrific attacks. Terrorism is usually an expression of weakness. Those who are militarily and politically inferior may be able to bring about isolated atrocious crimes, but not substantial change. At the same time, they also demonstrate their moral inferiority through their activities. Terrorism is only successful if it succeeds in generating maximum attention and provoking emotional overreactions. International road traffic and global environmental destruction kill more people every year than all the terrorist attacks of recent decades put together. Unfortunately, terrorist calculations benefit from a justified emotion: moral indignation. Road traffic and environmental destruction are many times more dangerous, but the suffering is not deliberately intended. That is why terrorists rightly deserve maximum moral contempt. Nevertheless, it is of central importance to distinguish between moral outrage and actionism born of a sense of threat. Otherwise, the terrorists have reached their goal and the escalation spiral begins.

The example of the USA shows how hysteria can be stirred up, resulting in the active violation and even abandonment of liberal principles.

The violation of its own principles not only damaged its international reputation, but also led to the erosion of its own normative self-image. These include the devastating and completely unlawful war in Iraq, the excesses in Abu Ghuraib prison, the systematic injustice of Guantánamo and the twenty-year war in Afghanistan, including the hasty withdrawal, leaving behind so-called "local forces". If it was Osama Bin Laden's intention to demonstrate the double standards of the so-called West and to unleash a clash of civilizations in Huntington's sense (see Chapter 3.6), he achieved many of his goals through the active support of George W. Bush and Donald Henry Rumsfeld. Of course, none of this is sufficient evidence to finally discredit the advantages of liberal social orders. Only the forms of political, journalistic and legal reappraisal and self-criticism clearly distinguish liberal constitutional states from authoritarian regimes. Examples of this are the countless press reports, advertisements and feature films in which American society critically examines its offenses. The same applies to the US Senate Committee of Inquiry, which found Donald Rumsfeld responsible for American torture practices.[122] Is it even remotely conceivable that Vladimir Putin or Mahmoud Ahmadinejad would have to face comparable proceedings in their own countries? The poison of double standards continues to work nonetheless. It would only be credibly neutralized if the former Secretary of Defense of the United States had to answer for war crimes and crimes against humanity before the International Criminal Court. The most influential nation in the free world has not yet even recognized the court in The Hague. It is not only the international credibility of the West that is suffering, but also the persuasive power of the Enlightenment. The impression quickly arises that the principles of the rule of law and international law are at best vague declarations of intent and clarification of a fair-weather practice.

What Islamist terrorism is unable to achieve on its own, liberal societies inflict on themselves when they betray the principles of Enlightenment. Such self-abolition ranges from disregarding their own legal principles to electing leaders who pursue a populist or even racist agenda.

However, self-abandonment manifests itself not only in racist or nationalist hardening, but also in a policy of appeasement that goes as far as self-denial.

When Ayatollah Khomeini called for the assassination of the writer Salman Rushdie in a fatwa in 1989, the reaction of the so-called free world was still quite robust. The call was firmly condemned by almost all heads of state, residence rights were promised and offers of protection were formulated. *The Satanic Verses* were available in bookshops and were often purchased simply

---

122 Cf.: "Secretary of Defense Donald Rumsfeld's authorization of aggressive interrogation techniques for use at Guantanamo Bay was a direct cause of detainee abuse there." – United States Senate Committee on Armed Services: Inquiry Into the Treatment of Detainees in US Custody. 20.11.2008 (Excerpt from the official, redacted publication of the report dated 22.04.2009, section "Unclassified". P. XXVIII).

to show solidarity. Six people died in the ensuing unrest and over a hundred were injured.[123]

17 years later, the picture had changed dramatically: in 2006, European heads of state and publishers were overflowing with apologies and expressions of regret when Danish cartoonists exercised their right to freedom of the press. In a hasty self-abandonment of freedom rights, numerous European countries even introduced laws to curtail religious criticism, which were only stopped thanks to legal intervention. Nevertheless, the protest against the Muhammad cartoons cost 139 lives and 823 injuries within a year.[124] Let us assume for a moment that the Danish Prime Minister had defended freedom of the press and freedom of opinion and that the so-called West had shown solidarity and hoisted the Danish flag on all public buildings. Such an act can be criticized with good reason as excessive, striking and undiplomatic. Nevertheless, it is legitimate to ask whether the outcome would have been worse. Such speculation relates not only to the number of victims, but also to the signal effect. The latter was devastating in any case. Instead of defending freedom of the press as a sacrosanct component of enlightened societies, it was degraded to a bargaining chip, while the hostility towards freedom of opinion was upgraded through understanding. None of this had anything to do with tolerance.

Genuine tolerance, on the other hand, would have been expressed through a clear commitment to freedom of the press and a simultaneous invitation to dialog. Tolerance does not mean renouncing everything that is an imposition. Tolerance means accepting that we owe each other a justification that strives for universality.[125]

Those who are able to provide this justification are allowed to impose hardships on their counterparts. On the other hand, those who argue solely from their conception of the good, without any intersubjective or intercultural mediation, have no right to recognition of their desires.

Neglecting this principle means nothing less than saying goodbye to democracy, the rule of law and human rights. Such a process takes place in stages, sometimes spectacularly, sometimes gradually.

Nine years after the Danish cartoon controversy, 12 employees of the French satirical magazine Charlie Hebdo were murdered and 11 others injured. Since

---

123 See: Eine Rushdie-Chronik. In: TAZ Archive https://taz.de/!1811095/ [Last accessed 15.08.2022].
124 See: S. Suzan J. Harkness, Mohamed Magid, Jameka Roberts, Michael Richardson: Crossing the Line? Freedom of Speech and Religious Sensibilities. In: *PS: Political Science & Politics*, 40(2), 2007. pp. 275–278.
125 Rainer Forst: *Toleranz im Konflikt: Geschichte, Gehalt und Gegenwart eines umstrittenen Begriffs*. Suhrkamp, Frankfurt am Main 2012. p. 171.

then, an entire genre of cartoons has almost disappeared. Following the reduction of press freedom, this process by no means came to a standstill, but was directed against the education system of the *Col de la République*. The cowardly and primitive murder of teacher Samuel Paty in 2020 is just the most prominent example to date. Across Europe, teachers are reporting that many subjects can no longer be taught without fear. In Germany, the German Teachers' Association recently warned of a "climate of intimidation"[126] based on a study that found that threats and insults against teachers are part of everyday life in 61% of German schools. Two years previously, the figure had been 48%.[127] At the same time, Samuel Paty's murderer was glorified on social networks as the "Lion of France"[128].

In the case of Samuel Paty, too, there was only fleeting consternation, not sustained support for schools as a place where opinions are formed free of dogma. In Germany, politicians, teachers and professors published an appeal calling for the Muhammad cartoons to be made a compulsory subject in German schools.[129] This explicitly called for the cartoons to be discussed, not viewed. The aim was to activate a necessary discourse and to give teachers the opportunity to reject responsibility for the choice of topic. After a brief discussion, the initiative petered out. A broad social solidarity could not be activated.

What will the consequences be if discursive teaching becomes as muted as parts of the press landscape? Where, if not at school, should democracy, a culture of debate and tolerance be reproduced?

Secularism is a cornerstone of enlightened ways of life. And it is fading. In America, fundamental Christians are calling for the abolition of the theory of evolution as a teaching subject and there are calls for Muslim prayer rooms in schools and for teachers that wear headscarves. Even the protection of physical integrity is being relativized in favor of religious traditions when parents

---

126 Lehrerverband warnt vor 'Klima der Einschüchterung', In: Frankfurter Allgemeine Zeitung, 20.10.2020.

127 Forsa Politik- und Sozialforschung GmbH on behalf of the Verband Bildung und Erziehung (ed.): *Die Schule aus Sicht der Schulleiterinnen und Schulleiter – Gewalt gegen Lehrkräfte*. Berlin March 27, 2020. p. 5. Digital at: https://www.vbe-bw.de/wp-content/uploads/2020/09/2020-04-07_forsa-Bericht_Gewalt_Baden-Wu%CC%88rttemberg.pdf [last accessed 15.08.2022].

128 Frank Jansen: "Für sie ist der Mörder aus Frankreich ein Idol – Radikalisierte Muslime in Deutschland". In: Der Tagesspiegel. 19.10.2020. Digital at: https://www.tagesspiegel.de/politik/radikalisierte-muslime-in-deutschland-fuer-sie-ist-der-moerder-aus-frankreich-einidol/26288138.html [last accessed 15.09.2022].

129 See: Tarek Badawia, Markus Tiedemann and Wolfgang Huber: Mohammed-Karrikaturen in die Schule? In: Die Zeit, 03.12.2020.

are allowed to have their sons circumcised for purely religious reasons without medical indication.

Discourses on tolerance can be conducted around all these questions. However, this means accepting the mutual duty of reciprocal and general justification.[130] In this context, the reference to traditions or cultural sensitivities can at best generate a very weak argument. Impositions are not sufficient evidence of intolerance. Anyone who is able to justify this can expect harshness from the other person. On the other hand, those who argue solely from their conception of the good without any intersubjective or intercultural communicability have no right to recognition of their desires.

It should be added that the infiltration of society by the views of fundamentalist Islam is progressing just as much as at the level of right-wing populism.

The vast majority of Koran schools in Germany are organized by Islamic associations that represent conservative Islam and do not shy away from playing martyrdom with young boys.[131]

"In my view, the ideological level is the most important and least considered level. It must [...] be said in all clarity that radicalization and Islamism go hand in hand with a certain understanding of Islam. "[132]

In North Rhine-Westphalia, the most populous federal state in Germany, between 47 and 57 percent of pupils at elementary school attended a Koran school in addition to Islamic religious education in 2019, and between 58 and 62 percent at secondary schools.[133] Authoritarian thinking and anti-Semitism are just as widespread among many Muslim students as among young people who would describe themselves as "right-wing".[134]

---

130 Rainer Forst: *Toleranz im Konflikt: Geschichte, Gehalt und Gegenwart eines umstrittenen Begriffs*. Suhrkamp, Frankfurt am Main 2012. p. 171.

131 See: Marc Röhlig: Türkische Gemeinden lassen Kinder in Deutschladn Krieg spielen. Soldat-Uniformen und "Märtyrer-Tode". In: SPIEGEL Panorama, 20.04.2018 https://www.spiegel.de/panorama/ditib-in-herford-und-wien-verkleidet-kinder-als-tuerkei-soldaten-a-00000000-0003-0001-0000-000002296792 [last accessed 15.08.2022];

Regina Mönch: Kleine Märtyrer. Updated. In: Frankfurter Allgemeine Zeitung, 28.04.2018. https://www.faz.net/aktuell/feuilleton/ditib-kommentar-kleine-maertyrer-spielen-krieg-in-moscheen-15563873.html [Last accessed 15.09.2022]

132 Ahmad Mansour: Eine nationale Strategie gegen Radikalisierung. In: Carsten Linnemann, Winfried Bausback (eds.): *Politischer Islam gehört nicht zu Deutschland*. Herder Verlag, Freiburg 2019. p. 128.

133 Cf.: Joachim Wagner: Die Koranschule ist starker als jeder Religionslehrer. In: Welt.de https://www.welt.de/debatte/kommentare/article201587404/Islam-Die-Koranschule-ist-staerker-als-jeder-Religionslehrer.html [Last accessed 15.08.2022].

134 Julia Bernstein et al, Mach mal keine Judenaktion! Herausforderungen und Lösungsansätze in der professionellen Bildung und Sozialarbeit gegen Antisemitismus, Frankfurt University of Applied Sciences 2018. Available online at: https://www. frankfurt-university.

There are also parallels to right-wing extremism at the level of political populism. One example is the so-called Denk party from Holland, which sees itself as a purely Islamic party, fundamentally rejects criticism of Erdoğan, denies the Armenian genocide and wants to introduce a racism register in which every Dutch citizen who makes "racist" comments in Denk's sense is to be recorded.[135]

Although the Denk-Partei describes the right-wing populist Geert Wilders as the "Hitler of our time", it shares his anti-democratic, anti-emancipatory thinking.[136]

In summary, it can be said that it is not religious or political terrorism that poses an existential threat to a society committed to the principles of Enlightenment. It is the danger of committing injustice ourselves through hysterical overreactions and devaluing our own normative foundations. Alternatively, there is the danger of a creeping self-abandonment through a diplomatically motivated appeasement based on a diffuse understanding of tolerance.

3.4.3 *Migration*

Migration and the Enlightenment have an intensive, reciprocal relationship. The great European emigration movements of the eighteenth and nineteenth centuries were driven both by economic hardship and the desire for political and intellectual freedom. States that guaranteed a free *"Pursuit of Happiness"* or at least promised that everyone could "be happy in their own way" benefited enormously in the medium term, both economically and spiritually. The

---

de/fileadmin/standard/Aktuelles/Pressemitteilungen/Mach_malkeine_Judenaktion Herausforderungen_und_Loesungsansaetze_in_der_professionellen_Bildungs-und_ Sozialarbeit_gegen_Anti.pdf [Last accessed 15.08.2022]. S. 345–346.

See: Roland Willareth: Diskriminierung durch Sprache. Antisemitismus an der Schule. In: Markus Tiedemann (ed.): *Migration, Menschenrechte und Rassismus. Herausforderungen ethischer Bildung*. Brill/Ferdinand Schöningh, Paderborn 2020. pp. 91–124.

135 Thomas Kirchner: Die Rassistenjäger. In: Süddeutsche.de https://www.sueddeutsche.de/ politik/niederlande-die-rassistenjaeger-1.3043002 [Last accessed 15.08.2022].

"That is why we want a so-called R-register (racism register) to be set up in which racist statements are recorded and [on the basis of which] it is made impossible for registered persons to work for a government organization." Denk (ed.): Politiek Manifest. Official Manifesto of the Denk Party. pp. 14–15 (translated from Dutch by the author).

136 Dirk Schümer: Europa hat jetzt eine erste reine Migrantenpartei. In: Welt.de https:// www.welt.de/politik/ausland/article155649010/Europa-hat-jetzt-eine-erste-reine-Migrantenpartei.html [last accessed 15.08.2022].

right to asylum that we know today is also a product of the Enlightenment. Its second root, church asylum, has always been limited to Christian charity and the institution of the church. Nevertheless, it is difficult to justify a right to migration on the basis of Enlightenment principles. Immanuel Kant is once again the forefather of the idea. In his treatises *On Perpetual Peace*, he points out that all citizens of the world are entitled to common ownership of "the surface of the earth, on which, as a spherical surface, they cannot disperse into infinity"[137]. However, this does not result in a general right of immigration. Even Kant could not ignore the fact that numerous long-term colonizations had already taken place. Appropriation, according to the liberal tradition since John Locke, takes place through work. Anyone who has developed a settlement area through labor owns it and cannot be forced to share it. The contract theory of the Enlightenment demands that others should not be harmed. Generosity is a moral imperative, not a legal one.

> "The right of world citizenship should [therefore] be restricted to conditions of general hospitality."
> Here, as in the previous articles, we are not talking about philanthropy, but about law, and h o s p i t a l i t y means the right of a stranger not to be treated hostilely by another because of his arrival on his land. The latter can refuse him if it can be done without his destruction; but as long as he behaves peacefully in his place, he cannot be treated hostilely. It is not a g u e s t r i g h t to which he can lay claim (for which a special benevolent contract would be required to make him a housemate for a certain time), but a right of visitation to which all men are entitled to offer themselves for company ...[138]

In this way, Kant had explicated a strong argument against colonization. European "discoverers" were allowed to introduce themselves and present themselves as company. Staying uninvited or even conquering were therefore morally and internationally reprehensible.

However, what enabled the justified criticism of colonialism in the eighteenth century makes it difficult to legitimize unlimited immigration to the global North today. After all, the principles of the right of asylum could also be won, because a rejection is only legitimate as long as this "can be done without his destruction"[139]. The distinction between the right of asylum and the desire to immigrate has arisen from this tradition. "Politically persecuted persons enjoy the right of asylum", for example, according to Article 16 (2) of the Basic Law of the Federal Republic of Germany. There is no right to immigration.

---

137 Kant: AA VIII, p. 358.
138 Kant: AA VIII, p. 357.
139 Kant: AA VIII, p. 358.

However, this legal distinction may provide clarity in theory, but is only of limited use in practice. Reducing the right to asylum to "political persecution" does not do justice to the plight of millions of refugees and falls short of the Kantian explanations. Hunger and misery, just like political persecution, can cause the "downfall" that Kant speaks of. Collectively turning a blind eye to these existential hardships also promotes ignorance and brutalization, which in turn have a negative impact on the foundations of liberal societies.

During the so-called "refugee crisis" of 2015 and 2016, this normative tension was particularly evident in Germany. The accompanying political rifts and radicalization processes were also caused by a lack of differentiation in demands and values. Part of the population succumbed to diffuse xenophobia, but was also reduced to this in public perception. In the opposite direction, the proponents were accused of breaking the constitution or even of a long-planned population exchange. How valuable it would have been if both sides had acknowledged the limits of their own justification and recognized acceptable arguments from the other side.

The assertion that the acceptance of millions of refugees without examining their motives is not covered by the asylum law of the Federal Republic of Germany is correct. The statement that this action by the federal government constitutes a breach of the constitution is false. Asylum law regulates the right to protection and care. It does not formulate a veto against assistance that goes beyond this. A freely elected government does not have the right to deny asylum to politically persecuted persons. However, it does have the right to come to the aid of other people. If this government is also re-elected in subsequent elections, it can feel vindicated in its decisions by the will of the voters. Of course, citizens have the right to demonstrate and take legal action against the government's policies. However, we must also remember our civic duty to recognize elections and judgments of the judiciary. In Germany, lawsuits against the government's "refugee policy" were rejected by the highest court[140].

The Herculean task of migration is not just about coping with registering, housing, feeding and integrating ever-increasing numbers of people in need of help. It also consists of acknowledging emotional and ethical paradoxes.

According to Eurostat, the statistical office of the European Union, around 2.4 million people fled to Europe in 2015 and 2016. 1.1 million of them came to Germany.[141] Six years later, Europe is experiencing the largest refugee move-

---

140   BVG: Ref. 2 BvE 1/18.
141   Eurostat press releases 44/2016 (p. 1ff); 46/2017 (p. 1ff).
      According to estimates that have been revised several times, the *Bundesamt für Migration und Flüchtlinge* put the actual number of asylum seekers who entered Germany

ment since the Second World War. Millions of Ukrainians left their homeland within a few weeks to seek safety from the Russian war of aggression. In both cases, an overwhelming culture of welcome emerged. At the same time, an astonishing discrepancy came to light. The very countries that refused to take in refugees from 2015 onwards and even refused to comply with pan-European resolutions showed impressive solidarity in 2022. The main burden of the first Ukrainian refugee movement was and still is borne by the neighboring states of Moldova, Romania, Slovakia, Hungary and Poland. In the first three weeks of the war, Poland alone managed to take in over 2 million people and provide them with humane care. An achievement that is politically and morally unparalleled. However, it is also true that just a few weeks earlier, families from Syria and Afghanistan, which the Belarusian dictator Lukashenko had used as leverage, were categorically rejected and left to fend for themselves in the border region during the winter. It is undisputed that there are serious differences between those seeking protection. It was mainly educated women, children and elderly people who fled Ukraine, while considerable numbers of men even entered Ukraine to take part in the country's defense. In 2015 and 2016, it was mainly young, uneducated men who came to Europe while women and children were often left behind and at the same time NATO soldiers were deployed for a free Afghanistan, among other things. Emotional differentiations are therefore perfectly understandable. Nevertheless, it remains the task of reason to insist on fairness and self-criticism. This includes the fact that the majority of refugees from Ukraine left by car or train. The refugees of 2015 and 2016 came on foot and often crossed continents. Women and children are not able to cope with these hardships to the same extent. Young men also have the right to flee from war. And: many of the people who were at risk of freezing to death in the winter of 2021/22 in the border region between Belarus and Poland were women and children. The concern is therefore not entirely unfounded that the cultural and religious background of the two refugee groups in particular has made a significant difference. Once again, the tremendous achievement of Polish society in particular in caring for Ukrainian refugees remains a historically outstanding example. Furthermore, it is only natural that the reception of people, of neighbors with a related cultural and linguistic background, is met with greater emotional readiness than that of people who, rightly or wrongly, appear foreign and unsettling. Nevertheless, these emotions should not be the sole guiding principle for action. Enlightened societies are committed to an egalitarian human right.

---

in 2015 and 2016 at around 890,000 and 280,000 people respectively (see: Jahresbericht des Bundesamtes für Migration und Flüchtlinge: *Das Bundesamt in Zahlen 2016*. p. 73ff).

The ethical paradoxes of the migration issue begin with a reductive understanding of borders and end with the dilemma of an unequal distribution of aid.

In the years 2016–2018, the evaluation of borders mutated into a test for European and North American societies. While one faction stylized state borders as an indispensable, identity-creating and identity-preserving value, the other faction reduced borders to a negation of freedom per se.

Why borders are supposed to be necessary guarantors of identity cannot be understood outside of nationalist ideologies. The Canadian-American border runs right through the *Haskell Free Library*. The library belongs to both the Canadian village of Stanstead and the American town of Derby Line. However, neither the existence nor the visit to the library jeopardizes the Canadian or American identity. The latter would only be challenged if customs and traditions were propagated and practiced in the other half of the library that would contradict the fundamental constitutional and ethical convictions of the visitors and the funding communities. However, where a common constitutional framework has been found, the dismantling of borders represents an increase in personal freedom without jeopardizing individual and collective identities. This is precisely what makes the European Community so beautiful.

However, a blanket discrediting of borders as a restriction of freedom also falls short. Thinkers on the so-called left spectrum in particular often neglect the fact that state borders also function as an expression of civic autonomy. This is easy to grasp when it comes to controlling the flow of goods. Free citizens want to have a say in deciding which goods should be imported or exported into their country. The sale of medical products is generally well received, while the import and export of weapons is unpopular. Green electricity is readily imported, while the import of drugs is to be prohibited. What applies to goods does not completely lose its validity when it comes to people. Visiting students from India are welcome, but Russian oligarchs or Colombian drug dealers should be denied entry. Enlightened ways of life strive for maturity and the ability to act. The rule of law has a dual function here. Firstly, it must protect the self-determination of its citizens in the best possible way and secondly, its organs and laws should themselves be an expression of civic self-determination. For this, a state needs the capacity to act, and this in turn requires a limited national territory in which the collective of citizens has the say. Julian Nida-Rümelin has worked out the extent to which control over state borders is linked to the idea of enlightened self-determination.

> This deontology of boundaries includes not only the rights of individuals to defend themselves against institutions on the part of the state, but also on

the part of other persons, as well as the constitutive conditions of collective authorship in the form of political institutions, states, cultural and otherwise constituted communities. Without structure, without legitimate and accepted boundaries, there is no authorship, no accountability, no responsibilities, no respect and no dignity. The sympathetic plea for borderlessness, the thesis that borders are fundamentally illegitimate because they maintain differences, cannot be ethically legitimized on closer inspection.[142]

Unfortunately, differentiated statements of this kind are rarely heard, which is why a continuing anti-Enlightenment polarization in the context of migration debates is to be feared. There is a lack of awareness of the fact that many aspects of the issue cannot be resolved satisfactorily.

In the context of so-called poverty migration, the problem escalates into an inescapable dilemma of culpable entanglement. Let's start with an almost unbearable example. Rescuing drowning people is a requirement of international maritime law and a moral duty. At the same time, it cannot be denied that so-called smugglers speculate on this operation and create "pull effects", as a result of which people drown. Suppose it could be proven that every person rescued from the Mediterranean would result in ten more, two of whom would then drown. Of course, the duty to rescue shipwrecked people would remain untouched. To deny this would be outrageous. At the same time, it is completely morally unacceptable to lure people to their deaths. This dilemma cannot be resolved, and a society that has to reject every possible course of action is faced with an existential ordeal.

No less dramatic is the weight of the numbers, which makes any satisfactory solution impossible even without the threat from oceans or deserts.

According to the UNHCR, 89.3 million people were displaced in 2021[143] (in 2020 it was 82.4)[144]. Between 2015 and 2021, around 495,000 asylum applications were submitted in Italy and 2.3 million in Germany.[145] Together, this corresponds to the total population of Rome or three-quarters of the population of Berlin.

---

142   Julian Nida-Rümelin: *Über Grenzen denken. Eine Ethik der Migration.* Edition Körber Foundation, Hamburg 2017. p. 165.
143   UNHCR: Global Trends – Forced Displacement in 2021. p. 2.
144   UNHCR: Global Trends – Forced Displacement in 2020. p. 2.
145   Data according to Eurostat, UNHCR – Statistical Surveys 2015–2021.
         Italy: https://www.unhcr.org/refugee-statistics/download/?url=K1aKu0 [Last accessed 15.08.2022];
         Germany: https://www.unhcr.org/refugee-statistics/download/?url=AdfF8x [Last accessed 15.08.2022].

Even if far more people apply for asylum than are later granted the right to stay or residence, the numbers are still impressive. In any case, humanity demands humane accommodation regardless of legal status. In practice, this is not the case in many places. The largest refugee camp financed by the European Union to date has been set up on the Greek island of Lesbos. The camp, which was fenced in with walls and barbed wire, was designed for 2,800 people and was temporarily occupied by up to 20,000 people.[146]

Inhumane practices in refugee camps, children at risk of dying of cold on the Polish border, drowning people in the Mediterranean, refugees dying of thirst in the Mexican-American border region: short-term solutions are possible. North America and Europe are among the richest regions in the world. It is possible to care for millions of refugees in a humane manner. Nor is it currently clear that these societies have reached their limits. Nevertheless, it can hardly be denied that an economic, social and political breaking point exists. According to the pan-African research network Afrobarometer, which surveyed 45,000 Africans in 34 countries over two years, 37 percent of the African population are considering emigrating. Of those willing to emigrate, 27 percent cite Europe as their desired destination.[147] The German Foundation for World Population currently puts Africa's rapidly growing population at 1.3 billion people[148]. On this basis, migrant numbers can be calculated that far exceed the population of Germany or France. The inhumane conditions in refugee camps such as Moria are inexcusable given the wealth of the northern hemisphere and the European Union's self-image as a Nobel Peace Prize winner. At the same time, it cannot be denied that the camps will fill up again and again and that the potential number of migrants exceeds the possibilities of economic, social and political compensation.

A utilitarian position could be taken that the rich countries of the North should take in at least as many people as it takes to level out living conditions in the North and South. Relieving the burden on the South and redistribution in the North would generate the greatest possible benefit for the greatest possible number. However, this solution has numerous pitfalls. First of all, it

---

146   Cf: Franziska Grillmeier: Der neue Alltag auf der Insel – gefährlich für Flüchtlinge und Helfer. In: *Tagesspiegel*.de. https://www.tagesspiegel.de/politik/fluechtlingskrise-auf-lesbos-der-neue-alltag-auf-der-insel-gefaehrlich-fuer-fluechtlinge-und-helfer/25606814.html [Last accessed 15.08.2022].

147   Josephine Appiah-Nyamekye, Carolyn Logan, E. Gyimah-Boadi: In search of opportunity: Young and educated Africans most likely to consider moving abroad. In: *Afrobarometer Dispatch No. 288*, 03/2019. p. 3.

148   Deutsche Stiftung Weltbevölkerung in cooperation with the Population Reference Bureau: *DSW-Datenreport 2021*. p. 8ff.

cannot be assumed that the population of the global North would be prepared to take this selfless step. Demanding it would very likely strengthen nationalist forces. In addition to the demise of liberal constitutional states, this would also mean a lack of development aid. Moreover, it remains questionable whether such a step could really generate the greatest benefit in the medium term. An economic decline in the global North would not only reduce the quality of life there, but also its productivity and aid to the global South.

In addition, there is a social and systematic problem of justice. The imperative to take in people in need ultimately results from the equality of human dignity. However, this dignity and the resulting entitlements do not only apply to those who reach the European or North American borders. It is equally due to those people who are left behind. In fact, the refugee movements themselves already reflect a social injustice. Those who make the journey usually have the health and financial means to cross continents and pay smugglers. The group of people who set off or are even poached also includes people with qualifications that are then sorely missed in their country of origin. This effect, known as the "brain drain", exacerbates global injustice and primarily affects the poorest countries in the world.[149] Among those left behind are the so-called "bottom trillion", those people who have to survive on less than one euro a day.[150] They represent the proportion of the world's population that needs help the most. If large numbers of the less destitute reach the global North and are fed there according to the usual standards, aid for the bottom trillion will decrease. In fact, the care, accommodation and education of refugees in North America and Europe require considerable sums of money.[151] With these sums, a much larger number of people in the Global South could be lifted out of poverty.

Reinhard Merkel has chosen a vivid example to illustrate the problem:

> Imagine a wealthy landowner with a thousand needy people crowding around his estate. To ten of them who have made it over the wall and up to the front door he grants admission, permanent housing and maintenance. This exhausts his resources to almost their limit. If he distributed them to all one thousand,

---

149 Cf: Frédéric Docquier, Hillel Rapoport: Globalisation, Brain Drain and Development. In: *Journal of Economic Literature*, 50/3, 2012. pp. 681–730.

150 Cf.: "The global rate of extreme poverty has risen for the first time since 1998, from 8.4% in 2019 to 9.5% in 2020. This means that almost one in ten people in the world is affected by extreme poverty." – Bundeszentrale für politische Bildung: Internationaler Tag für die Beseitigung der Armut. https://www.bpb.de/kurz-knapp/hintergrund-aktuell/342096/internationaler-tag-fuer-diebeseitigung-der-armut/ [Last accessed 15.08.2022].

151 In Germany alone, the so-called "refugee-related burdens" on the budget amounted to €22.9 billion in 2020 (Bundesfinanzministerium: *Finanzplan des Bundes 2021 bis 2025*. DS 19/31501, 08/2021. p. 40).

everyone would be helped. But as it is, with the best will in the world, he has hardly anything left for the 990 who have remained outside. It offers them nothing more than the famous drop in the ocean. If you want a symbol for the morality of German refugee policy: something like this.[152]

This picture certainly needs to be supplemented. It should be added that the ancestors of our landowner exploited the lands beyond his walls and that unfair trade relations still exist. One could also ask what criteria identify the dwindling resources. But even a more differentiated picture does not solve the problem: the wealth of our landowner is partly based on exploitation, but not only. A complete expropriation and distribution among the poor is therefore hardly justifiable. Taking in all those in need would be tantamount to this decision. Providing for only ten needy people without taking into account the misery beyond the walls is an unacceptable inequality of treatment. Minimal care for those who have arrived in favor of those in need beyond the walls would create a two-class society with racist potential within the borders. Moreover, it must not be forgotten that our landowner does not live alone. A massive increase in aid or intake numbers could lead to an uprising by the existing estate residents and thus to an end to all aid. Ignoring the misery on the other side of the wall is also not an option. The residents of the estate would become brutalized and would have to practice a self-imposed loss of reality. A society worth living in, striving for Enlightenment, will not last long in this way. The decision-making situation is much easier on the neighboring estates. There are totalitarian regimes there that only have the welfare of either the oligarchy or their own population in mind. There is no conflict with the all-dominant principle of national self-interest there and every little bit of help for people outside one's own borders can be seen as a generous benefit.

A simple syllogism, on the other hand, illustrates how great the ordeal is for societies that feel committed to the ideas of the Enlightenment.

P1: Societies that strive for Enlightenment are existentially threatened if they violate their own ethical principles.
P2: The refugee movements of the twenty-first century make it impossible not to violate normative principles of the Enlightenment.
K: Societies striving for Enlightenment are under existential threat.

---

152   Reinhard Merkel: Wir können allen helfen. In: Markus Tiedemann (ed.): *Migration, Menschenrechte und Rassismus. Herausforderungen ethischer Bildung.* Brill/Ferdinand Schöningh, Paderborn 2020. p. 17; see also Frankfurter Allgemeine Zeitung from 22.11.2017. p. 9.

3.5 The digital catalyst

It can be considered a commonplace that the digital revolution has brought about a media paradigm shift. No matter how you assess the development, the speed of dissemination and the exponential growth of those involved remains dizzying. In November 1990, Tim Berners-Lee made the world's first website available. Programming languages have long since ceased to be necessary. Billions of people navigate the World Wide Web effortlessly using user-friendly software. In the near future, satellite-based Internet access will be available anywhere in the world.

The development is capable of awakening utopian hopes as well as dystopian fears.

Is the Internet the realization of Comenius' dream of "teaching everyone everything"? To the encyclopaedists around Diderot, Wikipedia might appear to be the realization of a dream of mankind. The knowledge of all for all. "What is Enlightenment?" by Kant, *A Theory of Justice* by Rawls, *Critique of Black Reason* by Achille Mbembe: all of this is now available, along with competent introductions and controversial commentaries, to an unimaginable number of interested people. The same applies to political activity: the Arab Spring, the civil rights movement in Hong Kong, Fridays for Future, the international protest against the Russian war of aggression in Ukraine: all of this would be almost inconceivable without digital media.

However, digital media are also strengthening forces that have a destructive effect on the project of Enlightenment. The improved possibilities of international communication and information are countered by increasingly sophisticated methods and effects of manipulation and surveillance. For better or for worse, digitization is proving to be a powerful catalyst. The central question is: who will win the race?

At least two aspects promote the emergence of Post-Enlightenment Societies.

3.5.1 *The aestheticization of the living environment and the problem of unequal acceleration*

According to Ernst Cassirer's philosophy of symbolic forms, man is the symbolizing being and his specific forms of expression are either presentational or discursive in nature.

As far as we know, only we are capable of not only directly experiencing a river like the Vltava, but also painting it, paying homage to it in symphonies, praising it in poems, topographizing it, analyzing it chemically and much more. The classic representative of presentational forms is the iconic image.

Discursive forms are articulated in the medium of language and find their most abstract expression in formal logic. Of course, there are gray areas such as linguistic images, metaphors, etc. All these forms of expression are valuable components of human life forms.

Presentational symbolism enables the expression of feelings and ideas. Their spectrum ranges from expressionist representations of the unconscious to the cross-cultural power of music. However, only the discursive form is capable of formulating and testing truth claims. The struggle for objectivity, the unconstrained compulsion of the better argument, is manifested solely in the medium of discursive language, which struggles to provide coherent evidence. In this context, Karl Popper speaks of the *critical* or *argumentative function* of language, which alone enables a "critical discussion about the truth and falsity of propositions".[153] Images can provoke reflection and illustrate ideas, but they elude the criteria of justification. A picture is not true or wrong. It is not good or bad. A picture is a picture is a picture.

> Language is an abstraction from experience, while images are concrete representations of experience. A picture may be worth as much as a thousand words, but it is by no means an equivalent for a thousand or a hundred or even just two words. Words and images belong to different spheres of discourse, because a word is always and above all an idea, a product of the imagination, so to speak. Something like "cat", "work" or "wine" does not exist in nature. Such words are terms for regularities that we perceive in nature. Pictures do not show concepts, they show things. It cannot be repeated often enough: unlike a spoken or written sentence, a picture is irrefutable. It does not make an assertion, it does not refer to a opposite or the negation of itself, it does not have to satisfy any rules of plausibility or logic.[154]

This does not diminish the aesthetic value of presentational forms. Their legitimate realm is art, emotion and myth. Enlightenment, however, is dependent on the discursive form. Reflection requires conceptual abstraction from concrete experience in order to think the particular as contained in the general.[155] Only propositional language enables the formulation of truth claims. Sensory impressions are not true or false, not good or evil. These categories are reserved for conceptualization.

---

153 Cf.: Karl Popper: *Ausgangspunkte*. Ex Libris, Zurich 1981. pp. 104–109; Ders.: *Alles Leben ist Problemlösen*. Piper, Munich 1994. p. 120.
154 Neil Postman: Das Verschwinden der Kindheit. S. Fischer Verlag, Frankfurt am Main 1987. p. 87.
155 Cf.: Kant: AA V, p. 176.

It is therefore not insignificant for a society whether it communicates mainly in discursive or presentational forms, whether visual impressions or arguments exert a dominant influence in it.

The phases of the Enlightenment were always associated with the primacy of discursive forms. The sophists of ancient Greece may also have taught the art of rhetorical persuasion. However, the distinction between better and worse arguments was at least as important to them. In the manageable city states of antiquity, the exchange of positions and arguments could still be organized through direct discourse. The decisive medium for the expansion of the Enlightenment, however, was writing. Socrates and Pericles were contemporaries who both knew how to read and probably also how to write.[156] It is certain, however, that their teachings could never have had this culture-forming effect without the written tradition. The same applies to the second phase of the Enlightenment. The Declaration of Human Rights can be systematically traced back to the philosophy of Locke, Rousseau and Kant. However, without the written dissemination of these theories, human rights would never have been transferred into positive law. Written culture and Enlightenment are able to potentiate each other. The political Enlightenment has always promoted general literacy and the learning of reading and writing promotes important basic skills of Enlightenment.

> Anyone who learns to read also learns to engage with the rules of a complex logical and rhetorical tradition that forces you to weigh sentences carefully and thoroughly and to constantly modify meanings if new points of view arise as the text progresses. The reader must learn to proceed in a reflective and analytical manner, develop patience and receptivity and remain in a constant state of suspension, from which they can also say no to a text after careful consideration.[157]

Written culture is therefore not only able to archive knowledge across cultures, it also promotes the reader's power of judgment. The same applies to the promotion of humanity. "Books, the poet Jean Paul once remarked, are thicker letters to friends. With this sentence, he quintessentially and gracefully named the essence and function of humanism: it is friendly telecommunication in the

---

156 Socrates' literacy is attested in several sources, but whether he was also able to write is questionable. Cf.: Plato: Phaidon, [97b], Apology [26d f] and Xenophon: Erinnerungen an Sokrates [I 6,14].
157 Postman: p. 91.

medium of writing. What has been called *humanitas* since the days of Cicero belongs in the narrowest sense to the consequences of literacy."¹⁵⁸

Unfortunately, written culture is by no means a sufficient criterion for humanism and Enlightenment. This hope would fall short of the "dialectic of Enlightenment"¹⁵⁹. *Don Carlos* and *Mein Kampf* were both written and reproduced by the printing press. Nevertheless, the fact remains that Enlightenment requires the discursive medium of propositional language. Its essence finds its conclusion "in its own argumentative judgment [...], whereby it finally terminates in itself: as a critical or dialectical effort of the concept".¹⁶⁰

In order to gauge the effect of digitization on the continued existence of the Enlightenment, it is therefore necessary to assess whether discursive or presentational forms, whether images or concepts dominate the medium. Quantitative distribution alone is not decisive. At all times in cultural history, aesthetic perception and popular diversion are likely to have played a greater role in everyday life than reflection and the struggle for objectivity. So if the dissemination of conceptual debate also gains massively through digitization, the overall effect could be assessed positively despite unchanged proportions. There are several arguments for this. Never before in the history of mankind has there been such a extensive and easily accessible selection of information options, educational opportunities and discussion forums. Aestheticization can also be seen as an enrichment in many parts of life. Despite all the streams of tourists, only a fraction of humanity will be able to visit the Vatican Museums. Digital tours can help here.

However, there are also worrying signs of de-rationalization. Newspaper publishers around the world have come under massive pressure, even though they also offer their product digitally. The number of traditional newspaper subscribers is falling and is not being offset by the increase in online readers. Communication from citizens is also becoming shorter and tending towards the iconic. The maximum length of a tweet has been limited to 280 characters since November 2017. This is roughly the length of my last three sentences. A tightly written postcard is about twice as long. How much argument can be made in 280 characters? Comic-like depictions of feelings

---

158 Peter Sloterdijk: Regeln für den Menschenpark. Ein Antwortschreiben zum Brief über den Humanismus – die Elmauer Rede. In: *DIE ZEIT*, No. 38, 16.09.1999. p. 18.

159 See: Max Horkheimer and Theodor Wiesengrund Adorno: *Dialektik der Aufklärung. Philosophische Fragmente*. Querido, Amsterdam 1947.

160 Roland W. Henke: Ende der Kunst oder Ende der Philosophie? Ein Beitrag zur Diskussion um den Stellenwert präsentativer Materialien im Philosophie- und Ethikunterricht. In *Zeitschrift für Didaktik der Philosophie und Ethik*, 1/2012. pp. 59–66.

characterize a considerable part of the communication of children, young people and adults. The staging of impressions or self-portrayals characterize the everyday lives of millions. These are mostly photos that document trivial everyday activities.

In a society striving for Enlightenment, however, a clear distinction must be made between statement and depiction, between staging and justification. The growing dominance of presentational forms could pose a threat to individual and collective maturity. This is particularly true if the problem of unequal acceleration is also taken into account.

The problem can be described quite simply: the spread of doxa can be accelerated to almost the speed of light, whereas the emergence of episteme benefits much less from digital media. The reason for this is that the spread of mere states of excitement, opinions or prejudices neither requires an elaborate process of appropriation nor is it tied to a specific medium. They are sparked by slogans and rumors as well as visual impressions. Short messages and images can be disseminated very quickly and their consumption makes minimal intellectual demands. Knowledge, on the other hand, must always be actively acquired and internalized. Episteme requires reading, research, criticism and controversy. In short: it takes time. It arises from a long process of development that can only be accelerated to a very limited extent. Wikipedia may have made Diderot's dream come true. But the effort of reading and studying remains the same as it was centuries ago. Promises of happiness, prejudices and stereotypical patterns are multiplied by emotional impulses and simple repetition, creating real, as well as virtual masses. Even Gustav Le Bon did not consider it necessary for crowds to gather physically; it is sufficient for their members to reinforce each other through the media (see section 4.3.2). The digital age offers ideal conditions for this. The pursuit of episteme is linked to the search for the antithesis of criticism and the pressure to justify oneself. Doxa, on the other hand, seeks confirmation through association with like-minded people. In the real public space of a liberal society, salutary corrective measures take effect. There, bizarre and absurd opinions are quickly exposed to criticism and ridicule. This does not reliably prevent the mass acceptance of dangerous ideas, but at least makes it more difficult. In the digital world, critical voices have not disappeared, but they can be suppressed. Whether controlled by algorithms or consciously organized, the isolation in "echo chambers" to reinforce one's own basic assumptions has never been as effective as it is today. Unfortunately, this applies not only to trivial stupidities, but also to delusions and inhuman discrimination. Rational counter-arguments, if they are accepted at all, are rarely effective. One reason for this is that constant repetition quickly creates a robust illusion of truth. The factor of emotional attachment is at least as important. Statements and theses are not tested for their persuasive power. Rather, the decisive factor is that the sender and receiver share the same emotional state. Rule of thumb: whoever feels the way I do is right. This is exactly what pre-enlightened tribal behavior is.

In addition, the cultivation of judgment is made more difficult by the dominance of visual impressions. As explained above, logical criteria are ineffective in the face of images.

The unlimited possibilities of visual manipulation and deepfakes in the digital age are only mentioned here in passing. It is important to note that all images, as shown above, elude rational categories. Only in combination with concepts are they able to contribute to the acquisition of the epistemic through illustration. On their own, they have a tendency to incapacitate and overwhelm. This is particularly true of moving images, as they strain our neural networks to such an extent that simultaneous reflection and critical distancing become almost impossible. We have all watched bad movies to the end because the fast cuts kept our brains so busy that we were unable to ask ourselves: Do I even want what I am doing here right now? Is it worth paying attention to these things? Would it be better for me to turn my attention to other things? Are the information, role models and demands presented credible? Are they acceptable? The suppression of these questions is the essence of every media overload. While the processing of aesthetic data runs at full speed, the critical power of judgment lapses into passivity. However, unconscious learning from the model remains active. Neurologist Manfred Spitzer has provocatively summarized these aspects. "Studies have clearly shown that excessive continuous consumption of television, computer games, video games or the internet makes children and young people fat, stupid and violent."[161] Educators also warned of the negative effects of increasingly digital leisure activities for schoolchildren decades ago.[162] Back in 2001 – the smartphone was still a long way from being a mass product – four out of ten of the most frequently mentioned Christmas wishes from the age group between 6 and 12 were related to audiovisual media. Books or other print media were not mentioned at all.[163]

---

161 Cf.: Manfred Spitzer: "TV macht dumm, dick und gewalttätig", https://www.youtube.com/watch?v=LftI9pYDg7I, Min. 2.29 [last accessed 02.08.2022].

162 Cf.: Ruth Möller: Welche Defizite haben unsere Schulanfänger? Ein Gespräch mit der Rektorin einer Grundschule. In: *Kindergarten heute.* November/December 2002. pp. 20–23.

163 Cf: Institut der deutschen Wirtschaft Köln: Weihnachtsgeschenke: Viel Elektronik unterm Baum. Die beliebtesten Weihnachtswünsche von 6- bis 12-jährigen in Prozent. In: *Informationsdienst des Instituts der deutschen Wirtschaft*, No. 49. December 2002. p. 1.

All respondents at that time are now eligible to vote. Many of them will have children themselves and influence their media use.

As early as 1987, Neil Postman drew a gloomy conclusion based solely on the mass medium of remote viewing. His assessment seems more relevant today than ever:

> Taken together, the electronic and optical revolutions represent an uncoordinated but powerful threat to language and literacy, a remelting of the world of ideas into a world of 'light-switching' symbols and images. The scope of this development can hardly be overestimated. For while the speed of transmission made the controlled handling of information impossible, the mass-produced image changed the form of this information itself – from the discursive to the non-discursive, from the sentence form to the image form, from the intellectual to the emotional.[164]

If this diagnosis proves to be true, digitization will not be a neutral catalyst, but an accelerant in the demise of the Enlightenment. Unreflected opinions, prejudices and stereotypical ideas have always been fast and pandemic. The Enlightenment has had to deal with this dynamic by means of a laborious and lengthy educational process. Due to the one-sided digital acceleration, the race is in danger of being lost for good.

3.5.2 Structural loss of the public sphere

It makes you sit up and take notice when one of the most famous intellectual greats of our time feels compelled to add to his magnum opus at the age of 92. Under the title "Reflections and Hypotheses on a Renewed Structural Change in the Political Public Sphere", Jürgen Habermas places the social and political impact of digital media at the center of his reflections.[165] According to Habermas, it has not yet been decided whether destructive or negative potentials predominate. The "global organizational potential offered by the new media serves radical right-wing networks as well as the brave Belarusian women in their persistent protest against Lukashenko."[166] On the one hand, digital media has opened up an unprecedented quantity of opportunities for participation. On the other hand, it remains questionable whether this promotes, stagnates or erodes the rationality of public discourse.

---

164   Postman 1987, p. 87.
165   Jürgen Habermas: Überlegungen und Hypothesen zu einem erneuten Strukturwandel der politischen Öffentlichkeit. In: *Leviathan*, 49th vol., special volume 37/2021. pp. 470–500.
166   Ibid. p. 487.

Today, this great emancipatory promise is drowned out by the wild noises in fragmented, self-circling echo chambers." [...] "The self-empowerment of media users is one effect; the other is the price they pay for being released from the editorial tutelage of the old media as long as they have not yet sufficiently learned how to use the new media. Just as book printing turned everyone into potential readers, digitization is now turning everyone into potential authors. But how long did it take for everyone to learn to read?[167]

According to Habermas, one of the tasks of quality journalism during this transitional phase is to defend rationality standards in the formation of public opinion. Nevertheless, the analogy to book printing is a cause for concern. Centuries of fanaticism and cruelty passed before literariness – if at all – developed extensive humanistic effects. There is also another consideration: we may not be experiencing a paradigm shift towards a new structure of the public sphere. Perhaps we are experiencing a complete loss of structure. According to Hannah Arendt, a central structural achievement of the Enlightenment movements is the clear separation between the private and the public space. The separation between oikos and agora, academy or popular assembly, was already manifest in Attic democracy. In the house, the free Greek could do as he pleased.[168] In the public sphere, on the other hand, he was accountable to his counterpart. According to Arendt, this giving and taking of reasons in the political sphere is what makes specifically human action possible and is to be regarded as a central component of the *human condition*.

> To be political, to live in a polis, means that all matters are settled by means of words that can convince, and not by coercion or force.[169]

However, the obligation to justify oneself in the public sphere only gains contours through the existence of the private sphere. The private sphere is the legitimate place of the irrational, the intimate and the self-determined remembering or forgetting. Beate Rösser distinguishes between three levels of privacy.[170] Local privacy encompasses the exclusivity of spaces and places.

---

167 Ibid. pp. 487, 488.
168 The fact that women, children and slaves were rather defenseless victims of this private despotism is a deplorable lack of participation, but does not devalue the separation between private and public space.
169 Hannah Arendt: *Vita activa oder Vom tätigen Leben*. 20th edition. Piper, Munich 2019. p. 36.
170 Cf: Beate Rössler: *Der Wert des Privaten*. Suhrkamp Verlag, Frankfurt am Main 2001. p. 144ff.

Decisional privacy describes the right to personal lifestyles and stylistic perceptions without the need for justification. The third level is informal privacy.

> In essence, this is [...] about who knows what and how about a person, i.e. about control over information that concerns them; and control at least in the sense that they have control in many respects, in other respects they can at least estimate what other people know about them: that they can therefore have well-founded assumptions about what people or institutions with which they are involved [even unconsciously] know about them, and that they can then also have corresponding possibilities for sanctions or at least criticism in accordance with these assumptions and expectations.[171]

As much as citizens are committed to rational discourse in the public sphere, they have the right to exclude the public from the various levels of privacy. Sissela Bok defines "privacy as the condition of being protected from unwanted access by others – either physical access, personal information or attention. Claims to privacy are claims to control access (...)".[172] What the private individual "does or does not do is of no significance, has no consequences, and what concerns him is of no concern to anyone else. "[173]

The distinction between these two spheres is far more than the consideration of two human needs. It is a necessary basic structure of a liberal society.

> If nothing is private, there is nothing public. Wherever the boundary runs, it has an important public function: by indicating that some things are not public, it protects the integrity of the public sphere.[174]

Unfortunately, digital media in particular have contributed significantly to the erosion of this demarcation. The private sphere suffers from massive encroachments from outside and active divestment from within. At the same time, public discourse is being privatized and trivialized.

Let's start with the obvious encroachments from outside.

Hannah Arend cited the efforts of the tsarist secret police Ochrana to use a card index system to gather as much information as possible about as many citizens of the empire as possible as an early example of total rule.[175] Compared

---

171 Ibid. p. 201.
172 Sissela Bok: *Secrets: On the Ethics of Concealment & Revelation*. 2nd edition. Oxford University Press, Oxford 1984. pp. 10–11.
173 Rössler 2001, p. 73.
174 Ned O' Gorman: *Politk für alle – Hannah Arendt lesen in unsicheren Zeiten*. Nagel & Kimche, Munich 2021. p. 143.
175 Cf: Hannah Arendt: Die ungarische Revolution und der Totalitäre Imperialismus. Piper, Munich 1958.

to the working methods of subsequent organizations, Arendt's example seems downright primitive. However, even the surveillance strategies of the Gestapo, the KGB or the State Security are dwarfed by the new digital possibilities. What is currently being organized in the People's Republic of China seems like a breathtaking mixture of two dystopias. As in Huxley's *Brave New World*, citizens are to be given as much consumer satisfaction as possible. At the same time, media surveillance eclipses everything described by Orwell in *1984*. Not only are "telescreens" installed in countless places, citizens voluntarily carry them around with them. Technically, few people are aware that even switching off a device does not provide absolute security against the continuous recording of visual and acoustic data. To do this, it would be necessary to remove the battery or SIM card.

This is not just about real-time surveillance, but also about the good old index cards. Admittedly, the flood of data is enormous and the majority of information remains irrelevant. However, the digital card index offers almost unlimited storage capacity. Information that is not interesting today does not have to be so tomorrow. In addition, search functions enable countless compilations, depending on intentions and needs. The state infiltrates the private sphere and not only gains knowledge of the movement and communication profiles of its citizens, but also the authority to interpret their biographies.

It could now be argued that the misuse of digital technologies by authoritarian states was to be expected. Liberal societies, on the other hand, would have nothing to fear due to their organized separation of powers. There are good reasons to describe this idea as out of touch with reality. It is part of the nature of digital media not to be limited to governmental or social systems and to be locked in or out only by considerable technical and legal barriers. According to Clive Hamilton and Mareike Ohlberg, the Chinese telecommunications supplier Huawei, for example, is "an excellent example of how the CCP [Chinese Communist Party] combines espionage, intellectual property theft and influence operations."[176] It is also worth recalling the more than well-founded suspicion that the 2016 US presidential election was influenced by Russia in favor of the late President Donald Trump. In addition to the hacker attack on the US digital election system, millions of relevant posts were launched on social communication platforms.[177]

---

176 Clive Hamilton, Mareike Ohlberg: Die lautlose Eroberung. Wie China westliche Demokratien unterwandert und die Welt neu ordnet. 3rd edition. DVA, Munich 2020. p. 238.
177 See: Kathleen Hall Jamieson: Cyberwar: *How Russian Hackers and Trolls Helped Elect a President – What We Don't, Can't, and Do Know*. Oxford University Press, Oxford 2018.

Secondly, countries such as Poland and Hungary are demonstrating just how bad the separation of powers is in supposedly liberal forms of government. For example, Poland de facto abolished both press freedom and the independence of the judiciary in 2020 and 2021. So what should stop the rulers in Warsaw from installing a system of data surveillance? In the United States of America or the United Kingdom, all these instances were in place. Nevertheless, a global and suspicion-independent surveillance system, including a pre-council data repository, was set up under the leadership of the National Security Agency (NSA) from 2007 at the latest. This not only involved the surveillance of befriended heads of state such as the German Chancellor, but also the violation of the constitutional fundamental rights of the countries' own citizens.[178] The historical background of international terrorism and the intention to prevent further attacks may explain these attacks, but they do not justify them. Precisely because it was a secret action, it is possible to speak of a unilateral termination of the social contract, in which the use of force and adherence to the law is legitimized by the protection of fundamental rights.

Furthermore, the statement that blameless citizens have nothing to fear falls far short of the mark. Disregarding basic rights is also problematic if the injured party feels no psychological strain. A police officer who searches my private rooms without a warrant is violating the social contract. For this determination, it is irrelevant whether something was stolen, whether I did not even notice the intrusion or whether it does not bother me.

> Claiming that we do not care about our privacy because we have nothing to hide is ultimately the same as claiming that we do not care about freedom of expression because we have nothing to say. Or that we do not care about freedom of the press because we do not like to read. Or that we do not care about freedom of religion because we do not believe in God. Or that we do not care about the right to peaceful assembly because we are lazy and anti-social and suffer from agoraphobia. Just because one freedom or another is not important to us today does not mean that it will be unimportant to us or our neighbor tomorrow [...].[179]

In addition, the sphere of privacy is not only endangered by state access. According to Shoshana Zuboff, we are in the age of "surveillance capitalism", the essence of which is to "unilaterally extract human experience as raw

---

178 See: Glenn Greenwald: *No Place to Hide: Edward Snowden, the NSA, and the U.S. Surveillance State*. Henry Holt & Co, New York 2014.

179 Edward Snowden: *Permanent Record – Meine Geschichte*. S. Fischer Verlag, Frankfurt am Main 2019. p. 265.

material for conversion into behavioral data"[180]. As in every form of capitalism, it is about profit accumulation, which is achieved through low-cost access to raw materials and expanding mass production. Industrial capitalism has led to ever faster exploitation of natural resources. Surveillance capitalism accomplishes this process through data collection.

"So [...] every Google search produces a wake of collateral data such as the number and pattern of search terms, how a search is phrased, spelled, punctuated, dwell time, click patterns, location, etc. ... "[181] These can be quickly combined with chat histories, movement profiles, log-in data, Streetview information, facial recognition and many other sources. Just a few years ago, such a mass of information would have been impossible to archive and therefore volatile. Today's computer capacities allow an almost unlimited amount of data to be stored, while the associated software offers powerful analysis tools and search functions. The data collected in this way goes far beyond the possibilities of product improvement, targeted advertising or the creation of user profiles. The card index boxes lamented by Hannah Arendt are not only created by state organizations. Data collection penetrates numerous levels of the private sphere. Shoshana Zuboff cites the example of Google's Streetview program as its vehicles also record emails, passwords and other information from the surrounding private households.

> Technicians in Canada, France and the Netherlands found that this user data included names, phone numbers, credit card information, passwords, text messages, emails and transcripts of chats, as well as records of online dating, porn viewing, browser activity, medical information, photos and video and audio files. The specialists concluded that such data packages could be put together and used to create detailed profiles of clearly identifiable individuals.[182]

Above all, however, the sphere of privacy is not only being carelessly defended, it is also being actively abandoned. The mental paradigm shift can hardly be overlooked. In the 1980s, a census in Germany had to be postponed several times. Lawsuits were filed and rulings by the Federal Constitutional Court resulted in the questionnaires being amended in order to guarantee the fundamental right to informal self-determination. Nevertheless, numerous political and social organizations continued to call for a boycott. Today, citizens often disclose significantly more information than was ever collected in the census

---

180 Shoshana Zuboff: *Das Zeitalter des Überwachungskapitalismus*. Campus Verlag GmbH, Frankfurt am Main 2018. p. 22.
181 Ibid. p. 90.
182 Zuboff 2018, p. 171.

when signing up for a cell phone contract or accepting the data protection conditions of a website.

Just as the political and economic encroachments on the private sphere give rise to totalitarian structures, their voluntary disenfranchisement leads to political neglect.

According to Hannah Arendt, the specific feature of the private sphere is its absence. As far as confrontations with others in the public space are concerned, "the private person does not appear, and it is as if he did not exist at all."[183] In the public space of the present, the private is omnipresent. Asked or unasked, interested or uninterested, our perception is incessantly flooded with information about other people's private concerns and behavior. Fewer and fewer people are protected by shame or pride from sharing their most private experiences and trivial activities with an anonymous public. Instead, they are actively looking for opportunities to do so ever more quickly and extensively. The result is a form of capitalist blindness. The representation of privacy becomes a commodity and attention functions as a currency. However, attention should not be confused with recognition or even appreciation in this context. It is solely about registration, measured by the quantity of clicks or likes, which, however, do not allow any conclusions to be drawn about the intensity of the engagement or the sustainability of the impression. I heard Cindy Lauper say this in an interview years ago:

> When we were young we tried to do something that was worth being famous. But today, being famous is worth everything.

If this analysis is correct, it reveals both a dangerous addictive character and a loss of rationality in the public sphere. Trivial things remain trivial, even if they are publicized in the media; vulgar content or actions remain commonplace. It is therefore only natural that the attention achieved decays with the same speed with which it was generated. In order to compensate for the loss, an ever faster and more aggressive presentation of the self or provocation of the other is required. As habituation and brutalization progress at the same time, this attention also fades after a very short time and a new and even more intense impulse is required. A downward spiral that destroys people just like a drug habit. The futile hunt for reaction with simultaneous mutual reinforcement of provocation, habituation and blunting leads to the overstepping of moral boundaries. In most cases, the destructiveness is directed against oneself. For

---

183 Hannah Arendt: *Vita activa oder Vom tätigen Leben*. 20th edition. Piper, Munich 2019. p. 73.

a brief moment of apparent attention, people allow themselves to be instrumentalized by the media or grant the most intimate insights. At the same time, attacks on others also follow this dynamic. Self-injuries and injuries to others equally arouse the hope of attention. The spectrum ranges from a lack of reverence to verbal insults and massive physical violence.

The loss of rationality in the public sphere is also a result of this development. The struggle for attention in the sense of media regulation is increasingly replacing the struggle for recognition on the basis of rational justification. When quantitative registration outweighs argumentative persuasiveness, the willingness to cultivate the latter and regard it as obligatory dwindles. At the same time, the all-present presentation of private content creates the illusion of a relevance that goes beyond the private. This applies not only to the viewing of trivialities, but also to the claim to consideration of purely personal, unfounded views, opinions and feelings. The duty of reciprocal rational justification is replaced by the celebration and documentation of excitement. It degenerates into a private sphere with a public claim. The public space loses its constitutive rules.

The end result of this development is a total structural loss of the public sphere and an erosion of rational social organization that can hardly be compensated for.

> A democratic system as a whole suffers damage if the public infrastructure can no longer direct citizens' attention to the relevant issues that require decisions and can no longer guarantee the formation of competing public, which means. qualitatively filtered, opinions.[184]

---

184 Jürgen Habermas: Überlegungen und Hypothesen zu einem erneuten Strukturwandel der politischen Öffentlichkeit. In: *Leviathan*, 49th vol., special volume 37/2021. p. 498.

CHAPTER 4

And now? The Post-Enlightenment Society

4.1 The return of the classics

It should have become clear that enlightened ways of life are historically rare and have only ever been practiced by a minority of the world's population. A global triumph of forms of life and government shaped by the Enlightenment was not to be expected and has never taken place. Most recently, the political scientist Francis Fukuyama nurtured such hopes in his 1992 book *The End of History and the Last Man*. This book did not explicitly predict a bright future for the Enlightenment, but rather for liberal democracy as a way of life for humanity without alternatives.

On the one hand, according to Fukuyama, humanity has now exhausted all conceivable systems. New forms of government are not to be expected. On the other hand, according to the main thesis, the ideological dialectic of history came to a standstill after the collapse of the so-called Eastern Bloc. This process will lead to the final triumph of liberal democracy.

The first thesis is convincing. The canon of political models has not been expanded since Marxist theory. The realization of the individual models may be disputed. The experiences with actually existing socialism can be understood as a variety of despotism without reference to the theory of Marxism. Numerous liberal democracies can also be accused of being more of a sham than a reality. The Chinese combination of dictatorship and free market economy may seem exotic, but it has already been practiced by the fascist regimes of Europe and Latin America. The term communism alone is confusing. Word creations such as "illiberal democracy" do not present any conceptual innovations either. Rather, it is a euphemism intended to disguise the fact that democracies are degenerating into autocracies.[1] Digitization alone could give rise to entirely new forms of political organization. However, here too it is debatable whether the political models are really changing or whether it is just the forms of communication and ways of life within the conventional organizational models that are changing.

---

1 Cf: Fareed Zakaria: *The Future of Freedom: Illiberal Democracy at Home and Abroad*. W.W. Norton & Company, New York 2003.

However, Fukuyama's main thesis, according to which liberal democracies will continue to dominate the fate of humanity, has proven to be wrong. It was already based on a selective perception at the time of its creation. The end of the Cold War, the opening of the Eastern Bloc, the fall of the Berlin Wall, the overcoming of apartheid in South Africa or the handshake between Yitzchak Rabin and PLO leader Arafat in Oslo: all these events fed the illusion of a "wind of change" towards a global democratic and liberal family of nations. However, the war in Yugoslavia, nationalism and Islamophobia in India, the genocide in Rwanda and Burundi and the shooting of Yitzchak Rabin were also part of reality at the time. The massacre on Tiananmen Square, in which thousands of students peacefully striking for democracy and civil rights were murdered, should have made it clear that neither the systemic conflict nor the use of violence had become obsolete, at least from the point of view of the Chinese Communist Party. The attacks of September 11, 2001, at the latest, also made fanatical Islamism highly visible. The thesis of an irreversible triumph of liberal democracy was therefore never justified.

It remains undisputed that the political concepts of the second phase of the Enlightenment were extremely successful. Their achievements range from self-determined sexuality to collective bargaining autonomy and the United Nations General Assembly. To this day, the majority of authoritarian regimes shy away from openly declaring themselves as such, and considerable propaganda efforts are made to maintain a democratic façade.

However, the normative dominance of the motives of Enlightenment is coming to an end. Economic, military and demographic factors are strengthening regions of the world without corresponding traditions. Freedom as a guiding principle is losing its appeal. Promises of happiness, irrationality and national egoism are coming to the fore. Social forms based on the ideals of the Enlightenment are dissolving or being pushed to the periphery. The effort that an enlightened way of life demands from individuals and collectives reduces its appeal.

It is therefore to be expected that humanity will return to its standard models: collective organization under autocratic rule and the individual life form of the child-adult.

4.1.1 *Child-adults*

The child-adult is the usual human form of existence in which physical maturity is achieved, but not full mental maturity. Normative and epistemic orientation are primarily fed by the satisfaction of individual needs and the requirements of culturally traditional concepts. The striving for maturity and the struggle for objectivity play no or only a subordinate role, which is why there is no central difference between children and adults. Adults remain infantile in terms of their rational autonomy. One part results from paternalism without critically reflecting on existing guidelines. Another part demands freedom of action and decision-making, sometimes vehemently, without tying these demands to their own qualifications and without being willing to take lasting responsibility for the results. This lack of responsible adults also destroys the condition for the possibility of genuine childhood. This cannot exist without the protection of responsible adults. An everyday culture that does not differentiate between children and adults devalues adults and overburdens children. While some are not encouraged to be critically independent, others are exposed to experiences that destroy childhood as a protected social space. This is how humanity has lived in most epochs of its history and it is returning to this model as the ideals of Enlightenment fade. For the most part, the distinction between children and adults was and is made on the basis of biological characteristics. Those who grow faster also grow up faster. The everyday experience, legal status and knowledge of both groups differed only slightly. Whether old or young, the majority of people possessed and still possess marginal rights at best. This was and is particularly true for slaves, serfs, children and women. Of course, some evidence of at least a rudimentary understanding of childhood can also be found outside the Enlightenment epochs. For example, the classic career of a knight began at the age of seven as a page and rarely ended before the age of 20. However, this hardly documents any evidence of a differentiated understanding of childhood as a phenomenon worthy of protection. Before the age of seven, only a few boys would have been physically able to cope with the tasks of a page. Moreover, their tender age did not prevent them from having to leave the parental home and henceforth serve a foreign knight in his often bloody business. It was not uncommon for girls to be given in marriage to a stranger before they reached sexual maturity. It should also be mentioned that these examples represent a vanishingly small, privileged group. The impositions on children from non-noble classes often knew no restrictions at all. The *Sachsenspiegel*, written between 1220 and 1235 by Eike von Repgow, declared a free man to be of age at 21. This resulted in entitlements such as inheritance rights. There is no mention of duties of care towards women and children, for example.

In addition to being largely without rights, the majority of children and adults shared and still share the same living environment. This applies to possible punishments as well as to gainful employment or amusements. As soon as their physical development allows, children in societies without any claim to Enlightenment were and are assigned the same tasks as adults. In addition to hard physical labor, this also includes fighting and marriage. The same applied and still applies to movement in public spaces. Children and adults alike visited and viewed ceremonies, sacrificial cults, acts of war, etc. Even the knowledge of adults in these societies was and is only partially superior to that of children. The dominant information media in human history are the visual impression and oral tradition. Accordingly, the average educational hierarchies in societies without the influence of the Enlightenment were flat. Adults can only draw on a greater wealth of experience. They have heard and seen things more often. Nevertheless, the information media are egalitarian. Even small children can listen and watch just as well as adults. An average adult was probably only slightly superior to a child when it came to finding their way around a medieval town. When looking for a tailor, both would have looked for a sign with a pair of scissors. Should a blacksmith be found, both could ask passers-by or look for a sign with a horseshoe.

This egalitarianism was only interrupted with the Enlightenment. The central ideal of the Enlightenment was always the mature adult who, as an autonomous personality and citoyen, takes responsibility for his or her own life and the public sphere. The program that was to lead to this goal was education. The target group consisted of underage adults and equally underage children. This gave rise to an important differentiation. In the Kantian vocabulary, the average adult is "self-inflicted immature". They do not lack the ability to use their intellect without the guidance of another person, but lack courage and determination. Children, on the other hand, are not "self-inflicted immature". They do not lack courage, but rather rational capacity and information. Ergo, both groups also must be treated differently. This gave rise to the idea of an educational curriculum that would lead children step by step to maturity, taking into account their respective stage of development. The idea of childhood as a social space worthy of protection was born. Plato, Aristotle, Locke, Rousseau, Hume and Kant all tried to be pedagogous as well.

At the same time, every adult who developed maturity through processes of Enlightenment potentially contributed to making childhood possible. This applies primarily to protection and care, but also to empowerment. Educational concepts are empowerment programs (see chapter 5.3.3), the success of which depends largely on imparting knowledge and skills in a measured and age-appropriate manner. This requires a hierarchy of knowledge and skills that demands the adult to select information, prepare experiential spaces and offer exercises. Care and support can only be realized if there are adults who are able and willing to take responsibility for this.

The more capable adults take on this task, the more people can experience a childhood worthy of the name.

The culture of writing, which was closely linked to the Enlightenment, helped to reinforce the tendencies described above. The cultural techniques of reading and writing broke through the egalitarian access to information. As long as learning to read and access to writing was strictly limited, a further instrument of oppression and the consolidation of power was created. However, as soon as the aim was to achieve general literacy, the dynamics of the Enlightenment intensified. More and more people gained access to more and more information that went beyond their immediate sphere of experience. Complex, differentiated and critical thinking was promoted. Reading is not only an immanent intellectual training, it is also a constant challenge to think the particular as contained in the general.[2] At the same time, the medium of writing is not egalitarian. It requires an arduous qualification phase to gain access to the bound information. This concerns not only the ability to decipher a complicated code, but also imagination and the ability to abstract. Today, a literate person is far superior to an illiterate person. This applies not only to orientation in the city, but also to the acquisition of information and its verification. From an educational perspective, the medium of writing not only creates epistemic hierarchies, but also enables the careful selection of information. It is completely unproblematic to leave a printed work of Steven King or Marquis de Sade in a toddler's room. The information remains inaccessible, the danger of traumatization is averted.

Knowledge and skills have always been passed on to subsequent generations. However, the fact that adolescents need to be treated in a way that is tailored to them is something that was recognized during the Age of Enlightenment. In prehistoric times, it is highly likely that children and adults were taught the art of making fire or hunting in the same way. In the monastery schools of the Middle Ages, there was very little differentiation according to age. Everyone went through the same curriculum. It was only during the Enlightenment that pedagogy emerged as a critical struggle for the appropriate when, how and how much information to pass on. Its spectrum ranges from academic didactics to school curricula for different year groups and early childhood development support. These achievements spread and enjoyed worldwide success. Today, the right to education is established as a human right and has even been ratified as such by the United Nations.[3]

---

2 Kant: AA V, p. 179.
3 UN Social Covenant, Article 13.1; UN: Universal Declaration of Human Rights, Article 26.

Of course, it is also true that a huge proportion of humanity has only been reached by this progress very rudimentarily or not at all. A child who has to help his family survive in the slums of Manila benefits little from UNESCO's policy documents. His form of existence was and is that of a child-adult.

However, even in societies that have already established a differentiation between children and adults, an erosion can be observed that is gradually leading back to the child-adult. Although a reintroduction of child labor in the near future is not to be expected, the weekly program of children can already exceed the working hours of their parents. This is due to the shortening of school years, the need for extra tuition and the omnipresent pressure for self-optimization. Public executions have been abolished, which is why adolescents could be spared such impressions. However, the media paradigm shift has long since opened up access to traumatizing content again. Today, visual depictions of fictional or real atrocities are just a mouse click away. The Marquis de Sade must still be read, but sadistic depictions are available in abundance.[4]

Passing children on to others like objects will hopefully not become common practice again. However, capitalist delusions can contribute to children being viewed as commodities. The German phrase 'sich ein Kind anschaffen' (to acquire a child) alone is treacherous. It is a classic confusion of having and being in the sense of Erich Fromm. You want to have children as much as you want to buy a car, but do you also want to be a parent? A differentiated understanding of what it means to be a parent, as well as the emotional and intellectual maturity to make childhood possible, is rarely realized. Nor is this to be expected as a result of the common everyday media culture. After all, it is flooded with trivial, stereotypical superficiality, in which every conflict is compensated for by more consumption. "The stupidity that the cultural market counts on is reproduced and reinforced by it".[5]

The Frankfurter Allgemeine Zeitung published a ranking of the most successful female influencers in Germany in 2021.[6] These providers focused

---

4 My wife works as a speech therapist in various daycare centers. Speech acquisition also includes talking about feelings. When asked what scares them the children answer "zombies" with frightening regularity. If the children then imitate them, there is only one conclusion to be drawn: they have already seen such films. We are talking about pre-school children. They are 3–5 years old!
5 Theodor Wiesengrund Adorno: Theorie der Halbbildung. In: Hans-Ulrich Lessing, Volker Steenblock (eds.): *"Was den Menschen zum Menschen macht ..." Klassische Texte einer Philosophie der Bildung*. Published by Karl Alber. Freiburg im Breisgau 2010. p. 164.
6 Julia Anton: Reich dank Reichweite. In: FAZ.net https://www.faz.net/aktuell/stil/trends-nischen/das-sind-die-wertvollsten-deutschen-influencer-ganz-vorne-nur-frauen-17684153.html?utm_source=pocket-newtab-global-en-EN [last accessed 10.08.2022].

on cosmetics, lifestyle and fitness. The number of so-called "followers" is in the millions. A short film showing a professionally dressed influencer entering a hotel balcony received more than 84,000 likes within 14 hours. Just for comparison: at the height of the so-called Spiegel affair, the political magazine sold 437,000 copies. A statistic that records how many parents subscribe to a political magazine today and how many follow one of the influencers mentioned would be much more meaningful.

The return to being a child-adult will have very different effects. For the majority of the world's population, little will change. In any case, they have only marginally benefited from the achievements of Enlightenment. However, the erosion of Enlightenment will also affect their living situation. In countries that have committed themselves to the principles of Enlightenment, there are also countless forms of exploitation. However, there is still a labor law that explicitly protects minors in particular and should also be taken into account in international trade relations.

If awareness of these standards declines, the influence on the direct exploiters also decreases. In countries such as China or Qatar, forced labor is part of state doctrine. It is not as if the exploitation of foreign workers or entire population groups, which borders on slavery, is not known. Boycotts and criticism are a matter of course for a responsible consciousness. Nevertheless, they are not practiced. Consumption in front of the television at home is too comfortable. The media and industrial profit margins are too large. And the confrontation with injustice is too superficial to tarnish the beautiful appearance.

In the privileged parts of the world, the erosion of maturity is progressing steadily. A good that is not needed will not be missed. The children and adults of affluent regions will continue to demand freedom of consumption and the satisfaction of their needs. Political or intellectual freedoms are increasingly perceived as a burden and are gradually being pushed into the background.

This "ego weakness" in Adorno's sense causes a quickly activated aversion to personal responsibility, foreignness and diversity and strengthens their affinity for authoritarian structures.[7] This not only has consequences for their personal lifestyle, but also for collective political organization. Living democracy cannot be achieved with a majority of child-adults.

4.1.2 *Autocracy*

Autocratic forms of rule have always dominated human history. Systemic competition was rare. When enlightened societies come to an end, many an

---

7 Cf.: Theodor Wiesengrund Adorno: Studien zum autoritären Charakter. Suhrkamp, Frankfurt am Main, 1995. p. 53.

autocrat will smile with relief and carry on as before. Little will change for the majority of the world's population either. They were not allowed to be citizens anyway. They were and remain subjects.

In the context of this essay, it is not necessary to analyze the nature of autocracy in detail. It is sufficient to recall that the political principles of the Enlightenment are to be understood as a counter-proposal and thus make an ex negativo definition possible. Enlightenment strives for the autonomy of man. This applies to their personal and moral conduct as well as to their existence and activities as citizens. For the political sphere, therefore, a differentiated system of republican self-determination, democratic participation and constitutional control of power was devised. In autocracies, individuals or groups of individuals exercise political power without being substantially controlled and regulated by the separation of powers, constitutions, freedom of the press or free elections. The spectrum of manifestations ranges from mild patriarchal monarchies to totalitarian reigns of terror, the nature of which was described by Hannah Arendt.

Autocracies are therefore not necessarily synonymous with tyranny. According to Plato, every form of government turns ugly when the common good is neglected in favor of the self-interest, and of course autocrats who are committed to the common good are also conceivable. According to Sir Karl Popper, "Plato's political program is far from being superior to that of totalitarian systems [and] basically identical to it."[8] Nevertheless, Plato's philosopher-king can be thought of as the ideal of a selfless ruler who follows the idea of justice alone. Admittedly, historical examples are harder to find. Nevertheless, we do know that Cyrus II used his position as Persian God-king in the sixth century BC to declare slavery over. Marcus Aurelius went down in Roman history as a selfless emperor who practiced self-criticism on a daily basis and advocated cosmopolitan tolerance. "People are there for each other. So teach them or tolerate them."[9] Reference could also be made to Jigme Khesar Namgyel Wangchuck. The King of Bhutan worked on overcoming his own position of power and transformed his country into a democracy with a constitutional monarchy in 2008.

Autocracies do not necessarily have to pose a threat to international peace either. In his treatise *On Perpetual Peace*, Kant argued that the central step towards world peace must be to organize all states as republics. According to Kant, nations that govern themselves do not plunge into the cruel experience

---

8 Karl R. Popper: *Die offene Gesellschaft und ihre Feinde*. Volume 1: Der Zauber Platons, 7th edition, UTB, Tübingen 1992. p. 106.
9 Marcus Aurelius VIII, p. 59.

of war. Historically, however, this thesis is difficult to prove. The longest period of peace that the Roman Empire experienced, the Pax Augusta, was during the time of an autocrat. Unfortunately, it cannot be denied that colonialism and war also emanated from democracies.

Nevertheless, the Enlightenment movement's deep mistrust of all forms of autocratic concentration of power is anything but unfounded. There is a lack of political participation, control and regulation as well as fundamental rights that protect against arbitrary domestic and foreign policy. What makes autocracies so threatening is the reduction or even absence of the principle of justification. As explained in chapter 3.2, it is the insight that we owe each other general, intersubjective and reciprocal justification that makes it possible to proclaim moral and political human rights. As a rule, autocracies do not stand up to such a discourse of justification. They legitimize themselves on the basis of pure pragmatism, tradition, speculative ideological premises or egomaniacal personality cults.

Ideological and egomaniacal autocracies lack almost all rational predictability. Ideological worldviews defy the principle of justification. Anyone who doubts is attacked as unbelieving, counter-revolutionary or simply malicious. This becomes particularly threatening when the absolute claim to truth goes hand in hand with a radical willingness to destroy others and oneself. The history of the Third Reich demonstrated this radicalism in a terrifying way. But religions also have a tendency to see martyrdom, destruction and annihilation as a serious alternative to spreading their own way of life. From the believer's point of view, there is even a certain consistency. Those who accept the premise that all other values must be subordinated to the maximum demands of their own religion can consistently come to the conclusion that total annihilation is better than compromise or even renunciation. Only from an external perspective can this premise be exposed as an arbitrary setting and the conclusions drawn as irrational self-deception. The core competence of enlightened judgment lies in the ability to view one's own convictions critically from an outside perspective. Losing this ability is the nourishing evil of all fundamentalist movements. Ideological regimes confuse worldview with truth. In the years 2014 to 2019, the caliphate of the so-called Islamic State (الدولة الإسلامية) demonstrated the excesses that such fanaticism is capable of. But also Iran's theocracy is an example of this form of autocracy. There are many indications that the country is seeking to acquire nuclear weapons.

Egomaniac autocracies confuse personal sensitivities with rationality. Egomania is characterized by the lack of external reference systems such as science or ethics. Personal needs and feelings alone are consciously or unconsciously elevated to the central decision-making criterion. The North Korean dictator Kim Jong-un can be seen as a prime example of an egomaniacal autocrat. He is already in possession of nuclear weapons.

After all, pragmatic autocracies have a rationality of purpose. They are often oriented towards profane interests such as economic gain or geopolitical power. In this way, bargaining chips are created, a minimalist basis for understanding. During the Cold War, the minimalist consensus that one must live in order to have an advantage protected humanity from self-destruction. Today's autocracies in China and Russia can also hope for rationality of purpose. The profane interests of their own nation are the central point of reference. However, these dictatorships are also permeated by ideological and egomaniacal tendencies. These range from media stagings and constantly reorganized terms of office to the power to govern for life, which was transferred to Chinese party leader Xi Jinping by the National People's Congress on 11 March 2018 without a dissenting vote.[10] In the summer of 2020, a constitutional amendment in Russia enabled 67-year-old President Vladimir Putin to remain in office for a further 16 years after almost 20 years in office. The totalitarian suppression of domestic opposition and the aggressive expansion of spheres of influence, including aggressive war, characterize the image of these great powers. No one possesses more nuclear weapons.

There is little to suggest that the growing dominance and spread of authoritarian forms of government will be halted. The so-called "free world" did little to counter this development until the attack on Ukraine. The economic dependencies were too great, the normative self-image too eroded. The self-confidence and self-assertion of the principles of Enlightenment were not even enough to respond to the annexation of Hong Kong and the internment of hundreds of thousands of Uyghurs with a boycott of the Winter Olympics in China. Only the Russian war of aggression in Ukraine could bring about a turning point (see chapter 5.1).

Authoritarian regimes are spreading, liberal democracies are retreating or dissolving. This is particularly evident in the Islamic world. At the end of the hopeful Arab Spring, the choice seems to be between religious or military despotism. Developments in Egypt in particular have shown that democratic alternatives fail due to the dominance of the uneducated masses with little affinity for Enlightenment.

---

10   Chinesischer Präsident im Amt bestätigt – ohne Gegenstimme. In: Spiegel Online: https://www.spiegel.de/politik/ausland/china-xi-jinping-einstimmig-als-staatschef-bestaetigt-a-1198605.html [Last accessed 14.09.2022].

In Turkey, for example, autocracy took hold with the constitutional referendum on April 16, 2017[11]. The dismantling of democratic structures was announced, decided and carried out in public. Turkey's republican authorities were largely relieved of their duties and state power was tailored to the person of Erdoğan. At the same time, the ruler, whose egomaniacal self-aggrandizement is unparalleled,[12] ensured that religion returned as a formative authority in schools, universities and politics out of personal conviction or power-political calculation. Kemal Atatürk can certainly not be regarded unreservedly as a pioneer of the Enlightenment. Republicanism and secularism were, however, necessary components of his political program. His emblem still hangs in Turkish offices, only it no longer belongs there. European states such as Poland and Hungary have already subordinated the ideals of the Enlightenment to national egoism and a nationalist cult of identity. Italy fluctuates regularly. The social and political orientation of these states is now closer to the Erdoğan model than to the fundamental values of the European Union. This leads to the conclusion that an Europe dominated by right-wing populists is a realistic option for the future.

What is particularly dramatic is that there no longer seems to be a core political substance in which the principles of the Enlightenment can be considered secure. Nations such as Sweden, which were considered a safe haven for an enlightened self-image, are showing signs of disintegration. According to Samuel P. Huntington, Enlightenment is nothing more than a cultural expression without any claim to universalism (see chapter 3.6). But even if this were conceded, the Enlightenment would be no less exposed to decline. According to Huntington, humanity is characterized by eight cultural circles that cluster around core nations. If the core nation weakens, all members and the achievements of the cultural group weaken. In the case of the United

---

11 Cf: Auf dem Weg in die Autokratie? In: Tagesschau.de https://www.tagesschau.de/faktenfinder/ausland/tuerkei-referendum-117.html [last accessed 15.09.2022].

12 One manifestation of this is the lavishly extended presidential palace, inaugurated in 2014, which Erdogan commissioned to be built when he was still prime minister, despite numerous court rulings. With around 1,000 rooms, a pure construction area of 40,000 m² (in the middle of a nature reserve) and construction costs that were ultimately estimated at just under half a billion euros, Erdogan's "White Palace" is one of the largest state palaces in the world. (Cf.: Erdogans Palast kostet halbe Milliarden Euro. In: *Der Standard*. Online: https://www.derstandard.at/story/2000007722288/erdogans-palast-kostet-halbe-milliarde-euro [Last accessed 15.08.2022]; 1000 illegal rooms for Erdogan. In: *Spiegel Online* https://www.spiegel.de/politik/ausland/tuerkei-erdogan-bezieht-praesidentenpalast-mit-1000-zimmern-a-999881.html [last accessed 15.08.2022].

States of America, which according to Huntington undoubtedly constitutes the core nation of the so-called 'West', the signs of erosion are unmistakable. Of course, the USA will not simply disappear from international politics and, as a nuclear power, will remain an important factor in the long term. Nevertheless, Huntington already lamented the steadily declining vitality and innovative strength of American culture and population, which also implies a willingness for critical and self-critical citizenship. In 2016, eight years after Huntington's death, his fears were confirmed. Consciously or unconsciously, the voting majority of the American population has decided to no longer submit to the strenuous project of Enlightenment and instead explicitly rely on feelings, personal nimbus and immaturity. This is a human paradigm shift that, after everyday culture, has now also affected political life. It is about consumption instead of freedom, about prejudice instead of maturity, about gut feeling instead of rational differentiation. The project of Enlightenment has been hit hard in the USA. It is still unclear whether it is dying. But even if it manages to recover, a powerful leadership role is still a long way off. An enlightened, modern democracy rests on two pillars. A resilient and well thought-out constitution and a population that lives up to its responsibility as an electorate. The American constitution still separates right from wrong, rationality from delusion and has prevented the worst from happening during Donald Trump's presidency. However, one pillar alone cannot support democracy, and the second pillar of democracy, civil society, which strives for maturity, has been deeply shaken or broken away. It cannot be emphasized enough: the frightening thing is not that the 45th president of the USA used lies, insults and propaganda during his election campaign and his reign. That has happened many times before. The drama is that this presidential candidate did not even attempt to give his statements the appearance of objectivity and he was still elected. Few things have illustrated the mental shift better than the formulation of alternative facts. Let us remember: facts are those proven realities that separate episteme and doxa. In the history of mankind, there are numerous people who have claimed to be able to subject reality to their will. The examples range from antiquity to modern times. Persian King Xerxes believed he could subjugate the sea by lashing it after it had prevented a bridge from being built on the Bosporus. In the 17th century, the French King Henri IV still practiced the healing of illnesses by laying his royal hands on the patient. It was not until the Enlightenment that such practices were identified as reverie, propaganda or madness.

When a US president makes the recognition of scientific facts, fundamental rights or election results dependent on his personal sensitivities, we can only speak of a relapse into pre-Enlightenment times or the beginning of a

Post-Enlightenment Society. The simple refusal to take note of realities, scientific data, financial, legal or political arguments, if they do not correspond to one's own wishes, is a novelty in American government history in its extent and impertinence. Once again: of course, individuals will always suffer from a loss of reality. However, the hope of the Enlightenment was that responsible citizens would neither trust these individuals nor transfer power to them. The national and international damage can easily be limited. One experience, however, is irreversible: in the United States, a person can be elected president at any time who blatantly admits that they do not want to be guided by facts, realities, objectivity – in short, epistemes. For a decisive proportion of Americans, living in an enlightened society is no longer important. The remaining core nations of liberal democracy, England and France, have also been badly hit. England has shown little interest in multilateral responsibility by leaving the European Union and elected Boris Johnson as Prime Minister in 2019. His former employer Max Hastings from the *Daily Telegraph* attested to Johnson's broken relationship with the truth. According to Hastings, the UK now has an entertainer as head of government, just like Ukraine or the USA.[13]

In France, a victory for right-wing populist Marine le Pen was narrowly prevented in the 2017 presidential elections. President Macron did indeed take on the Herculean task of revitalizing the European Union project and committing it to the shared values of the Enlightenment. There was no support from Germany for a long time. The country spent a whole five months trying to form a government. In the Netherlands, it took a whole nine months in 2021 for a government to find a parliamentary majority. Perhaps France will succeed in rallying a smaller number of states around it and remain committed to the principles of the Enlightenment in a residual union. If, on the other hand, a right-wing populist wins the reins of government in France, this hope will also be lost. In 2022, Emmanuel Macron and his *La République en Marche* party lost their majority in the National Assembly. Left and right-wing populists grew. Elections will be held again in France in 2027. It is therefore more than questionable whether France has the strength to keep the ideas of the Enlightenment alive and rally other states around it.

Autocracies therefore have almost free rein. However, there are good reasons to hope that the formative totalitarian ideologies of the twentieth century – fascism and communism – will not experience an absolute renaissance. At least in Europe, the collective memory is probably still too sensitized on this

---

13   Max Hastings: I was Boris Johnson's boss: he is utterly unfit to be prime minister. In: *The Guardian Online.* https://www.theguardian.com/commentisfree/2019/jun/24/boris-johnson-prime-minister-tory-party-britain [last accessed 15.08.2022].

point. A world revolution or a dictatorship of the proletariat is only propagated by marginal minorities. Openly fascist or even National Socialist voices also only have limited majority support. However, in Europe and North America, a political right with a national to nationalist profile is gaining ground. Although it does not espouse open racism, it advocates ethnic tradition and identity. Enlightenment values such as freedom of religion, separation of powers and freedom of the press are also subordinated to this goal.

Furthermore, a theocracy in Europe, North America, Australia, Japan or New Zealand is unlikely. The hurdles of many constitutional texts are too high, the associations with medieval conditions too absurd. However, there is a proximity between the nationalist movements and many representatives of the majority religions. National movements use religions as projection surfaces for a national identity, and quite a few religious representatives use the opportunity to lend political weight to their beliefs. In Germany, the PEGIDA movement in particular invokes the defense of the Judeo-Christian West. The common call for a state church as a moral and political authority is not far away from this perspective. This has long been a reality in Poland and Hungary. In Russia, the Orthodox Church is already in league with the regime and does not shy away from participating in war propaganda.[14]

In summary, it can be assumed that liberal democracies are eroding, while existing autocracies are gaining influence and self-confidence. How authoritarian or even totalitarian these become is determined by geopolitical distributions of power and the vitality of the remaining democracies.

4.2 Marginal existence: surviving on the periphery

The future of modern, secular and constitutional democracies lies on the periphery, understood as global political significance and geographic location. If Hong Kong were an island state, far away from mainland China, democracy, human rights and freedom of the press could perhaps still exist there. But two factors sealed its demise. The immediate proximity to the authoritarian "brother" and the lack of support from a weakening "free world". It is likely that even at the end of the twenty-first century there will

---

[14] Regina Elsner: "Verfolgte" Kirche in der Ukraine – Kriegspropaganda, Kirchenkonflikt und globale Konsequenzen. In: *MONITOR – Analyse & Beratung der Konrad Adenauer Stiftung*, Issue 4/22.

still be states that are explicitly and credibly committed to the ideas of Enlightenment, universalism and democracy. However, there is little to suggest that there will be many of them and that they will be able to play a significant role in world politics. The more periphery, the greater the chances of survival for the enlightened way of life. Norway, Canada and New Zealand can be regarded as model countries, i.e. nations in which a relatively small population lives at a great distance from the geopolitical trouble spots. Geographical distance primarily reduces external stress factors such as wars, refugee movements, environmental destruction and overpopulation, even if these naturally also have an impact on the periphery. A small population also has a positive effect on the relationship between the masses and the elite discussed above (section 4.3.2.). Whether this is enough to withstand the internal stress factors remains to be seen. Other nations have a much harder time. Although external stress factors can be reduced through isolation, border controls and lockdowns, this cannot be done without undermining their own principles of human rights and cosmopolitanism (see section 4.4.3). This can be observed in the refugee policies of Europe, America and Australia. Can a nation credibly claim to be committed to human rights and at the same time maintain gulag-like refugee camps on tropical islands? In an imperfect world, the desire to control one's own territory is the legitimate concern of all states in order to preserve the self-determination of their citizens. However, self-determination without self-discipline is based on the confusion of egoism and freedom. Those who seek to preserve the rule of law and liberal freedoms in a *fortress Europe* overlook the fact that global citizenship and international justice are also among the imperatives of the Enlightenment. These values have never survived for long behind walls.

States on the geopolitical periphery could reduce these stress factors. During the coronavirus pandemic, New Zealand demonstrated that even in the twenty-first century it is possible to practice almost complete isolation from foreign countries. Nevertheless, these are not islands of the blessed. International power relations, capitalist blindness and digital distortion of reality are also having an effect on the periphery. Nevertheless, it may be possible to maintain the vitality of the principles of political Enlightenment there. Everything depends on electoral majorities submitting to the exhausting and often frustrating project of differentiation, the search for truth and intersubjective justification. The democracies of Canada, New Zealand and Norway have so far shown a gratifying resilience to right-wing populism, conspiracy narratives, religious fanaticism and even terrorism (see section 4.4.2). They are all on the periphery.

4.3 Speculative consolation

The Post-Enlightenment Society is a pessimistic forecast. The organization of child-adults by authoritarian leadership cadres evokes unpleasant associations. Nevertheless, it should be remembered that we are not talking about the apocalypse here, but about a return to normality. In addition, three considerations are presented below that can be understood as speculative hope or consolation.

4.3.1 *Speculation 1: Putin, the savior of the West*

Let's try a thought experiment: let's assume we are unscrupulous advisors to the Russian president in 2020. Our task is to inflict as much damage as possible on the model of liberal democracy and strengthen Russia's autocracy. Expanding democratic structures in our immediate neighbors cannot be in our interest. Would we support a war of aggression against Ukraine in this situation? Probably yes. An occupation of Ukraine would end its geopolitical alignment with Western Europe, secure natural resources and prevent the spread of democratic ideas on the soil of former Soviet republics. Up to now, we have achieved success with military operations, warlike destabilization and annexation from Chechnya to Donbass and Syria to Crimea, and have only suffered minor disadvantages as a result of sanctions. The situation is also extremely favorable. Thanks in part to our media interventions, the United States of America and the United Kingdom are governed by easily manipulated egomaniacs. Germany and France were only able to prevent the rise of right-wing populists with their last strength. Poland and Hungary are already gradually abolishing democracy. If the incumbent US president could be helped back into office, an attack on Ukraine would even have the potential to bring down the entire so-called West. America would hold back and perhaps even, as already announced, end its membership of NATO. The usual hysterical chaos could be expected from the Europeans. Britain has already left the EU and the British Prime Minister is mainly concerned with self-promotion. It is even possible that the heated atmosphere in the French elections in April 2022 could help the nationalists and EU sceptics into office. Added to this is Europe's dependence on our gas exports. Flows of refugees would contribute to a general destabilization. The Eastern European members of NATO and the EU would complain about a lack of economic and military support and harden their nationalism. Yes, spring 2022 would be a good time. However, we should wait until the Olympic Games in Beijing are over. We do not want to upset China. After all, it is our most important strategic partner in the destruction of the liberal social model. If everything works out, our president will triumph over the liberal democracies and this Enlightenment nonsense will go down in history.

A comparable planning scenario somewhere in the depths of the Kremlin is not unrealistic. However, there is hope that the analysts have miscalculated. They may even have achieved the opposite of what they intended. Not only did the re-election of the 45th President of the United States fail, the invasion of Ukraine created a historically surprising unity of NATO and the European Union in the first weeks of the war. If this cohesion continues, liberal forms of society could even emerge stronger from the crisis. Those who are made aware of what they stand to lose will once again appreciate freedoms that were previously taken for granted. The confrontation with suffering and hardship is able to break through capitalist blindness and activate individual energy. The direct comparison of propaganda and free reporting could revive the power of judgment and critical faculties. Of course it is possible that all these hopes will prove to be a flash in the pan. However, if the shock is deep enough, a turn-around towards the ideals of Enlightenment is within the realm of possibility. In the end, according to Francis Fukuyama in a speech in March 2022, "there could be a rebirth of freedom that extends to Taiwan."[15] In this case, too, the Russian president would go down in history, albeit reluctantly as the savior of enlightened ways of life.

4.3.2 *Speculation 2: bad for freedom, but good for the climate*
The Post-Enlightenment Society means a massive loss of individual freedom, rational objectivity, institutional justice and political participation, but it could help to limit the destruction of natural resources. Liberal forms of society have proven to be highly ecologically destructive. As shown in chapter 4.4.1, there is no necessary relationship between capitalism and Enlightenment. Nevertheless, they have generally favored each other. The ideals of individualism and autonomy form the basis of moral responsibility and political aspirations for freedom. So far, however, they have always unleashed economic forces that have contributed massively to the destruction of the natural foundations of life. Changes in the lifestyles of free and self-determined citizens can only be brought about very slowly in liberal societies and democratic structures. It is necessary to convince people, go through legal legitimization processes and win parliamentary majorities. These obstacles are significantly reduced

---

15   Francis Fukuyama: Putin wird die Niederlage seiner Armee nicht überleben. – 12 Thesen zum Krieg in der Ukraine. In: Neu Zürcher Zeitung Online. https://www.nzz.ch/feuilleton/francis-fukuyama-russia-will-lose-this-war-and-further-12-forecasts-ld.1674933 [Last accessed 15.08.2022].

in autocracies. They therefore have enormous potential to prevent humanity from destroying its own basis of existence in an act of freedom. It is currently the western democracies that are reporting the biggest CO_2 reductions at the world climate conferences. Fairness demands that we add that these are often the biggest emitters of the past. In addition, further savings and the necessary expansion of renewable energies are increasingly coming up against the obstacles mentioned above. Where there are hardly any civil rights, however, these frictional losses are minimal. Gigantic wind farms, dammed lakes across many gorges, forced resettlement, birth control: all this can be organized quickly in authoritarian states. It might be bad for the Enlightenment, but perhaps it is good for the climate.

This is particularly true when the authoritarian management style makes use of the new digital possibilities. One example is the social points system introduced in China. Professional, social, medical and economic privileges are linked to the achievement of social points. Technologies such as facial recognition or profile analysis open up unimagined possibilities for registering socially desirable behavior and sanctioning undesirable behavior. For example, in some test cities, citizens are warned by name in real time if they cross the road at a red light.[16] Currently, social points are primarily linked to socially compliant behavior and political statements in line with the government. However, it would be easy to expand the canon to include criteria such as CO_2 emissions, organic reproduction or resource consumption. Authoritarian forms of government do not come into conflict with their normative principles. And what applies to national policy can also be applied to international policy. At present, China's pragmatically oriented development aid links investments and development aid primarily to access to natural resources and agricultural production areas. In the near future, aid could also be linked to falling birth rates or officially certified sterilizations. What appears to be a horror scenario in terms of human and civil rights could help to prevent the currently unchecked ecological self-destruction of humanity.

4.3.3 *Speculation 3: digital options*

Let's take this speculation to the extreme and transport ourselves to the year 2040. As shown, key aspects of digitization will play into the hands of autocrats to maintain their power (see section 4.5). However, this does not necessarily have to lead to an Orwellian dystopia. A dictatorship that nobody notices and

---

16 Christoph Giesen: Ein ganzes Land als Testgelände. In: Sueddeutsche.de. https://www.sueddeutsche.de/politik/china-ein-ganzes-land-als-testgelaende-1.4664052 [Last accessed 15.08.2022].

at the same time helps to preserve the ecosystem of planet Earth would also be conceivable.

In 2040, digitization and automation will have taken over most of the professions we know today. Fields are planted, watered and harvested fully automatically, cars drive autonomously and the majority of medical and social services have been taken over by robots and programs.

In response to economic change, a basic supply of food, housing and digital spaces was established. Since then, the majority of the world's population has spent the majority of their lives in virtual reality. Digital cures are particularly popular, allowing people to spend several days in the digital world while all their physical needs are taken care of. Different types of delivery make it possible to minimize the interruption of the digital experience. This development has had two significant effects. A significant decline in the birth rate and CO_2 emissions. As virtual realities enable a previously unimagined level of intense and unprecedented experiences, the importance of travel, sport, cultural events, comfort, space requirements, calorie consumption and much more has dramatically decreased. Added to this is a steadily declining birth rate. On the one hand, virtual sexuality cannot be identified as such during the simulation and, on the other, the sensory intensity exceeds reality many times over. In addition, the birth and rearing of children is perceived by many citizens as a protracted, unpleasant abstinence from digital worlds. Autocratic regimes have actively encouraged these tendencies. Indispensable human labor in the real world is extracted through coercion. At the same time, numerous ecological problems are overcome. The biological reproduction rate and resource consumption per capita have been halved. Overpopulation in dependent developing countries is also being counteracted by the massive expansion of 'virtual reality villages'. In these, digital illusion is offered in return for either the sale of resources or sterilization, while at the same time providing basic physical care. The global population is falling, global warming has been kept below 2 degrees Celsius and numerous ecosystems are in the process of regeneration.

There is also an option that does not have to be understood as authoritarian. In 2040, many industrialized nations still describe themselves as bourgeois democracies. However, the possibilities of a primarily digital way of life have also found their way here. They have not been promoted or even decreed by the state, but have been spread by numerous international corporations. The same applies to the loss of physical work, which was compensated for by the introduction of an unconditional citizen's income. Quite a few people have used the resulting freedom for intensive artistic, sporting or political activity. However, a clear majority of the population also describes itself primarily as a virtual citizen. As this majority gradually loses interest in forming political opinions and spends their lives in digital worlds, the ideal of a democracy shaped by empowerment and co-determination is under threat. The danger of authoritarian overpowering is great. However, a committed minority with a focus on the common good still dominates the political scene. The term aristocratic democracy seems appropriate. The rule of the people is fizzling out due to a growing lack of interest in the real world, while at the same time an elite is trying to save what can be saved. These true aristocrats in Plato's sense are not interested in personal power, but in the common good. They take over the reins of government because no one else wants this responsibility. Their aim is to rebalance masses and resources in order to reactivate freedom and democracy on this basis.

In aristocratic democracy, power and political organization are theoretically in the hands of all and de facto in the hands of a few. However, these do not seek to maintain the status quo or use it to their personal advantage. There is no closed oligarchy. Rather, the aim is to prevent worse things from happening and to keep the conditions for a return to an enlightened way of life alive. Access to power remains permeable. Everyone who is willing to participate in the arduous political and social work is welcome. There is no system of oppression. The aristocrats merely recognize that a growing proportion of people are less and less interested in authenticity, truth and freedom. People who have forgotten how to distinguish between doxa and episteme, between propaganda and information, between assertion and justification, are an enormous danger to peace and humanism. Dictatorships potentiate and control this problem by depriving people of their right to political co-determination. The elite of aristocratic democracy merely tries to channel the self-inflicted immaturity of the masses. The increasing number of child-adults is not wanted, but rather regretfully acknowledged. The largest possible number of citoyens is still desired. Free and secret elections still take place. It is striking that voting is still organized as a physical ballot despite all the digital possibilities. This necessary interruption to virtual life has caused voter turnout to fall to 20–35%. Nevertheless, citizens are still expected to bear this burden in order to guarantee a minimum level of engagement and interest and to avoid confusion with digital games. There is free access to information, discussions and political participation at all times. Developments are controversially discussed in the democratic forums that still formally exist. Awareness campaigns are trying to convince citizens to become 'full reality citizens'.

Attractive tasks with creative power and unimagined leisure opportunities beckon. In addition to responsible jobs and effective political co-determination, leisure activities have changed fundamentally. Overcrowded national parks, queues at ski lifts, cultural events with uninterested audiences – all this is a thing of the past. Nevertheless, the success rates of awareness campaigns remain modest. Radical voices are calling for a ban or at least severe restrictions on virtual reality. However, these initiatives are not successful. Whenever a corresponding proposal is put to the vote, there is an unusually high turnout with categorical rejection. On the other hand, the introduction of a 'reality service' is being discussed pragmatically in order to guarantee the work and administrative processes that are still necessary in the real world.

Visionaries, however, are thinking much further ahead. At some point, the earth's population is likely to have fallen to an ecologically healthy level due to the low reproduction rate of virtual citizens. Numerous regions of the earth would offer attractive living space. War, terror and flight would be unlikely. This situation would offer ideal conditions for a powerful revival of enlightened life forms. Until then, however, we must prevent the vast majority of humanity from completely losing interest in non-digital identities. Can we trust that a recovered Earth will arouse enough fascination and interest? Must there be a violent liberation from the digital cave if necessary?

It is to be hoped that an elite of enlightened, aristocratic democrats is already working on these issues.

Ciao Bella

We are witnessing the decline of a guiding principle—grand and sublime, yet too demanding to prevail in mass society. It was a privilege to be able to participate in one of these rare eras. The future is not hopeless. The guiding ideas of truth and freedom are too good to be forgotten forever. It is up to the followers of the Enlightenment to preserve as many embers as possible in order to rekindle the flame when the time comes. Unfortunately, it is uncertain how long it will remain dark.

Those who embrace Enlightenment ideals may find solace in comparing it to a great love. What remains is the gratitude of having experienced something so beautiful and rare. It is a shame that we could not keep it. It is leaving and we who are alive now will not see it again.

Postface to the second German edition

The prediction of an emerging Post-Enlightenment Society has elicited an astonishing response. The revised new edition is being published just one and a half years after the first edition.

Current political and social developments are likely to have fueled this interest. In Ukraine, a success of the imperialist Russian war of aggression and a blueprint for the dictatorships of this world are to be feared. The terrorist massacre of 7 October 2023 threatens to be just as successful as 11 September 2001 from the point of view of the attackers. Once again, a traumatized society will not find the strength to distinguish between *jus ad bellum* and *jus in bello*. In the United States, the Post-Enlightenment Society has already begun. The majority of Americans have once again elected a man who considers neither scientific knowledge nor the principles of the Constitution to be relevant. The establishment of an authoritarian hereditary monarchy is much more likely than a return to genuine democracy.

In Germany, we can expect a secure far-right party to become the strongest party in several federal states and perhaps even the state government, while in France a right-wing populist has a good chance of moving into the Élysée Palace. At the same time, an exponentially growing proportion of eligible voters inform themselves with an attention span of just a few seconds via a Chinese entertainment app. The necessary measures to avert a global climate catastrophe are falling behind schedule, while migration movements are anticipated to intensify. The list of concerns is long.

However, the thesis of the Post-Enlightenment Society is based on a fundamental approach: talk of the crisis is omnipresent. We talk about the crisis of democracy, of science, of institutions, and so on. However, we do this in a very selective way. A crisis represents a period of hardship and challenges that is ultimately expected to be overcome. Afterwards, the implicit hope is that we will carry on as before and continue with our way of life and society. Crises are much less often understood and articulated as the beginning of a downfall. This is probably due to unconscious processes. This essay attempts to avoid these processes of repression. It takes seriously the option that the current crises herald a downfall and that we are witnessing the transition to a Post-Enlightenment Society. If this analysis is correct, the question arises as to what exactly we are losing and what exactly is the essence of our way of life.

One suggestion would be to see the core of our way of life in economic freedom and material prosperity. However, this is only partially convincing. On the one hand, it is debatable whether these are necessary conditions of our way of life. On the other hand, there is only a limited danger. In other forms of society, such as authoritarian China, economic freedoms are not under threat. Capitalist opportunities for development are even encouraged.

The majority of people therefore consider democracy to be the essence of our way of life. It is democracy that is being lost in the Post-Enlightenment Society. However, even this diagnosis is still too imprecise. Democracy can be understood and practiced in a very vulgar way as the tyranny of the majority. The rapidly growing model of illiberal democracies testifies to precisely this understanding. So it is not democracy as such, but a particular form of democracy that characterizes the essence of our form of society. It is a democracy that is committed to the ideals of the Enlightenment.

This raises the question of the essence of Enlightenment. This essay argues that there is a double consensus. The first part of the consensus says: objectivity exists. Truth and facts exist. It is unspeakably difficult and rare to recognize them, and even more challenging to prove them to others, but they exist. The second part of the consensus has a normative character. Since we are among the beings who are able to recognize objectivity, we possess a dignity that must be respected. This happens through the right and the duty of reciprocal and general justification. In legal and political terms, this idea gives rise to human rights, the democratic constitutional state and international law. The Post-Enlightenment Society is characterized by the loss of this consensus.

There were enough calls for Cassandras. When Samuel P. Huntington's *The Clash of Civilizations* appeared, it was often rejected as a reactionary program. The idea of leaving behind the ideological conflicts of the twentieth century only to stumble into a clash of civilizations was too disappointing. Fukuyama's dream of the end of history, according to which humanity would henceforth organize itself more and more peacefully in democratic constitutional states with a multicultural society, was too tempting. What was overlooked was that Huntington in no way advocates the confrontation of cultures, but considers it inevitable on the basis of uncomfortable but astute analyses. Anyone who picks up Huntington's works will find an accurate prediction of the Ukraine war, including information on social fault lines and front lines. You can also read about migration without assimilation and right-wing populist counter-movements.

However, the dominance of culturally shaped identity, which is presented as having no alternative, deserves to be contradicted. Enlightenment must go into opposition here. Its aim was always to focus on personal autonomy and to push back cultural identity bit by bit. It was breathtakingly ambitious, but there were considerable successes, ranging from individual liberation to the

United Nations. Huntington counters these objections with pessimism. Ethical universalism, human rights, international law and other achievements of the Enlightenment may not be theoretical fallacies, but their persuasive power remains limited to the "Davos culture" of an intellectually and economically privileged minority. Moreover, Huntington shares John Locke's fear that societies without a common cultural identity are threatened with disintegration. At the latest in his Letters on Toleration, Locke had worked out that it was ethically imperative to grant all citizens maximum freedom with regard to their religious and secular lives and to insist only on compliance with the social contract. Nevertheless, he feared that this could break the cohesion of society.

The optimism of the Enlightenment, on the other hand, emphasizes the model of cosmopolitanism and the program of humanistic education. The doxastic cultural influences are countered by the striving for objectivity and intercultural justification. At the same time, it cannot be denied how fragile and crisis-prone the project of Enlightenment is and how much commitment and care it requires. The obvious conclusion would be increased vigilance and a sustained and passionate commitment to the ideals of Enlightenment. Unfortunately, this is exactly what did not happen. Rather than addressing the impending clash of civilizations with dedicated educational efforts, many societies retreated into the naïve belief in self-sustaining multiculturalism. This development opened the door to numerous forms of negative dialectics, but above all once again served the toxic primacy of cultural identity.

The lifeblood of Enlightenment, the pursuit of objectivity and the duty of reciprocal and universal justification is in a bad state. Internationally, there is an increasing lack of power and determination to enforce international law and peaceful conflict resolution. At the level of nation states, a differentiated picture emerges. Most of the world's population has never experienced the political and intellectual benefits of the Enlightenment. In the few privileged societies, there is an increasing lack of appreciation and commitment.

Perhaps future generations will demand a justification for the existing lack of freedom. The population of China or Russia would probably succeed in this explanation. They could only offer isolated signs of heroic resistance to the continued existence of the dictatorships. This excuse does not apply to the people of North America and Western Europe. Rather, freedom was renounced in an act of freedom. Egomaniacal leadership, denial of science, apathy or refusal of discourse were not without alternative. This was true both in personal choices and at the ballot box. The demise of the second Enlightenment and the beginning of the Post-Enlightenment Society is also the product of external influences. However, it is primarily an act of self-abandonment.

Literature

Adichie, Chimamanda Ngozi (2009): The danger of a single story [Video]. In: *TED Talks*. Online: https://www.ted.com/talks/chimamanda_ngozi_adichie_the_danger_of_a_single_story [abgerufen am 04.10.2022].

Adorno, Theodor W. (1970): Erziehung nach Auschwitz. In: Gerd Kadelbach (Hg.): *Erziehung zur Mündigkeit. Vorträge und Gespräche mit Hellmut Becker 1959–1969*. 25. Auflage. Frankfurt a. M.: Suhrkamp.

Adorno, Theodor W. (2010): Theorie der Halbbildung. In: Hans-Ulrich Lessing / Volker Steenblock (Hg.): *„Was den Menschen zum Menschen macht …". Klassische Texte einer Philosophie der Bildung*. Freiburg i. B.: Karl Alber.

Adorno, Theodor W. (1995): *Studien zum autoritären Charakter*. Frankfurt a. M.: Suhrkamp.

Anders, Günther (1981): *Die atomare Drohung*. München: Verlag C.H. Beck.

Anderson, Luvell / Lepore, Ernie (2013): Slurring words. In: *Noûs*, 47(1). S. 25–48.

Anderson, Luvell / Lepore, Ernie (2013): What Did You Call Me? Slurs as prohibited words: Setting things up. In: *Analytic Philosophy*, 54(3). S. 350–363.

Anton, Julia (2021): Ranking deutscher Influencer: Reich dank Reichweite. In: *Faz.net*, 14.12.2021. Online: https://www.faz.net/aktuell/stil/trends-nischen/das-sind-die-wertvollsten-deutschen-influencer-ganz-vorne-nur-frauen-17684153.html?utm_source=pocket-newtab-global-de-DE [abgerufen am 04.10.2022].

Appiah-Nyamekye, Josephine / Logan, Carolyn / Gyimah-Boadi, E. (2019): In search of opportunity: Young and educated Africans most likely to consider moving abroad. In: *Afrobarometer Dispatch* No. 288, 03/2019. Online: https://www.africaportal.org/publications/search-opportunity-young-and-educated-africans-more-likely-consider-moving-abroad/ [abgerufen am 05.10.2022].

Arendt, Hannah (1958): *Die Ungarische Revolution und der Totalitäre Imperialismus*. München: Piper.

Arendt, Hannah (1963): *Über die Revolution*. München: Piper.

Arendt, Hannah (1969): *Macht und Gewalt*. München: Piper.

Arendt, Hannah (2019): *Vita activa oder Vom tätigen Leben*. 20. Auflage. München: Piper.

Aßmann, Lothar / Bergmann, Reiner / Henke, Roland Wolfgang / Schulz, Matthias / Sewing, Eva-Maria (2002): *Zugänge zur Philosophie – Grundband für die Oberstufe*. Berlin: Cornelsen.

Badawia, Tarek / Tiedemann, Markus / Huber, Wolfgang (2020): Mohammed-Karikaturen in die Schule? In: *Die Zeit*, 03.12.2020.

Bartlett, Robert C. (2001): *The idea of Enlightenment: a post-mortem study*. Toronto: University of Toronto Press.

Beck, Ulrich (1989): Risikogesellschaft. Überlebensfragen, Sozialstruktur und ökologische Aufklärung. In: *Aus Politik und Zeitgeschichte. Beilage zur Wochenzeitung Das Parlament.* S. 4–7.

Bernstein, Julia (o. J.): Mach mal keine Judenaktion! Herausforderungen und Lösungsansätze in der professionellen Bildung und Sozialarbeit gegen Antisemitismus. Frankfurt University of Applied Sciences 2018. Online: https://www.frankfurt-university.de/fileadmin/standard/Aktuelles/Pressemitteilungen/Mach_mal_keine_Judenaktion__Herausforderungen_und_Loesungsansaetze_in_der_professionellen_Bildungs-_und_Sozialarbeit_gegen_Anti.pdf [abgerufen am 01.08.2021]. S. 345–346.

Beutelsbacher Konsens (o. D.): [online] https://www.lpb-bw.de/beutelsbacher-konsens/ [abgerufen am 05.10.2022].

Bieri, Peter (2003): *Das Handwerk der Freiheit. Über die Entdeckung des eigenen Willens.* Frankfurt a. M.: Fischer.

Bieri, Peter (2010): Wie wäre es, gebildet zu sein? In: Hans-Ullrich Lessing / Volker Steenblock (Hg.): *„Was den Menschen eigentlich zum Menschen macht ...". Klassische Texte einer Philosophie der Bildung.* Freiburg i. B.: Karl Albert.

Birnbacher, Dieter (2018): Religion und Religionskritik – eine Einführung. In: *Zeitschrift für Didaktik der Philosophie und Ethik (ZDPE).* 40(1). S. 3–8.

Böckenförde, Ernst-Wolfgang (1991): Die Entstehung des Staates als Vorgang der Säkularisation. In: Ders.: *Recht, Staat, Freiheit. Studien zur Rechtsphilosophie, Staatstheorie und Verfassungsgeschichte.* Frankfurt a. M.: Suhrkamp.

Bok, Sissela (1984): *Secrets: On the Ethics of Concealment & Revelation.* 2. Auflage. Oxford: Oxford University Press.

Borger, Rykle (1985): Der Kyros-Zylinder. In: Otto Kaiser (Hg.): *Texte aus der Umwelt des Alten Testaments.* Band 1: Alte Folge. Gütersloh: Gütersloher Verlagshaus. S. 407–410.

Bruckner, Pascal (2007): Fundamentalismus der Aufklärung oder Rassismus der Antirassisten? In: Thierry Chervel / Anja Seeliger (Hg.): *Islam in Europa. Eine internationale Debatte.* Frankfurt a. M.: Suhrkamp.

Bubner, Rüdiger (1989): Rousseau, Hegel und die Dialektik der Aufklarung. In: Jochen Schmidt (Hg.): *Aufklärung und Gegenaufklärung in der europäischen Literatur, Philosophie und Politik von der Antike bis zur Gegenwart.* Darmstadt: Wissenschaftliche Buchgesellschaft.

Bundesamt für Migration und Flüchtlinge (BAMF) (Hg.): Jahresbericht. Das Bundesamt in Zahlen 2016. Online: https://www.bamf.de/SharedDocs/Anlagen/DE/Statistik/BundesamtinZahlen/bundesamt-in-zahlen-2016.html;jsessionid=839E95ED55FC6D9AEF6CBA66F4E71195.intranet262?view=renderPdfViewer&nn=284738 [abgerufen am 05.10.2022].

Bundesverfassungsgericht (BVerfG) (2009): Urteil des Zweiten Senats vom 30. Juni 2009- 2 BvE 2/08 -, Rn. 1–421, Absatz 364. Online: https://www.bundesverfassungsgericht.de/SharedDocs/Entscheidungen/DE/2009/06/es20090630_2bve000208.html [abgerufen am 05.10.2022].

Bundesverfassungsgericht (BVerfG) (2018): Beschluss des Zweiten Senats vom 11. Dezember 2018 - 2 BvE 1/18 -, Rn. 1–29. Online: https://www.bundesverfassungsgericht.de/SharedDocs/Entscheidungen/DE/2018/12/es20181211_2bve000118.html [abgerufen am 05.10.2022].

Collier, Roger (2012): Ugly, messy and nasty debate surrounds circumcision. In: *CMAJ: Canadian Medical Association journal = journal de l'Association medicale canadienne*, 184(1). S. 25–26.

Cook, John / Oreskes, Naomi / Doran, Peter T. / Anderegg, William R. L. / Verheggen, Bart / Maibach, Ed W. / Carlton, J. Stuart / Lewandowsky, Stephan / Skuce, Andrew G. / Green, Sarah A. / Nuccitelli, Dana / Jacobs, Peter / Richardson, Mark / Winkler, Bärbel / Painting, Rob / Rice, Ken (2016): Consensus on consensus: a synthesis of consensus estimates on human-caused global warming. In: *Environmental Research Letters*, 11(4). S. 048002.

Dahrendorf, Ralf (2003): Über Populismus. Acht Anmerkungen zum Populismus. In: *Transit*, 25. S. 156–163.

Docquier, Frédéric / Rapoport, Hillel (2012): Globalisation, Brain Drain und Development. In: *Journal of Economic Literature*, 50(3). S. 681–730.

Draken, Klaus / Schulze, Matthias (2022): Im Gespräch: Über den Umgang mit kontroversen Beispielen im Philosophie- und Ethikunterricht. In: *Zeitschrift für Didaktik der Philosophie und Ethik*, 4/2022. Im Druck.

Die Bibel nach der Übersetzung Martin Luthers, Stuttgart 2017.

Diels, Hermann / Kranz, Walther (Hg.) (1951/1952): *Die Fragmente der Vorsokratiker*. 3 Bände. 6. Auflage. Berlin: Weidmann.

Der Spiegel (2013): Samuel L. Jackson und das N-Wort. In: *Der Spiegel*, 03.01.2013. Online: https://www.spiegel.de/panorama/django-unchained-samuel-l-jackson-diskutiert-das-n-wort-a-875552.html [abgerufen am 21.06.2022].

Der Spiegel (2018): Chinesischer Präsident Xi im Amt bestätigt - ohne Gegenstimme. In: Der Spiegel, 17.03.2018. Online: https://www.spiegel.de/politik/ausland/china-xi-jinping-einstimmig-als-staatschef-bestaetigt-a-1198605.html [abgerufen am 20.01.2022].

dpa (2019): Proteste für mehr Klimaschutz: Globaler Klimastreik geht in die zweite Runde. In: *Faz.net*, 27.09.2019. Online: https://www.faz.net/aktuell/politik/ausland/klimastreik-globale-fridays-for-future-demos-gehen-weiter-16406182.html [abgerufen am 05.10.2022].

Deutsche Stiftung Weltbevölkerung (Hg.) (2021): DSW-Datenreport 2021. Soziale und demografische Daten weltweit. Online: https://www.dsw.org/wp-content/uploads/2021/10/DSW-Datenreport_2021_web.pdf [abgerufen am 05.10.2022].

Elias, Norbert (1939): *Über den Prozeß der Zivilisation*. Basel: Haus zum Falken.

Elsner, Regina (2022) „Verfolgte" Kirche in der Ukraine - Kriegspropaganda, Kirchenkonflikt und globale Konsequenzen. In: *MONITOR – Analyse & Beratung der Konrad Adenauer Stiftung*, 04.04.2022. Online: https://www.kas.de/de/monitor/detail/-/content/verfolgte-kirche-in-der-ukraine [abgerufen am 05.10.2022].

El-Mafaalani, Aladin / Waleciak, Julian / Weitzel, Gerrit (2017): Tatsächliche, messbare und subjektiv wahrgenommene Diskriminierung. In Albert Scherr / Aladin El-Mafaalani / Gökçen Yüksel (Hg.): *Handbuch Diskriminierung*. Wiesbaden: Springer VS Wiesbaden.

Escobar, Herton (2021): 'A hostile environment.' Brazilian scientists face rising attacks from Bolsonaro's regime. In: *Science.org*, 07.04.2021. Online: https://www.science.org/content/article/hostile-environment-brazilian-scientists-face-rising-attacks-bolsonaro-s-regime [abgerufen am: 05.10.2022].

Esser, Hartmut (2001): Integration und ethnische Schichtung. In: *Arbeitspapiere - Mannheimer Zentrum für Europäische Sozialforschung*, 40. S. 3–68.

Fachverband Philosophie e.V. / Fachverband Ethik e.V. / Forum für Didaktik der Philosophie und Ethik (Hg.) (2016): Dresdener Konsens. Online: https://www.fachverband-ethik.de/fileadmin/user_upload/Baden-Wu%CC%88rttemberg/dateien/aktuelles/DRESDENER_KONSENS.pdf [abgerufen am 23.06.2022].

Fachverband Philosophie e.V. / Landesverband NRW (Hg.) (2022): Stellungnahme des Fachverbands Philosophie (NRW) zur Diskussion um die Aufgaben im Philosophiebuch „Zugänge". Online: https://fv-philosophie.de/wp-content/uploads/2022/03/FVNRWBrief-Aufgabe-Zugaenge-2.pdf [abgerufen am 23.06.2022].

Falkenburg, Brigitte (2012): *Mythos Determinismus: Wieviel erklärt uns die Hirnforschung?* Berlin: Springer.

Flaßpöhler, Svenja (2021): *Sensibel. Über moderne Empfindlichkeit und die Grenzen des Zumutbaren*. Stuttgart: Klett-Cotta.

Forst, Rainer (2003): *Toleranz im Konflikt. Geschichte, Gehalt und Gegenwart eines umstrittenen Begriffs*. 4. Auflage. Frankfurt a. M.: Suhrkamp.

Forst, Rainer (2007): *Das Recht auf Rechtfertigung*. Frankfurt a. M.: Suhrkamp.

Foucault, Michel (1978): *Was ist Kritik?* (Übers.: Walter Seitter, 1992). Berlin: Merve Verlag.

Foucault, Michel (1980): Truth and Power. In Colin Gordon (Hg.): *Power/Knowledge: Selected Interviews and Other Writings, 1972–1977*. New York: Pantheon Books.

Forsa Politik- und Sozialforschung GmbH im Auftrag des Verbands Bildung und Erziehung (Hg.): Die Schule aus Sicht der Schulleiterinnen und Schulleiter – Gewalt gegen Lehrkräfte. Berlin, 27. März 2020. S. 5. Online: https://www.

vbe-bw.de/wp-content/uploads/2020/09/2020-04-07_forsa-Bericht_Gewalt_Baden-Wu%CC%88rttemberg.pdf. [abgerufen am 20.09.2021].

Frankfurt, Harry G. (1971): Freedom of the Will and the Concept of a Person. In: *Journal of Philosophy* 68. S. 5–20.

Frankl, Viktor Emil (1997): *Der Wille zum Sinn. Ausgewählte Vorträge über Logotherapie.* München: Piper.

Freud, Sigmund (1921): *Massenpsychologie und Ich-Analyse.* Leipzig, Wien, Zürich: Internationaler Psychoanalytischer Verlag GmbH.

Frege, Gottlob (2003): Der Gedanke – Eine logische Untersuchung. In Logische Untersuchungen. Vandenhoeck & Ruprecht, Göttingen.

Fromm, Erich (1957): Die autoritäre Persönlichkeit. In: *Deutsche Universitätszeitschrift*, 12(9). S. 3f.

Fromm, Erich (1965): *Escape from Freedom.* 18. Auflage. New York: Avon Books.

Fromm, Erich (1980): Die Flucht vor der Freiheit. In Rainer Funke (Hg.): *Gesamtausgabe in zwölf Bänden, Bd. I: Sozialpsychologie.* Stuttgart: DVA. S. 299–314.

Fukuyama, Francis (1992): *Das Ende der Geschichte: Wo stehen wir?* München: Kindler.

Fukuyama, Francis (2022): Putin wird die Niederlage seiner Armee nicht überleben. 12 Thesen zum Krieg in der Ukraine. In: *Neue Zürcher Zeitung*, 21.03.2022. Online: https://www.nzz.ch/feuilleton/francis-fukuyama-russland-wird-diesen-krieg-verlieren-und-weitere-12-prognosen-ld.1674933 [abgerufen am 15.08.2022].

Gabriel, Markus (2013): Kritik am radikalen Konstruktivismus. In: Ders.: *Warum es die Welt nicht gibt.* Berlin: Ullstein.

Gadamer, Hans-Georg (1960): *Wahrheit und Methode – Grundzüge einer Philosophischen Hermeneutik.* 7. Auflage [2010]. Tübingen: Mohr Siebeck.

Gathen, Peter / Mönikes, Martin (2022): Eltern überlassen Erziehung der Schule. In: *Rheinische Post*, 22.01.2022.

Gauck, Joachim Bundespräsident a.D. (2021): „Menschen, die Freiheit, Demokratie und Menschenrechte lieben, fragen nicht danach, ob jemand schwarz ist oder weiß". In: *Die Zeit*, 31.03.2021. S. 56.

Gasset, José Ortega y (1970): *Der Aufstand der Massen.* Hamburg: Rowohlt.

Gerhard Roth, Gerhard (2004): Worüber dürfen Hirnforscher reden–und in welcher Weise? In: Christian Geyer (Hg.): *Hirnforschung und Willensfreiheit.* Frankfurt a. M.: Suhrkamp. S. 66–85.

Geschäftsstelle des Zentrums für transdisziplinäre Geschlechterstudien der Humboldt-Universität zu Berlin (Hg.) (2005): *Bulletin – Texte 28.* Online: https://www.gender.hu-berlin.de/de/publikationen/gender-bulletin-broschueren/bulletin-texte/texte-28/bulletin-texte-28 [letzter Zugriff am 04.10.2021]

Geyer, Christian (Hg.) (2004): *Hirnforschung und Willensfreiheit. Zur Deutung der neuesten Experimente.* Frankfurt a. M.: Suhrkamp.

Giesen, Christoph (2019): Ein ganzes Land als Testgelände. In: *Süddeutsche.de*, 07.11.2019. Online: https://www.sueddeutsche.de/politik/china-ein-ganzes-land-als-testgelaende-1.4664052 [abgerufen am 05.10.2022].

Global Campaign for Peaceducation (Hg.): „Liebe exportieren"–Imam im Zentrum des Terroranschlags von Christchurch verbreitet weiterhin Friedensbotschaft, 25.03.2020. Online: https://www.peace-ed-campaign.org/de/export-love-imam-at-centre-of-christchurch-terrorist-attack-continues-to-spread-message-of-peace/ [abgerufen am 15.09.2022].

Goergen, Klaus (2018): Wider den grassierenden Konstruktivismus unter Lehrkräften. In: Hans-Ulrich Lessing / Markus Tiedemann / Joachim Siebert (Hg.): *Kultur der philosophischen Bildung. Volker Steenblock zum 60. Geburtstag*. Hannover: Siebert-Verlag. S. 232–244.

Goergen, Klaus (2021): Einleitung. In: Dieter Birnbacher / Klaus Goergen / Markus Tiedemann (Hg.): *Normative Integration. Kulturkampf im Klassenzimmer und netzgeprägte Schülerschaft*. Paderborn: Schöningh.

Göpel, Maja (2021): *Unsere Welt neu denken: Eine Einladung*. Berlin: Ullstein.

Gosepath, Stefan (1992): *Aufgeklärtes Eigeninteresse – Eine Theorie theoretischer und praktischer Rationalität*. Frankfurt a. M.: Suhrkamp.

Greenwald, Glenn (2014): *No Place to Hide: Edward Snowden, the NSA, and the U.S. Surveillance State*. New York: Henry Holt & Co.

Grillmeier, Franziska (2020): Der neue Alltag auf der Insel–gefährlich für Flüchtlinge und Helfer. In: *Tagesspiegel.de*, 04.03.2020. Online: https://www.tagesspiegel.de/politik/fluechtlingskrise-auf-lesbos-der-neue-alltag-auf-der-insel-gefaehrlich-fuer-fluechtlinge-und-helfer/25606814.html [abgerufen am 15.08.2022].

Habermas, Jürgen (1996): *Die Einbeziehung des Anderen. Studien zur politischen Theorie*. Frankfurt a. M.: Suhrkamp.

Habermas, Jürgen (2021): Überlegungen und Hypothesen zu einem erneuten Strukturwandel der politischen Öffentlichkeit. In: *Leviathan*, 49(37). S. 470–500.

Hall Jamieson, Kathleen (2018): *Cyberwar: How Russian Hackers and Trolls Helped Elect a President—What We Don't, Can't, and Do Know*. Oxford: Oxford University Press.

Hampe, Michael (2018): *Die Dritte Aufklärung*. Berlin: Nicolai Publishing & Intelligence GmbH.

Hamilton, Clive / Ohlberg, Mareike (2020): *Die lautlose Eroberung. Wie China westliche Demokratien unterwandert und die Welt neu ordnet*. 3. Auflage. München: DVA.

Harari, Yuval Noah (2015): *Eine kurze Geschichte der Menschheit*. München: Pantheon.

Harkness, S. Suzan J. / Magid, Mohamed / Roberts, Jameka / Richardson, Michael (2007): Crossing the Line? Freedom of Speech and Religious Sensibilities. *PS: Political Science & Politics*, 40(2). S. 275–278.

Hartmann, Udo (2002): Geist im Exil. Römische Philosophen am Hof der Sasaniden. In: Monika Schuol u. a. (Hg.): *Grenzüberschreitungen. Formen des Kontakts zwischen Orient und Okzident im Altertum*. Stuttgart: Franz Steiner Verlag. S. 123–160.

Hasters, Alice (2020): *Was weisse Menschen nicht über Rassismus hören wollen aber wissen sollten*. München: hanserblau.

Hastings, Max (2020): I was Boris Johnson's boss: he is utterly unfit to be prime minister. In: *The Guardian*, 03.02.2020. Online: https://www.theguardian.com/commentisfree/2019/jun/24/boris-johnson-prime-minister-tory-party-britain [abgerufen am 15.08.2022].

Hassel, Florian (2015): Polen - Geistliche schüren Ängste vor Flüchtlingen. In: *Süddeutsche.de*, 10.09.2015. Online: https://www.sueddeutsche.de/politik/polen-angst-und-kalkuel-1.2640725 [abgerufen am 05.10.2022].

Hauser, Claudia (2022): Schulaufgabe sorgt für Entrüstung. In: *Bonner Generalanzeiger*, 14.02.2022.

Henke, Roland W. (2012): Ende der Kunst oder Ende der Philosophie? Ein Beitrag zur Diskussion um den Stellenwert präsentativer Materialien im Philosophie- und Ethikunterricht. In: *Zeitschrift für Didaktik der Philosophie und Ethik*, 34(1). S. 59–66

Herder, Johann Gottfried (1784): *Ideen zur Philosophie der Geschichte der Menschheit. Bd. 1*. Leipzig: Johann Friedrich Hartknoch.

Hermann, A. (1965): Haber und Bosch: Brot aus Luft–Die Ammoniaksynthese. In: *Physikalische Blätter*, 21(4). S. 168–171.

Höffe, Otfried (1996): Menschenrechte. In: Ders. (Hg.): *Vernunft und Recht. Bausteine zu einem interkulturellen Rechtsdiskurs*. Berlin: Suhrkamp. S. 49–82.

Horne, Gerald (2014): *The Counter-Revolution of 1776: Slave Resistance and the Origins of the United States of America*. New York: New York University Press.

Horkheimer, Max / Adorno, Theodor W. (1987): Dialektik der Aufklärung. In: M. Horkheimer: *Gesammelte Schriften. Bd. 5*. Frankfurt a. M.: Fischer.

Humboldt, Wilhelm von (1792/1966): Ideen zu einem Versuch, die Gränzen der Wirksamkeit des Staates zu bestimmen. In: *Humboldt-Werke, Bd. I*. Darmstadt: WBG [Abt. Verlag].

Huntington, Samuel P. (1996): *Kampf der Kulturen – The Clash of Civilizations. Die Neugestaltung der Weltpolitik im 21. Jahrhundert*. München: Siedler.

Informationsbüro des Staatsrats der Volksrepublik China (1991): Human rights in China. Beijing. Online: https://www.china.org.cn/e-white/7/index.htm [abgerufen am 05.10.2022].

Institut der deutschen Wirtschaft Köln (Hg.) (2002): Weihnachtsgeschenke: Viel Elektronik unterm Baum. Die beliebtesten Weihnachtswünsche von 6– bis 12-jährigen in Prozent. In: Informationsdienst des Instituts der deutschen Wirtschaft, Nr. 49, 12/2002.

Jansen, Frank (2020): Für sie ist der Mörder aus Frankreich ein Idol – Radikalisierte Muslime in Deutschland. In: *Der Tagesspiegel*, 19.10.2020. Online: https://www.tagesspiegel.de/politik/radikalisierte-muslime-in-deutschland-fuer-sie-ist-der-moerder-aus-frankreich-einidol/26288138.html [abgerufen am 07.09.2021].

Jaspers, Karl (1949): *Vom Ursprung und Ziel der Geschichte*. München: Piper.

Jefferson, Thomas (1824): Brief an Major John Cartwright vom 05.06.1824. Online: http://www.let.rug.nl/usa/presidents/thomas-jefferson/letters-of-thomas-jefferson/jefl278.php [abgerufen am 01.09.2022].

Jensen, Steven (2016): *The Making of International Human Rights: The 1960s, Decolonization, and the Reconstruction of Global Values*. Cambridge: Cambridge University Press.

Jonas, Hans (1984): *Das Prinzip Verantwortung - Versuch einer Ethik für die technologische Zivilisation*. Frankfurt a. M.: Suhrkamp.

Kant, Immanuel [AA] (1966ff): *Kant's gesammelte Schriften*. Hg. Von der Königlich Preußischen Akademie der Wissenschaften. Berlin 1900–1955, Nachdruck 1966 ff.

Kant, Immanuel (1785): Bestimmung des Begriffs einer Menschenrace. In: *Berlinische Monatsschrift* 06. S. 390–417.

Kazim, Hasnain (2014): 1000 Illegale Zimmer für Erdogan. In: *Der Spiegel*, 29.10.2014. Online: https://www.spiegel.de/politik/ausland/tuerkei-erdogan-bezieht-praesidentenpalast-mit-1000-zimmern-a-999881.html [abgerufen am 05.10.2022].

Klaiber, Tilo (2018): Die Macht des Beispiels beim Philosophieren (Lehren und Lernen). In: *Zeitschrift für Didaktik der Philosophie und Ethik*, 40(4). S. 80–94.

Kleingeld, Pauline (2007): Kant's Second Thought on Race. In: *The Philosophical Quarterly*, 57(229). S. 573–592.

Kiesewetter, Bernd (2021): 1. Mai Bochum: „Querdenker" stellen Grablichter vors Gericht. In: *Westdeutsche Allgemeine Zeitung*, 01.05.2021. Online: https://www.waz.de/staedte/bochum/1-mai-bochum-querdenker-stellen-grablichter-vors-gericht-id232186527.html [abgerufen am 05.10.2022].

Kirchner, Thomas (2016): Niederländische Einwanderpartei Denk. Die Rassistenjäger. In: *Süddeutsche.de*, 22.06.2016. Online: https://www.sueddeutsche.de/politik/niederlande-die-rassistenjaeger-1.3043002 [abgerufen am 05.10.2022].

KNA (2020): Brennpunktschulen im Visier: Lehrerverband warnt vor „Klima der Einschüchterung". In: *Faz.net*, 20.10.2020. Online: https://www.faz.net/aktuell/politik/inland/lehrerverband-beklagt-klima-der-einschuechterung-17010582.html [abgerufen am 05.10.2022].

Knobloch, Eberhard (2004): Naturgenuss und Weltgemälde. Gedanken zu Humboldts Kosmos. In: *Internationale Zeitschrift für Humboldtstudien*, 5(09). S. 30–43.

Kultusministerkonferenz (2006): Einheitliche Prüfungsanforderungen in der Abiturprüfung Philosophie (Beschluss der Kultusministerkonferenz vom 01.12.1989

i. d. F. vom 16.11.2006). Online: https://www.kmk.org/fileadmin/veroeffentlichungen_beschluesse/1989/1989_12_01-EPA-Philosophie.pdf [abgerufen am 23.06.2022].

Le Bon, Gustave (1982): *Psychologie der Massen* (Übersetzung: Rudolf Eisler). Stuttgart: Alfred Kröner Verlag.

Levitsky, Steven / Ziblatt, Daniel (2018): *Wie Demokratien sterben: Und was wir dagegen tun können.* München: Deutsche Verlags-Anstalt.

Libet, Benjamin (1985): Unconscious cerebral initiative and the role of conscious will in voluntary action. In: *The Behavioral and Brain Sciences*, 8(4). S. 529–539.

Lincoln, Abraham (1863): Gettysburg Address [Rede]. Gettysburg, 19.11.1863.

Locke, John (1689/1996): *Ein Brief über Toleranz.* Hamburg: Meiner Verlag.

Lyotard, Jean-François (2015): *Das postmoderne Wissen: Ein Bericht.* Wien: Passagen Verlag.

Lynas, Mark / Houlton, Benjamin Z. / Perry, Simon (2021): Greater than 99% consensus on human caused climate change in the peer-reviewed scientific literature. In *Environmental Research Letters*, 16(11). S. 114005.

Mansour, Ahmad (2019): Eine nationale Strategie gegen Radikalisierung. In: Carsten Linnemann / Winfried Bausback (Hg.): *Der politische Islam gehört nicht zu Deutschland.* Freiburg: Herder Verlag. S. 142–158.

Markwardt, Nils (2019): Pappkameraden des Ökopaternalismus. In: *Zeit Online*, 22.01.2019. Online: https://www.zeit.de/kultur/2019-01/umweltpolitik-klimawandel-klasse-sozialpolitik-vereinbarkeit?page=5 [abgerufen am 05.10.2022].

Martens, Ekkehard (1992): *Die Sache des Sokrates.* Stuttgart: Reclam.

Martens, Ekkehard (2017): Philosophie als Kulturtechnik humaner Lebensgestaltung. In: Julian Nida-Rümelin / Irina Spiegel / Markus Tiedemann (Hg.): *Handbuch der Philosophie und Ethik.* Band I: Didaktik und Methodik, 2. Auflage. Paderborn: Schöningh.

Mantyla, Kyle (2018). Rick Joyner: Sin, Not Climate Change, Is Responsible for Hurricane Florence. In: *Right Wing Watch*, 13.09.2018. Online: https://www.rightwingwatch.org/post/rick-joyner-sin-not-climate-change-is-responsible-for-hurricane-florence/ [abgerufen am 05.10.2022].

Mbembe, Achille (2013): *Kritik der schwarzen Vernunft.* Berlin: Suhrkamp.

McWhorter, John (2021): *Die Erwählten. Wie der neue Antirassismus die Gesellschaft spaltet* (Übers.: K. Riesselmann). Hamburg: Hoffmann und Campe.

McWhorter, John / Ridderbusch, Katja (2022): Schattenseite des Antirassismus - Ein unorthodoxer Blick auf die identitätspolitische Debatte. In: *Deutschlandfunk*, 31.01.2022. Online: https://www.deutschlandfunk.de/john-mcwhorter-die-erwaehlten-100.html/ [abgerufen am 05.10.2022].

Merkel, R. (2020): Wir können allen helfen. In: M. Tiedemann (Hg.): *Migration, Menschenrechte und Rassismus. Herausforderungen ethischer Bildung.* Paderborn: Brill/Ferdinand Schöningh.

Mills, Charles W. (2005): Kant's Untermenschen. In A. Valls (Hg.): *Race and Racism in Modern Philosophy*. New York: Cornell University Press.

Mills, Charles W. (2017): *Black Rights/White Wrongs: The Critique of Racial Liberalism*. Oxford: Oxford University Press.

Möller, Ruth (2022): Welche Defizite haben unsere Schulanfänger? Ein Gespräch mit der Rektorin einer Grundschule. In: *Kindergarten heute*. November/Dezember 2002. S. 20–23.

Mönch, Regina (2018): Ditib-Kommentar: Kleine Märtyrer. In: *Frankfurter Allgemeine Zeitung*, 28.04.2018. Online: https://www.faz.net/aktuell/feuilleton/ditib-kommentar-kleine-maertyrer-spielen-krieg-in-moscheen-15563873.html [abgerufen am 16.09.2022].

Moses, A. Dirk (2021): *The Problems of Genocide: Permanent Security and the Language of Transgression*. Cambridge: Cambridge University Press.

Murray, Douglas (2019): *Wahnsinn der Massen – Wie Meinungsmache und Hysterie unsere Gesellschaft vergiften* (Übers.: Birgit Schöbitz). München: FinanzBuch Verlag.

Mücke, Peter / Roelcke, Eckhard (2021): Debatte um „New York Times" – Political Correctness oder „Gesinnungsterror"? In: Deutschlandfunk Kultur, 15.02.2021. Online: https://www.deutschlandfunkkultur.de/debatte-um-new-york-times-political-correctness-oder-100.html [abgerufen am 23.04.2022].

Neiman, Susan (2017): *Widerstand der Vernunft. Ein Manifest in postfaktischen Zeiten*. Salzburg: Ecowin.

Nguyen-Kim, Mai Thi / Tutmann, Linda (2021): Wissenschaft ist keine Demokratie. In: *Zeit.de*. Online: https://www.zeit.de/gesellschaft/zeitgeschehen/2021-05/mai-thi-nguyen-kim-hass-internet-wissenschaftsjournalismus-pressefreiheit) [abgerufen am 15.08.2022].

Nida-Rümelin, Julian (2006): *Demokratie und Wahrheit*. München: C.H. Beck.

Nida-Rümelin, Julian (2013): *Philosophie einer humanen Bildung*. Hamburg: Edition Körber-Stiftung.

Nida-Rümelin, Julian (2015): *Unaufgeregter Realismus. Eine politische Streitschrift*. Paderborn: Brill/mentis.

Nida-Rümelin, Julian (2016): Veritas Filia Temporis. In: Ders.: *Humanistische Reflexionen*. Frankfurt a. M.: Suhrkamp.

Nida-Rümelin, Julian (2017): *Über Grenzen denken. Eine Ethik der Migration*. Hamburg: Edition Körber-Stiftung.

Nida-Rümelin, Julian (2021): Demokratie als Lebensform. In: Dieter Birnbacher / Klaus Goergen / Markus Tiedemann (Hg.): *Normative Integration. Kulturkampf im Klassenzimmer und netzgeprägte Schülerschaft*. Paderborn: Brill/Schönigh.

Nozick, Robert (1974): *Anarchy, State, and Utopia*. New York: Basic Books.

O' Gorman, Ned (2021): *Politik für alle – Hannah Arendt lesen in unsicheren Zeiten*. München: Nagel & Kimche.

LITERATURE

Orwell, George (1984/2002): 1984. 23. Auflage. München: Ullstein.
Paris, Rainer (2003): Autorität- Führung- Eliten: Eine Abgrenzung. In: Stefan Hradil, Peter Imbusch (Hg.): *Oberschichten - Eliten- Herrschende Klassen. Reihe Sozialstrukturanalyse*, Bd. 17. Opladen: Leske + Budrich.
Peşmen, Azadê (2018): Wie Tausende kleine Mückenstiche - Rassismus macht den Körper krank. *Deutschlandfunk Kultur*, 05.07.2022. Online: https://www.deutschlandfunkkultur.de/rassismus-macht-den-koerper-krank-wie-tausende-kleine-100.html [Abgerufen am 20.04.2022].
Pfordten, Dietmar von der (2015): *Moralischer Realismus? Zur kohärentistischen Metaethik Julian Nida-Rümelins*. Paderborn: Brill/mentis.
Pico della Mirandola, Giovanni (2010): Über die Würde des Menschen. In: Hans-Ulrich Lessing / Volker Steenblock (Hg.): *„Was den Menschen zum Menschen macht ...". Klassische Texte der Philosophie der Bildung*. Freiburg i. B.: Karl Alber.
Piggott, Steven (2016): Is Breitbart.com Becoming the Media Arm of the 'Alt-Right'? In: *Southern Poverty Law Center*, 28.04.2016. Online: https://www.splcenter.org/hatewatch/2016/04/28/breitbartcom-becoming-media-arm-alt-right [abgerufen am 05.10.2022].
Pinker, Steven (2018): *Aufklärung Jetzt – Für Vernunft, Wissenschaft, Humanismus und Fortschritt* (Übersetzung: Martina Wieser). Frankfurt a. M.: S. Fischer.
Pinker, Steven (2018): Die Welt war noch nie so gut wie heute! In: *Philosophiemagazin*, 2/2018. S. 66–71.
Platon (1977): *Werke in acht Bänden*. Hg. von Gunther Eigler. gr./dt., Übersetzung: Friedrich Schleiermacher (revidiert). 2. Auflage, 1999. Darmstadt: Wissenschaftliche Buchgesellschaft.
Pluckrose, Helen / Lindsay, James (2022): *Zynische Theorien. Wie aktivistische Wissenschaft Race, Gender und Identität über alles stellt - und warum das niemandem nützt*. München: C.H. Beck.
Popper, Karl R. (1992): *Die offene Gesellschaft und ihre Feinde*. Band 1: Der Zauber Platons. 7. Auflage. Tübingen: UTB.
Popper, Karl R. (1981): *Ausgangspunkte*. Zürich: Ex Libris.
Popper, Karl R. (1994): *Alles Leben ist Problemlösen*. München: Piper.
Postman, Neil (1987): *Das Verschwinden der Kindheit*. Frankfurt a. M.: S. Fischer.
Powell, James (2019): Scientists Reach 100% Consensus on Anthropogenic Global Warming. In: *Bulletin of Science, Technology & Society*, 37(4). S. 183–184.
Putnam, Hilary (1998): *Reason, Truth and History*. Cambridge: Cambridge University Press.
Rawls, John (1971): *A Theory of Justice*. Cambridge: Harvard University Press.
Rawls, John (1979): *Eine Theorie der Gerechtigkeit* (Übersetzung: Hermann Vetter). Frankfurt a. M.: Suhrkamp.

Rawls, John (1993): Gerechtigkeit als Fairneß: politisch und nicht metaphysisch. In: Axel Honneth (Hg.): *Kommunitarismus*. Frankfurt a. M.: Campus. S. 37–67.

Reich, Kersten (1996): Systemisch-konstruktivistische Didaktik. In: Rudolf Voß (Hg.): *Die Schule neu erfinden*. Neuwied: Luchterhand. S. 70–91.

Reich, Kersten (1998): Konstruktivistische Unterrichtsmethoden. Lehrtheoretische Voraussetzungen und ausgewählte Beispiele. In: *System Schule*, 2(1). S. 20–26.

Reich, Kersten (2010): *Systemisch-konstruktivistische Pädagogik*. Weinheim: Beltz.

Renz, Ursula (2019): *Was denn bitte ist kulturelle Identität? Eine Orientierung in Zeiten des Populismus*. Basel: Schwabe.

Rinner, Stefan / Hieke, Alexander (2022): Slurs under quotation. In: *Philosophical Studies,* 179(5). S. 1483–1494.

Ritter, Joachim (Hg.) (1971): *Historisches Wörterbuch der Philosophie*. Band 1 A-C. Darmstadt: Wissenschaftliche Buchgesellschaft. S. 622–632.

Rohbeck, Johannes (2021): Zur Aktualität der Aufklärung. In: *Zeitschrift für Didaktik der Philosophie und Ethik*, 43(1). S. 4–19.

Rohs, Peter (2016): *Geist und Gegenwart. Entwurf einer analytischen Transzendentalphilosophie*. Paderborn: Brill/mentis.

Rolf, Bernd / Peters, Jörg (Hg.) (2014): philo – NRW. Einführungsphase. Unterrichtswerk für Philosophie in der Sekundarstufe II, erarbeitet von Klaus Draken, Matthias Gillissen, Jörg Peters, Martina Peters und Bernd Rolf. Bamberg: C.C. Buchner Verlag.

Röhlig, Marc (2018): Türkische Gemeinden lassen Kinder in Deutschland Krieg spielen. Soldat-Uniformen und „Märtyrer-Tode". In: *SPIEGEL Panorama*, 20.04.2018. Online: https://www.spiegel.de/panorama/ditib-in-herford-und-wien-verkleidet-kinder-als-tuerkei-soldaten-a-00000000-0003-0001-0000-000002296792 [abgerufen am 15.08.2022].

Rössler, Beate (2001): *Der Wert des Privaten*. Frankfurt a. M.: Suhrkamp.

Rousseau, Jean-Jacques (1755): *Discours sur l'origine et les fondemens de l'inegalité parmi les hommes*. Amsterdam: Marc Michel Rey.

Ruhloff, Jörg (1993): Vom Gottesknecht zum Selbstliebhaber. Ausblicke auf Individualität, Subjektivität und Autonomie in Interpretationen des Menschen in Renaissance und Aufklärung. In: *Bildung und Erziehung* 46(2). S. 167–182.

Ruhloff, Jörg (2010): Die Tradition der humanistischen Bildung seit der Renaissance und die gegenwärtige Neudefinition der „Bildung". In: Hans-Ulrich Lessing / Volker Steenblock (Hg.): *„Was den Menschen zum Menschen macht ..."*. *Klassische Texte der Philosophie der Bildung*. Freiburg i. B.: Karl Alber.

Rüesch, Andreas (2022): Ukraine: Russlands Luftwaffe erleidet bisher schwerste Verluste. In: *Neue Zürcher Zeitung*, 17.03.2022. Online: https://www.nzz.ch/international/ukraine-russlands-luftwaffe-erleidet-bisher-schwerste-verluste-ld.1674908?reduced=true [abgerufen am 05.10.2022].

Sächsisches Integrations- und Teilhabegesetz (SITG). Online: https://www.zik.sachsen.de/integrationsgesetz.html [abgerufen am 20.04.2022].

Schelsky, Helmut (1975): *Die Arbeit tun die anderen. Klassenkampf und Priesterherrschaft der Intellektuellen.* Leverkusen: Westdeutscher Verlag.

Schiller, Friedrich (1962): Xenien – 388. Gewissensskrupel. In: *Sämtliche Werke, Band 1.* München: Hanser.

Schmidt, Arno (2003): *Die Geburt des Logos bei den alten Griechen.* Berlin: Logos Verlag.

Schmidt, Thomas E. (2021): Ist der Rassismus etwa unüberwindbar? In: *Die Zeit*, 22.07.2021. Online: https://www.zeit.de/2021/30/postkolonialismus-rassismus-linke-holocaust-antisemitismus [abgerufen am 05.10.2022].

Schnädelbach, Herbert (1985): Philosophie. In: Ekkehard Martens / Herbert Schnädelbach (Hg.): *Philosophie. Ein Grundkurs.* Band 1. (Überarbeitete und erweiterte Neuausgabe, 1991). Reinbek bei Hamburg: Rowohlt.

Schopenhauer, Arthur (1841): *Die beiden Grundprobleme der Ethik.* Frankfurt a. M.: Joh. Christ. Hermannsche Buchhandlung.

Schrey, Heinz-Horst / Hoche, Hans-Ulrich (1992): Regel, goldene. In: Joachim Ritter / Karlfried Gründer (Hg.): *Historisches Wörterbuch der Philosophie.* Band 8. Basel: Schwabe & Co. S. 450–464.

Schuessler, Jennifer (2020): Poetry Foundation Leadership Resigns After Black Lives Matter Statement. In: *The New York Times*, 10.06.2020. Online: https://www.nytimes.com/2020/06/09/books/poetry-foundation-black-lives-matter.html [abgerufen am 05.10.2022].

Schulte von Drach, Marcus C. (2016): Muslime und Migranten: Gibt es Parallelgesellschaften in Deutschland? In: *Süddeutsche Zeitung*, 10.08.2016.

Schultze-Kraft, Matthias / Birman, Daniel / Rusconi, Marco / Allefeld, Carsten / Kai Görgen / Dähne, Sven / Blankertz, Benjamin / Haynes, John-Dylan (2016): Point of no return in vetoing movements. In: *Proceedings of the National Academy of Sciences of the United States of America.* 113(4). S. 1080–1085.

Schümer, Dirk (2016): Europa hat jetzt eine erste reine Migrantenpartei. In: *Welt.de*, 24.05.2016. Online: https://www.welt.de/politik/ausland/article155649010/Europa-hat-jetzt-eine-erste-reine-Migrantenpartei.html [abgerufen am 15.08.2022].

Sloterdijk, Peter (1999): Regeln für den Menschenpark. Ein Antwortschreiben zum Brief über den Humanismus – die Elmauer Rede. In: *Die Zeit*, Nr. 38, 16.09.1999.

Snowden, Edward (2019): *Permanent Record – Meine Geschichte.* Frankfurt a. M.: S. Fischer Verlag.

Southern Poverty Law Center (Hg.) (2017): Breitbart exposé confirms: far-right news site a platform for the white nationalist „alt-right". In: *Southern Poverty Law Center*, 06.10.2017. Online: https://www.splcenter.org/hatewatch/2017/10/06/breitbart-exposé-confirms-far-right-news-site-platform-white-nationalist-alt-right [abgerufen am 15.08.2022].

Spitzer, Manfred (2013): TV macht dumm, dick und gewalttätig [Video]. Online: https://www.youtube.com/watch?v=LftI9pYDg7I [abgerufen am 07.12.2021]. Min. 2.29.

Stegemann, Bernd (2017): *Das Gespenst des Populismus*. Berlin: Verlag Theater der Zeit.

Steinmetz, George (1904): Von der „Eingeborenenpolitik" zur Vernichtungsstrategie: Deutsch-Südwestafrika. In: *Peripherie: Zeitschrift für Politik und Ökonomie in der Dritten Welt*. 24(97–98).

Stelzer, Hubertus (2015): Lebensweltbezug. In: Julian Nida-Rümelin / Irina Spiegel / Markus Tiedemann (Hg.): *Handbuch der Philosophie und Ethik. Band I: Didaktik und Methodik*. 2. Auflage. Paderborn: Schöningh.

Süddeutsche Zeitung (2021): Pädagogik-Professor: „Über 40 Prozent der Lehrer ungeeignet". Online: https://www.sueddeutsche.de/bildung/bildung-paedagogik-professor-ueber-40-prozent-der-lehrer-ungeeignet-dpa.urn-newsml-dpa-com-20090101-210924-99-339532 [abgerufen am 17.06.2022].

Swanson, Kevin (2017): Hurricane Harvey - What's the Message? In: *Generations*, 31.08.2017. Online: https://www.generations.org/programs/743 [abgerufen am 05.10.2022].

Szöllösi-Janze, Margit (1998): *Fritz Haber 1868–1934. Eine Biographie*. München: C.H. Beck.

TAZ (Hg.) (1989): Eine Rushdie-Chronik. In: *TAZ*, 26.05.1989.

Tannenberger, Christoph / Pasch, Nele (2017): Verfassungsreform in der Türkei. Auf dem Weg in die Autokratie? In: *tagesschau.de*, 17.04.2017. Online: https://www.tagesschau.de/faktenfinder/ausland/tuerkei-referendum-117.html [abgerufen am 05.10.2022].

The White House (o. J.): Remarks by President Trump on Infrastructure. In: *The White House*. Online: https://web.archive.org/web/20180113052441/https://www.whitehouse.gov/briefings-statements/remarks-president-trump-infrastructure/ [abgerufen am 05.10.2022].

Thiel, Rainer (1999): *Simplikios und das Ende der neuplatonischen Schule in Athen*. Stuttgart: Franz Steiner Verlag.

Tenta, Sabine (2022): Nach Rassismus-Vorwurf: Ministerium bemängelt Schulbuch als diskriminierend. In: *Landespolitik - Nachrichten – WDR*. Online: https://www1.wdr.de/nachrichten/landespolitik/siegburg-schulbuch-ethik-diskussion-100.html [abgerufen am 05.10.2022].

Tetens, Holm (2004): *Philosophisches Argumentieren*. München: Verlag C.H. Beck.

Terre des Femmes (2022): Polizeiliche Kriminalstatistik für 2021 veröffentlicht: 73 Fälle von versuchter oder vollzogener Zwangsverheiratung in Deutschland. Online: https://www.zwangsheirat.de/aktuelles/469-polizeiliche-kriminalstatistik-fuer-2021-veroeffentlicht-73-faelle-von-versuchter-oder-vollzogener-zwangsverheiratung-in-deutschland [abgerufen am 23.06.2022].

Tiedemann, Markus / Tinawi, Constanze (2021): Verzerrtes Normalitätsempfinden und toxische Toleranz. In: *Bundeszentrale für politische Bildung*, 22.11.2022. Online: https://www.bpb.de/themen/islamismus/dossier-islamismus/343155/verzerrtes-normalitaetsempfinden-und-toxische-toleranz/ [abgerufen am 05.10.2022].

Tugendhat, Ernst (1993): *Vorlesungen über Ethik*, Frankfurt a. M.: Suhrkamp.

United Nation High Commissioner for Refugees (UNHCR) (Hg.) (2021): Global Trends – Forced Displacement in 2020. Online: https://www.unhcr.org/statistics/unhcrstats/60b638e37/global-trends-forced-displacement-2020.html [abgerufen am 05.10.2022].

United Nation High Commissioner for Refugees (UNHCR) (Hg.) (2022): Global Trends – Forced Displacement in 2021. Online: https://www.unhcr.org/publications/brochures/62a9d1494/global-trends-report-2021.html [abgerufen am 05.10.2022].

United Nations (Hg.) (2022): World Population Prospects. Online: https://population.un.org/wpp/ [abgerufen am 05.10.2022].

United Nations High Commissioner for Refugees (UNHCR) (o. D.): Refugee Statistics. Online: https://www.unhcr.org/refugee-statistics/download/?url=K1aKuo [abgerufen am 05.10.2022].

United States Senate Committee on Armed Services (Hg.) (2008): Inquiry Into the Treatment of Detainees in US Custody. 20.11.2008 (Auszug aus der offiziellen, geschwärzten Veröffentlichung des Reports vom 22.04.2009, Sektion „Unclassified", S. XXVIII). Online: https://www.govinfo.gov/content/pkg/CHRG-110shrg47298/html/CHRG-110shrg47298.htm [abgerufen am 05.10.2022].

Venohr, Wolfgang (2000): *Stauffenberg: Symbol des Widerstands*. 3. Auflage. München: Herbig.

Wagner, Joachim (2019): Islam: Die Koranschule ist stärker als jeder Religionslehrer. In: *Die Welt*, 11.10.2019. Online: https://www.welt.de/debatte/kommentare/article201587404/Islam-Die-Koranschule-ist-staerker-als-jeder-Religionslehrer.html [abgerufen am 05.10.2022].

Watson, Kathryn (2020): Trump says „I don't think science knows" about climate. In: *CBS News*, 15.09.2020. Online: https://www.cbsnews.com/news/trump-western-wildfires-science-climate-change/ [abgerufen am 05.10.2022].

Watts, Edward (2004): Justinian, Malalas, and the End of Athenian Philosophical Teaching in A.D. 529. In: *The Journal of Roman Studies*, 94. S. 168–182.

Westdeutscher Rundfunk (Hg.) (2020): Im Gespräch mit Janine Kunze und Thomas Gottschalk. Die letzte Instanz [Video]. *YouTube*, 02.12.2020. Online: https://www.youtube.com/watch?v=vazgNVl_3jA&t=1120s [abgerufen am 05.10.2022].

Weizsäcker, Carl Friedrich von (1987): Der Mensch im wissenschaftlich-technischen Zeitalter. In: Ders.: *Ausgewählte Texte*. München: Goldmann.

Whalen, Andrew (2020): California Curator Resigns After Saying Museum Would Continue Collecting White Artists. In: *Newsweek*, 15.07.2020. Online: https://www.newsweek.com/sfmoma-curator-gary-garrels-san-francisco-museum-modern-art-reverse-discrimination-racism-1517984 [abgerufen am 05.10.2022].

Whitehead, Alfred North (1979): *Process and Reality*. New York: The Free Press.

Willareth, Roland (2020): Diskriminierung durch Sprache. Antisemitismus an der Schule. In: Markus Tiedemann (Hg.): *Migration, Menschenrechte und Rassismus. Herausforderungen ethischer Bildung*. Paderborn: Brill/Ferdinand Schöningh. S. 91–124.

Wilson, Jason (2018): Who are the Proud Boys, „western chauvinists" involved in political violence? In: *The Guardian*, 14.07.2018. Online: https://www.theguardian.com/world/2018/jul/14/proud-boys-far-right-portland-oregon [abgerufen am 05.10.2022].

Wittgenstein, Ludwig (1984): *Werke*. 8 Bände. Frankfurt a. M.: Suhrkamp.

Wöchentliche Hallische Frage- und Anzeigungs-Nachrichten. 28. November 1729. S. 271–274.

Wolff, Christian (1721/1985): *Oratio de sinarum philosophia practica - Rede über die praktische Philosophie der Chinesen* (Übersetzung: Michael Albrecht). Hamburg: Meiner.

Yaghoobifarah, Hengameh (2016): Fusion Revisited: Karneval der Kulturlosen. In: *Missy Magazine*, 11.07.2016. Online: https://missy-magazine.de/blog/2016/07/05/fusion-revisited-karneval-der-kulturlosen/ [abgerufen am 05.10.2022].

Zabriskie, Matt (2021): Read: Former President Donald Trump's January 6 speech, in: *CNN*, 09.02.2021. Online: https://edition.cnn.com/2021/02/08/politics/trump-january-6-speech-transcript/index.html [abgerufen am 05.10.2022].

Zakaria, Fareed (2003): *The Future of Freedom: Illiberal Democracy at Home and Abroad*. New York: W. W. Norton & Company.

Zuboff, Shoshana (2018): *Das Zeitalter des Überwachungskapitalismus*. Frankfurt a. M.: Campus Verlag.